THE EZ66 GUIDE
FOR TRAVELERS
2ND EDITION

Written and illustrated by
JERRY McCLANAHAN

Published by the

'NATIONAL HISTORIC ROUTE 66 FEDERATION

Cover paintings by Jerry McClanahan

ISBN 978-0-9709951-6-2

CONTENTS

*Pages are divided into TEXT pages in the front and back,
and STATE pages in the middle of the guide.*

FOR FREE UPDATES to the *EZ66 GUIDE For Travelers* go to
mcjerry66.com or the link at www.national66.org

AUTHOR'S INTRODUCTION

Route 66 consists of a community of friends, fans and fanatics from virtually every corner of the civilized world. It spans eight states (IL, MO, KS, OK, TX, NM, AZ and CA) and over 2,000 miles. Fueled by nostalgia and fired by preservation-minded folk, Route 66 is a magical cross section of the nation; from the massive skyscrapers of Chicago, over the green hills of the Ozarks, the grassy plains, the awesome deserts and mountains, then down into the fascinating mosaic of the Los Angeles basin. There's something for everyone here - the embodiment of freedom, the legendary emblem of 20th century roadside America.

Born in 1926, US 66 was pieced together from an existing network of promoted trails and unnamed roads, most of which were ornery dirt paths at the time. Despite the inexorable invasion of the interstates, at least 85 percent of old 66, in one guise or another, remains to be easily explored.

The road gained national attention in 1946 with the Bobby Troup song; · "Get Your Kicks on Route 66," a timeless tune that captured the heart of the country, then was covered by hundreds of artists over the decades. Also enhancing the road's popularity was the TV series of the 1960s, "Route 66," wherein Todd and Buzz traveled the country in a Corvette, seeking adventure (in reality, almost never on '66).

Change has always been a part of the Mother Road. The late 1920s and 1930s watched "Dirt 66" rapidly transform into a paved, all weather highway by 1938. Dirt roads gave way to narrow, twisty 2-lanes, which in turn were straightened and widened, some becoming 4-lane superhighways before the Interstate Highway System began taking over in the late 1950's. Much of old 66 hung on during the 1960s as the Interstate began to usurp the route's path across the country, digging up old pavement and stranding towns with cruel bypasses.

Finally, 1984 brought the final bypass in Williams, AZ. The next year, Route 66 was decertified. No longer an "official" US Hwy, authorities and commentators expected the old road to fade into history like the Oregon Trail, the Chisolm Trail and so many other once famous byways.

Widely eulogized in the press, Route 66 began a surprising comeback, sparked by volunteers who formed state associations. Before long, positive books and articles were published about '66, and people began traveling the old road, hoping to find what was left of the glory days. Books, videos, merchandise, magazines and films all point to the continuing, grass roots resurgence. Route 66 marked about 59 years as a US Hwy, but almost 8 decades as an American icon, and it is still going strong.

TEXT 2

As you explore the Mother Road with the EZ66 GUIDE, take the time to stop and visit with the people you'll encounter. They are the greatest resource the highway has to offer, a treasure to be shared with the world.

THE EZ66 GUIDE PHILOSOPHY

I'm known in Route 66 circles for articles covering EVERY abandoned and obliterated fragment and dead end of Route 66, in exacting detail. Fortunately, the EZ66 GUIDE won't subject you to that level of obsession. Instead, you'll find a fun, EZ to follow tour that will take you down Route 66 with as few problems as possible, in a friendly, informal fashion.

To make it EZ for you to follow and enjoy Route 66, the EZ66 Guide includes DETAIL MAPS of most Route 66 towns (or tricky areas), along with larger-area SECTION MAPS.

The TOUR ROUTE given in the DIRECTION BOXES (distilled from the many versions of US 66) was selected to route you on as much vintage, quality 66 as possible without the bother of dead ends, dirt roads or very rough conditions. As always, conditions may change due to road construction, street changes, etc. Be prepared to navigate around any such obstacles.

I have not gone into the history of most towns and areas (for that, see the books listed in the reference section). This is a guide to Route 66 as it is TODAY (with the caveat that it is always changing).

HOW TO FOLLOW THE EZ66 TOUR

The book switches to a horizontal format for the actual TOUR GUIDE section to better showcase the mostly horizontal maps (the spiral binding makes it EZ to flip thru the pages in your car).

Read the boxed WB (westbound) and EB (eastbound) directions to follow the MAIN TOUR ROUTE. The WB and EB directions are on the SAME page, along with DETAIL MAPS where needed. The route is divided by STATE, and each state is broken up into SECTIONS. At the beginning of each state is an INTRO page, and at the start of each section is a SECTION MAP. Each state has its own page number sequence (ex: AZ Page-1 thru AZ page-25).

WESTBOUND drivers (those headed in the direction of the LA area): read thru the book as normal, following the directions in the WB direction boxes at the TOP of each page. Flip BACK to refer to section maps.

EASTBOUND drivers (headed towards Chicago): begin at the BACK of the book (or of the section you are traveling) following the EB direction boxes on the

BOTTOM of each page. Follow the page-number cues (below the EB directions on certain pages) to flip FORWARD to the SECTION MAPS and STATE INTRO (read the latter FIRST when entering a new state).

In the directions and text, I also refer to the compass points (east, north, etc.) when a specific direction of travel is indicated.

The informative TEXT for the towns and attractions on each page is located in between the direction boxes (separated so you don't have to wade thru the text to find your next turn). This text is generally arranged from west to east, reading down. EB drivers, look thru each page's info text to see what is ahead, noting that the lowest items will generally be encountered first (there is an unavoidable WB bias, but I've tried to soften this whenever possible).

Use the frequent DETAIL MAPS to help navigate thru towns and junctions and refer to the SECTION MAPS to get a picture of upcoming towns and turns. It's a good idea to read ahead a section or two for long-range planning, highlighting items of interest. When following the directions, street signs will sometimes be absent. In that case, refer to the detail maps (note: street grids are shown only to indicate the town area, use a local map to navigate off '66). A good atlas is also handy to have.

In the directions, I have purposely avoided too much reference to mileage points. You don't want to spend the whole trip with your head in a book (and odometer calibrations vary). Mileage references (or landmarks) are given in cases where they are especially helpful.

On the section maps, the mileage between main points is given in a box at the bottom. In addition, interstate highway exit numbers correspond to mileage from the state line, so it's EZ to figure your mileage to towns anywhere along the route (except for CA, which is slowly phasing in exit numbers).

"HISTORIC 66" SIGNS: Many of the eight states (and communities) have done a nice job of marking the old alignments with "Historic 66" signs. The problem is that these signs tend to "disappear" (except for those painted on the road) and a few mislead or lead to a section that is NOT a part of the EZ66 TOUR. Since you can't count on having a "Historic 66" sign before every turn, use the signs when they appear to reassure you, but follow the directions in your EZ66 GUIDE.

USING THE MAPS

The BOLDEST lines mark the OFFICIAL TOUR ROUTE, as described in the direction boxes. The NEXT BOLDEST lines are OPTIONS or SIDE TRIPS. Thinner lines are NON-66 roads, while sections of interstates or some divided roads that are NOT a part of the TOUR are shown with thin parallel lines. The width of line does not indicate the width of road. In other words, a narrow 2-lane section of Route 66 will appear BOLDER than a 4-lane NON-66 street.

The scale of the maps is exaggerated/modified to show detail. Some maps have been stretched or condensed to fit the page. The general scale of the section maps is mostly consistent within states (except where noted). The detail map scales vary depending on the area that needed to be shown. You can tell by the comparative size of roads and details. To fit the page efficiently, I have tilted the North-South orientation slightly on many section maps (as noted on the compass rose).

ABOUT THE DIRECTIONS

You'll encounter the following terms in the direction boxes:

• **BL 15, BL 40, etc. equals:** Business Loop. These are loops from one exit to another thru the business district of bypassed towns, usually along 66, but not always. So don't follow them blindly, use the EZ directions to know when to deviate from the business loops.

• **HWY (shown on the maps as circles or ovals):** Used to indicate any designated highway other than US highways or Interstates. Example: HWY 3. Those state highways numbered "66" are referred to as MO 66, KS 66, OK 66 and CA 66.

• **JCT:** Junction or intersection.

• **"Y":** A JCT shaped like a Y where two roads diverge.

• **"T":** A JCT like a T, where one road ends at a crossroad.

• **SLANT, VEER or ANGLE:** Describe variations of turns that are not 90 degrees.

• **BEAR LEFT or RIGHT:** Usually at a "Y" junction.

• **CURVE LEFT or RIGHT:** Used for curved transitions at corners.

• **QUICK LEFT / RIGHT or QUICK EXIT:** Means an "immediate" turn.

• **JOG LEFT or RIGHT:** Used in cases where the route turns off one road, then quickly turns again onto a parallel road (or similar quick change in direction).

• **STAY AHEAD:** Do not turn off the road you are traveling. Usually used at junctions, intersections, underpasses and exits.

• **MERGE AHEAD:** As above, but indicates you are joining another highway number or street name.

NOTE: No matter how EZ you try to make it, some parts of Route 66 are unavoidably complex (think St Louis, OKC or LA). If you get confused, stop and look over the maps and text again (skimming ahead to study a city beforehand helps a lot).

ABOUT THE TEXT:

• **OPTIONS:** You can have a great trip by sticking ONLY to the MAIN TOUR, but the EZ66 GUIDE also has plenty of alternate OPTIONAL ROUTES to explore.

These are detailed in the text or detail maps, not the direction boxes. In some cases the OPTIONS are more interesting than the tour route, but were handled separately, due to complexity. These OPTIONS are especially recommended in the text. In a few cases, like in Oklahoma City or the Santa Fe Loop, the Main Tour Route breaks into TWO OPTIONS. Read the text to choose which you prefer.

• **SIDE TRIP:** These either lead to cool places on sections of Old 66 or are non-66 local attractions. Generally, an OPTION can replace the MAIN TOUR, while a SIDE TRIP is suggested as "in addition to."

• **DIRT 66 OPTIONS:** Early 66 was mostly dirt road (some paved sections have devolved to dirt). I have selected some of those prime "Dirt 66" sections as options (if you don't mind a rock chip or two). AVOID these roads when they are muddy (or if rain threatens). Drive slowly and watch for oncoming vehicles (dust and gravel) and be careful of soft shoulders or ruts. DON'T drive into standing or running water!

• **NON-RECOMMENDED SECTIONS:** Some abandoned or extremely ROUGH (huge potholes, washouts, cross-ditches, broken pavement, etc) sections of old 66 are presented in the text or on the maps (as dashed lines) purely for historic information. These are NOT part of the EZ TOUR. If you decide to drive any of these rough sections, do so AT YOU OWN RISK. DO NOT TRESPASS.

ALERTS SPOTLIGHTING FUN STUFF

• **GIANT ALERTS:** Old 66 is full of larger than life people, animals and things (ignore inflated purple gorillas) such as Illinois' famous Muffler Men triplets.

• **PHOTO OP:** An especially cool or touristy thing to photograph or pose by. Historic 66 signs, state line markers and "Dip in Road" signs are all photo ops!

• **GIFT SHOP ALERTS:** Gift shops are everywhere, of course. But these highlight gift shops that have really cool stuff, or that are especially deserving of business, such as museums. Try to buy from the small guy when possible. You may wish to ship your new-bought treasures home at intervals, to save room!

• **FOLK ART ALERTS:** Interesting roadside assemblages or sculptures.

• **SCAVENGER HUNTS:** To encourage taking your time while driving old 66, try to find the answers to these questions. I tried to pick things that have some permanence (like the plaques on old bridges). The answers will be found on the Federation's web site *www.national66.org* (for FUN only, folks!). CAUTION: you may have to pull off and walk on the roadside to find some answers, so please BE CAREFUL!

• **MUSEUMS AND ATTRACTIONS:** Fun, interesting or historic places in towns along the road. Hours vary with season, holidays, etc. (and space was often limited in the text) so I have included phone numbers or web sites of most of the listed museums or attractions. Call ahead to check on hours of operation and price of admission, if any (some are open during the week, others only one day a week or by appt). There are many more museums along '66 than I could include, and you won't be able to see them all. Do try some of the small town history museums, for the flavor of America, but make sure to visit ALL the museums dedicated to Route 66!

• **CAR GAMES:** To encourage your kids to get their heads out of the video games, scattered thru the book are simple little games requiring observation of features along '66 (don't blame ME for arguments over who won!). Feel free to make up your own rules. Encourage your kids to make a trip scrapbook with photos (let them take some), business cards, postcards, flyers, drawings, notes, and leaves. Perhaps they could "interview" some of the living legends of '66.

• **SPOT OLD 66:** I do point out many sections of abandoned road, but keep your eyes open for more. Lines of old poles or fences, old bridges, swaths of different soil or vegetation, rows of trees, old fences and roads running straight from curves all can be clues to an old alignment of 66. If you want to explore every bit of old 66, check out the fine books in the resources section.

• **ROUTE 66 ETIQUETTE:** PLEASE respect the road and its treasures. Take only photographs, leave only tire tracks. There are plenty of souvenirs to be bought along the route, so please leave those tempting signs along the way for others to see. Don't trash the route, and the ONLY place you should leave your name is in guest books, or on the  unofficial "Public Art Corridor" between Essex and Amboy, CA.

Business owners along the route are delighted to have you stop by, and most are friendly and happy to chat. Many have sunk much love and money into their corner of Route 66, so whenever possible, please PATRONIZE those businesses that are preserving the history of the Mother Road. By the way, it is a good idea to ask first before taking very many photos at an active business. It is polite, and most owners are happy to let you snap away (and you might make a new friend!).

• **CAUTIONS:** Your author and publisher have made a conscientious effort to produce an accurate guide, but we cannot be held responsible for any accidents, casualties or incidents resulting while using this book. Don't read this guide while driving. Appoint a navigator, or pull over and read ahead. Obey the speed limit (especially in small towns and school zones). Laws and streets change, so if a traffic sign is in opposition to the directions in this guide, OBEY the SIGN!

This guide is as accurate as possible at the date of publication. Conditions along 66 are in constant flux. Road conditions may change for the worse. Roads may close or be widened, streets may change name or become One-Way, and businesses may close or change management. Look for specific cautions and advisories in the text.

• **URBAN AREAS:** Avoid driving in questionable areas after dark. If a neighborhood gives you a bad feeling, drive on to the next area. Use the freeways as needed to bypass city traffic or neighborhoods. Tune to local radio for traffic bulletins. Hide cameras and other valuables from sight in your vehicle, and don't leave valuables in motel rooms. If a motel's neighborhood bothers you (bars, X-rated book stores, transients), move on.

• **DESERTS AND MOUNTAINS:** Carry some bottled water and a cell phone (AAA or other such membership is helpful). Stay with your car if it breaks down. Slow down on steep grades, and use a lower gear downhill to save on brakes. Don't crowd the centerline on blind curves. Avoid driving thru running water in flash flood-prone areas.

• **ADVISORIES:** Some sections of '66 are a bit rough (especially those with asphalt patches). I note many of them in the text (muscle car owners take note).

• **RV ALERTS:** My experience with RV's is limited to VW Campers, but I have noted in the text some areas on '66 that may prove problematic to big RVs. Much of Old 66 is narrow, so use care.

DON'T let all of the above scare you off Route 66. Its just common sense.

TRIP PREP

It's YOUR trip, so plan it the way you want. Some like to plan everything in advance, some just take off and hope for the best with very little forethought. I recommend taking the middle road. Allow for serendipity but put together a plan to visit the things you want to enjoy (phone numbers or websites are provided for most attractions along the way, please call ahead for hours of operation and fees). Make your motel reservations well in advance, or call ahead from the road a day or two ahead (or even that afternoon if you feel lucky!). It's up to you.

HOW LONG WILL IT TAKE?

Two weeks, one way, is rushing it if you want to see very much of what 66 has to offer. A good idea, if time is short, is to pick a section to explore, then hit another area next time (you WILL be back!). Or, use the guide to plan ahead, and skip and choose what sections you drive (expect your well-made plans to be changed by unexpected enjoyment).

TEXT 8

WHEN TO TRAVEL 66

The traditional travel season is April/May thru September (give or take). Too early in the spring risks ice and snow (especially in higher elevations). Spring is also prime time for thunderstorms (keep an ear out for local weather reports). The snow-threat resumes in late fall. Usually the main roads clear quickly, but you may have to wait out a heavy snowfall. Summer is vacation time, but expect heat (and humidity in the east). Winter is the off-season. There's less tourists, but many museums and business have limited (or no) winter hours. You're driving a great distance across a continent, from a northerly region of the Midwest down into the desert southwest, so conditions may range from one extreme to another. Higher elevations bring cooler weather (even in summer).

FOOD AND LODGING

While this is not primarily a guide to dining and lodging, (I recommend the Federation's *Route 66 Dining & Lodging Guide*), I have indicated some places to eat or sleep in towns that are noteworthy. These may be famous road icons or places that I have enjoyed. Since one person cannot stop at every place, I also mention some that trusty sources have recommended. None of this constitutes an endorsement. I haven't been paid by anyone, and omission does not necessarily mean disapproval. Some sections of Route 66  have a wealth of suitable vintage motels, others none. A few have gotten mixed reviews, so in those cases, I do not include a phone, and suggest that you check them out in person. Other motels I mention for their nice signs or history, with no recommendations one way or the other. When in doubt, ask nicely to check out the room FIRST (a proud owner won't refuse). If you must stay at a chain, I've found Super 8 Motels to be quite inexpensive and good, as well as the newer, 3-story Motel 6 properties (like the fine one in Springfield, IL). If you would like to step up a few notches, consider Hampton Inns. They have contibuted to the preservation of the route.

Now that you've prepared for your dream trip along Route 66, what are you waiting for? The road starts on the next page!

ROUTE 66 ACROSS ILLINOIS

CHICAGO, ILLINOIS is the **Eastern Terminus** of fabled **Route 66**. Whether you **begin** or **end** your journey of roadside discovery here, the great state of **ILLINOIS** has a bounteous harvest to offer, from the hustle and bustle of downtown Chi-town, to the peace and quiet of an old concrete slab road zigzagging across the prairie. Roadside icons abound along the almost **300 miles** of **ILLINOIS Mother Road**: Odell Station, the Pig Hip Museum, Soulsby's Shell, friendly giants at **WILMINGTON, ATLANTA** and **SPRINGFIELD**, historic **Abraham Lincoln** sites, big cities and small towns, farmland and prairie and woods, Funks Sirip and Cozy Dogs.

Illinois's Route 66 was blessed with pavement early on. A major change occurred in the route when the "temporary" routing along Illinois 4 south from **SPRINGFIELD** to **STAUNTON** was bypassed in favor of the direct route thru **LITCHFIELD** (alongside current 1-55) in 1930. Another change in the '30s was the bypassing of **JOLIET** for the route along and near current I-55 thru **PLAINFIELD**. The **Joliet** route became "Alt 66" and is the traditional tour route today.

Beginning in the 1940s, **4-Lane 66** bypassed the earlier 2-lane road thru towns. So, by the mid fifties, many sections of early **Route 66** lost their traffic, and their roadside businesses. Those road-icons that remain are cherished gems. Today, long stretches of the ultimate 4-lane 66 have lost their extra lanes, devolving back to 2-lane status. Along these extensive 2 and 4-Lane remnants are **friendly towns** filled with the history of the Midwest and the lure of the **open road**.

CHICAGO
JOLIET
WILMINGTON
DWIGHT
PONTIAC
ODELL
NORMAL
BLOOMINGTON
ATLANTA
McLEAN
LINCOLN
SPRINGFIELD
AUBURN
CARLIN-
VILLE
LITCHFIELD
MT OLIVE
STAUNTON
EDWARDSVILLE
MITCHELL
GRANITE CITY
ST LOUIS
MO

IL page-1

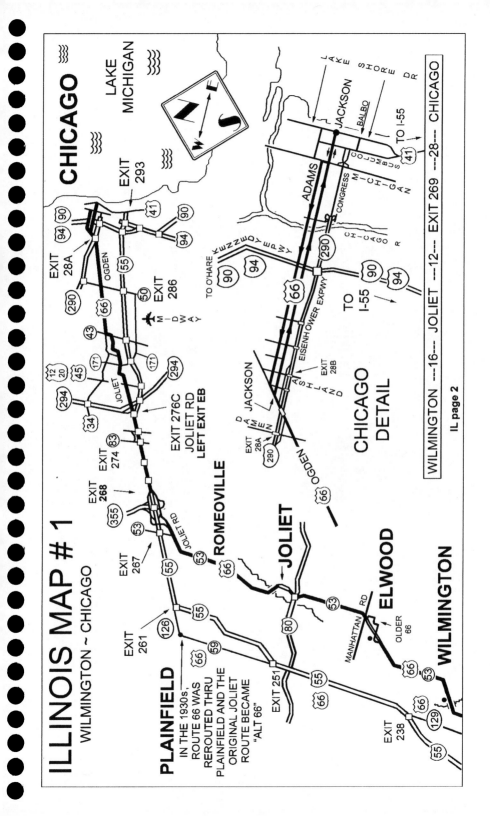

ILLINOIS MAP # 1

WILMINGTON ~ CHICAGO

CHICAGO

LAKE MICHIGAN

EXIT 293

EXIT 28A

OGDEN

EXIT 286

EXIT 276C
JOLIET RD
LEFT EXIT EB

EXIT 274

EXIT 268

EXIT 267

EXIT 261

EXIT 251

EXIT 238

PLAINFIELD

IN THE 1930s,
ROUTE 66 WAS
REROUTED THRU
PLAINFIELD AND THE
ORIGINAL JOLIET
ROUTE BECAME
"ALT 66"

ROMEOVILLE

JOLIET

ELWOOD

OLDER 66

MANHATTAN RD

WILMINGTON

TO O'HARE

KENNEDY EXPWY

EISENHOWER EXPWY

ADAMS

CONGRESS

JACKSON

BALBO

TO I-55

COLUMBUS

MICHIGAN

CHICAGO R

LAKE SHORE DR

ADAMS

JACKSON

EXIT 28A

EXIT 28B

OGDEN

TO I-55

CHICAGO DETAIL

WILMINGTON ---16--- JOLIET ---12--- EXIT 269 ---28--- CHICAGO

IL page 2

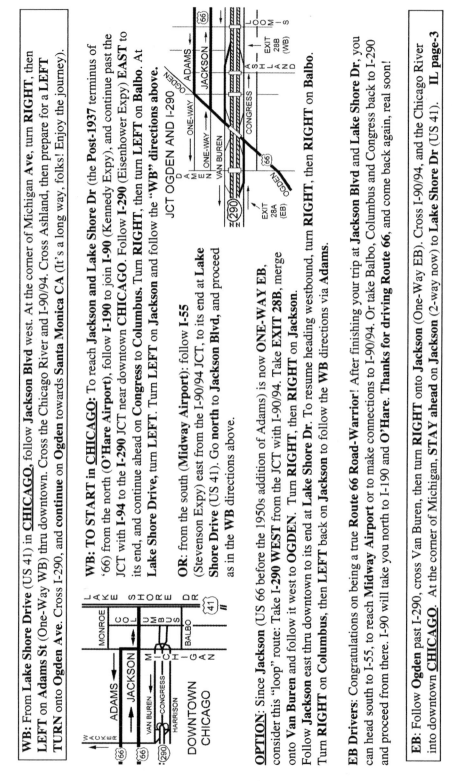

WB: From Lake Shore Drive (US 41) in <u>CHICAGO</u>, follow **Jackson Blvd** west. At the corner of Michigan Ave, turn **RIGHT**, then **LEFT** on **Adams St** (One-Way WB) thru downtown. Cross the Chicago River and I-90/94. Cross Ashland, then prepare for a **LEFT TURN** onto **Ogden** Ave. Cross I-290, and **continue** on **Ogden** towards **Santa Monica CA** (It's a long way, folks! Enjoy the journey).

WB: TO START in <u>CHICAGO</u>: To reach **Jackson and Lake Shore Dr** (the **Post-1937** terminus of '66) from the north (**O'Hare Airport**), follow **I-190** to join **I-90** (Kennedy Expy), and continue past the JCT with **I-94** to the **I-290** JCT near downtown **CHICAGO**. Follow **I-290** (Eisenhower Expy) **EAST** to its end, and continue ahead on **Congress** to **Columbus**. Turn **RIGHT**, then turn **LEFT** on **Balbo**. At **Lake Shore Drive**, turn **LEFT**. Turn **LEFT** on **Jackson** and follow the **"WB"** directions above.

OR: from the south (**Midway Airport**): follow **I-55** (Stevenson Expy) east from the I-90/94 JCT, to its end at **Lake Shore Drive** (US 41). Go north to **Jackson** Blvd, and proceed as in the **WB** directions above.

<u>**OPTION**</u>: Since **Jackson** (US 66 before the 1950s addition of Adams) is now **ONE-WAY EB**, consider this "loop" route: Take **I-290 WEST** from the JCT with I-90/94. Take **EXIT 28B**, merge onto **Van Buren** and follow it west to **OGDEN**. Turn **RIGHT**, then **RIGHT** on **Jackson**. Follow **Jackson** east thru downtown to its end at **Lake Shore Dr**. To resume heading westbound, turn **RIGHT**, then **RIGHT** on **Balbo**. Turn **RIGHT** on **Columbus**, then **LEFT** back on **Jackson** to follow the **WB** directions via **Adams**.

EB Drivers: Congratulations on being a true **Route 66 Road-Warrior!** After finishing your trip at **Jackson Blvd and Lake Shore Dr**, you can head south to I-55, to reach **Midway Airport** or to make connections to I-90/94. Or take Balbo, Columbus and Congress back to I-290 and proceed from there. I-90 will take you north to I-190 and **O'Hare. Thanks for driving Route 66**, and come back again, real soon!

EB: Follow **Ogden** past I-290, cross Van Buren, then turn **RIGHT** onto **Jackson** (One-Way EB). Cross I-90/94, and the Chicago River into downtown <u>**CHICAGO**</u>. At the corner of Michigan, **STAY ahead** on **Jackson** (2-way now) to **Lake Shore Dr** (US 41).   **IL page-3**

THINGS to SEE and DO in CHICAGO: Whether your trip begins or ends in __CHICAGO__, there's plenty to do and see. So much so, you could spend days here. Since there are miles of Route 66 waiting, here's a sampling of some of the sites on or near the Mother Road, from **Grant Park** thru the downtown "canyons" of the "Loop" and under the 'EL." **Chicagoland Chamber of Commerce**: www.chicagolandchamber.org or (312) 494-6700.

Jackson Blvd, the original US 66 thru downtown, has been **ONE-WAY** eastbound since the 1950s, when **Adams St** took over the westbound chores. The current "**END 66**" sign at Jackson and Michigan is only partially correct. Route 66 first began/ended there, but in 1937, the terminus moved out to **Lake Shore Drive**. Anchoring the eastern end of '66 is **Grant Park**, home since 1927 to **Buckingham Fountain** (between Columbus and Lake Shore, south of Jackson). Watch for the daily water show from April thru November, with lights and music at night. Try meter parking on Columbus, or the underground **Grant Park South Parking Garage** (pay) off Michigan, south of Jackson.

<u>SCAVENGER HUNT!</u> What fierce creatures guard the **Art Institute** just north of Jackson on Michigan Ave?

You'll need to crane your neck to see all of the **Sears Tower**, the **tallest building on US 66** (once tallest in the world!) A public observation deck is reached from the Jackson Blvd entrance. If the skyscrapers of downtown intrigue you, then check with the **Architecture Foundation** (www.architecture.org), which offers excellent narrated tours from their tour center in the **Railway Exchange Building**, on Jackson just before Michigan (check out the "**Santa Fe**" sign on the roof, a harbinger of the close association that 66 will have with that railroad further west).

Hungry? For breakfast or lunch try **Lou Mitchells** restaurant, at 565 W Jackson (near Jefferson St), which began on this same block in 1923. Or try the **Berghoff** on Adams St, with their great neon sign, or the many restaurants of "**Greektown**," west of the Kennedy Expwy.

West of downtown, between Ashland and Laflin, is the **Jackson Blvd Historic District**. There's much more to see on __CHICAGO__'s 66.

WB: Take **Ogden Ave** southwest thru **CICERO** and **BERWYN**. At **Harlem Ave** (Hwy 43), turn **LEFT**. Turn **RIGHT** at **41st St** into **LYONS** (becomes **43rd St**). Follow the boulevard as it curves left on **Prescott Ave** and right on **Joliet Rd** to **McCOOK**. Pass Hwy 171. Cross the RR tracks, then turn **RIGHT** on **55th St** (a detour). Turn **LEFT** on **East Ave**, then **RIGHT** back onto **Joliet Rd** thru **COUNTRYSIDE** and **INDIAN HEAD PARK**. Cross under I-294 (avoid "**right-turn only**"), then merge **AHEAD** onto **I-55 WB**.

Ogden Ave cuts a wide swath thru a partly industrial, partly "economically disadvantaged" section of **CHICAGO**. Keep an eye out on the south at 3801 for the defunct **Castle Car Wash** with its unique architecture. Across IL Hwy 50 in **CICERO** are more roadside goodies including **Henry's Drive In** ("It's a Meal in itself") with its **GIANT HOT DOG** sign. Neighboring **BERWYN** honors '66 with lighted glass-block "entry" signs and US 66 banners.

OPTION: ALT Route: Until **1928**, older US 66 followed **Ogden** (US34) into **LYONS**, instead of turning south on Harlem. Before then, there was no road thru what once was marshland, home to Gypsies. On the north at "Joliet Ave" (NOT Joliet Rd) is the **Hoffman Tower**, a castle-like structure built in 1908. At the corner of **Lawndale**, stop at the **Snowflake Drive** in (60 years young) for a treat before taking **Lawndale** back down to **Joliet Rd**.

The current route is forced into a **DETOUR** because of a quarry that dug too close to the skirts of the Mother Road! You can catch glimpses of the abyss from **55th St**, before heading thru **McCOOK**, **COUNTRYSIDE** and **INDIAN HEAD PARK** towards a forced join-up with **I-55**.

EB: Take **EXIT 276C** (LEFT EXIT) from I-55 onto **Joliet Rd**. Cross under I-294 into **INDIAN HEAD PARK**, and stay **AHEAD** thru **COUNTRYSIDE**. Cross La Grange Rd. Turn **LEFT** on **East Ave** (a detour), then **RIGHT** on **55th St** and **LEFT** back onto **Joliet Rd** in **McCOOK**. Cross Hwy 171 and then Lawndale Ave. Curve **LEFT** with the main blvd onto **Prescott Ave** in **LYONS**, then curve **RIGHT** onto **43rd St**, (becomes **41st St**). At **Harlem Ave** (Hwy 43), turn **LEFT**. Turn **RIGHT** onto **Ogden Rd** and continue thru **BERWYN** and **CICERO** to the JCT of I-290 in **CHICAGO**. (see **IL page-3** to continue)

IL page-5

WB: Follow **I-55** southwest from **EXIT 276**. Take **EXIT 268** (S Joliet Rd). Follow the **"Joliet Rd"** signs (do NOT rejoin I-55) and curve under I-55 onto **Joliet Rd**, continuing thru **ROMEOVILLE** (where HWY 53 joins). **Joliet Rd** soon becomes **Broadway**. Nearing **JOLIET**, be in the left lane at the **Ruby St** stoplight, and turn **LEFT** with **Hwy 53** across the **Des Plaines River** into **JOLIET**.

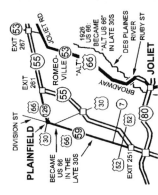

SIDE TRIP: In **WILLOWBROOK**, take **EXIT 274** to visit **Dell Rhea's Chicken Basket**, a great roadfood stop since 1946, often featuring live music. Briefly join **Kingery Rd** (Hwy 83) north, then turn **RIGHT** on **Midway Drive**, and follow the curve back right, then left alongside I-55 onto **Joliet Rd** (which is a sundered section of old 66) to the 'Basket.

On the main route south from EXIT 269, notice **Montana Charlie's Little America Flea Market**, open from April thru October on weekends. Also look for the neon sign and rooster that mark **White Fence Farms**, which not only offers fried chicken, but a petting zoo, antique cars and machines, plus rides and games. **Scavenger Hunt!** The **Illinois State Police Headquarters** building on Hwy 53 is vintage. What **DISTRICT** does it serve? ____

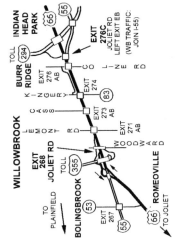

SIDE TRIP: In the 1930's, US 66 was re-routed thru **PLAINFIELD**, while Joliet Rd became "Alt 66". Our tour covers the **JOLIET** route, because the newer alignment was largely replaced by I-55, but use the detail map to visit **PLAINFIELD** if you can. The brief section of **Hwy 59** that is co-signed as **US 30**, south of town, was at one time both the **Lincoln Highway AND US 66**.

EB: From **JOLIET**, turn **RIGHT** at the light onto **Broadway** (Hwy **53**) and continue (becomes **Joliet Rd**) thru **ROMEOVILLE**. When Hwy 53 turns, stay **AHEAD** with **Joliet Rd**. Nearing **I-55**, follow the signs **"To Chicago"** and merge onto **I-55 EB**. Nearing EXIT 276AB, move to the **LEFT LANE**. At **EXIT 276C**, take the **LEFT EXIT** onto **Joliet Rd.**

WB: From **Broadway**, cross the **Des Plaines River** on **Ruby**, then curve **RIGHT** onto **Chicago St**. Stay with **Hwy 53** as it angles right onto **Ottawa** (becomes one-way SB). Follow **Ottawa/Hwy 53** south past downtown **JOLIET**. Stay with **Hwy 53** as it veers from Ottawa to rejoin the other lanes as **MLK Blvd**, then south on **Hwy 53** past I-80 and thru **ELWOOD** to **WILMINGTON**.

Across the drawbridge (WB) over the **Des Plaines River** lies **JOLIET**. The **Joliet Museum** at 214 N Ottawa houses a new **Route 66 Welcome Center and Gift Shop** (815) 723-5201. **ART ALERT!** See my big **ROUTE 66 MURAL!** Pick up a brochure detailing their "Community Public Art Tour."

OPTION: To follow **original 66:** From the north, stay **AHEAD** on **Chicago St** INSTEAD of following Hwy 53 onto Ottawa. Follow Chicago St straight south into downtown. This will take you past the majestic **Rialto Square Theatre** at 102 N Chicago, built in 1926 (the same year that 66 was born!). It has an amazing architectural presence, inside and out. At **Jefferson**, you'll have to turn **LEFT**, then detour back north on **Scott** to **Clinton**, which will take you over to **Ottawa** to continue south. If headed **NORTH**, just turn **LEFT** from **Scott** onto **Van Buren**, then follow **Chicago** north to **Ruby**.

GIANT ALERT! A cousin of the three famous "Illinois 66 Giants" stands proud just off the route. You can see the **Joliet Jackhammer's** mascot from Clinton, east of Scott, at Silver Cross Field ballpark. South of town, save the speed for **Route 66 Raceway** and enjoy the drive thru the **Joliet Arsenal** region, with its conservation areas. **OPTION:** I recommend you follow the **detail map** to drive the old 2-lane 66 thru the **ELWOOD** area (from the stoplight for **Manhattan Rd** to the south JCT with **Elwood Rd**).

EB: Follow **Hwy 53** north from **WILMINGTON**, thru **ELWOOD** and past I-80 into **JOLIET**, entering on **MLK Blvd**. Approaching downtown, turn **RIGHT** (only) on **Washington**, then **LEFT** on **Scott** (one-way NB). Pass downtown, then follow **Hwy 53** as it turns **LEFT** on **Columbia** and joins **Ruby St** across the **Des Plaines River** to the stoplight at **Broadway**.

(see MAP # 1 on IL page-2)

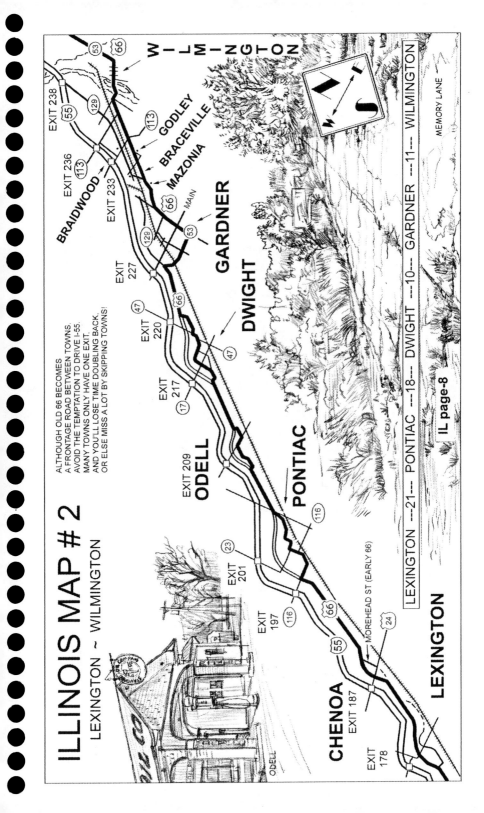

ILLINOIS MAP # 2

LEXINGTON ~ WILMINGTON

ALTHOUGH OLD 66 BECOMES
A FRONTAGE ROAD BETWEEN TOWNS.
AVOID THE TEMPTATION TO DRIVE I-55.
MANY TOWNS ONLY HAVE ONE EXIT.
AND YOU'LL LOSE TIME DOUBLING BACK.
OR ELSE MISS A LOT BY SKIPPING TOWNS!

LEXINGTON ---21--- PONTIAC ---18--- DWIGHT ---10--- GARDNER ---11--- WILMINGTON

IL page-8

MEMORY LANE

WILMINGTON

GODLEY
BRACEVILLE
MAZONIA

BRAIDWOOD

GARDNER

DWIGHT

PONTIAC

ODELL

CHENOA

LEXINGTON

MOREHEAD ST (EARLY 66)

MAIN

EXIT 238
EXIT 236
EXIT 233
EXIT 227
EXIT 220
EXIT 217
EXIT 209
EXIT 201
EXIT 197
EXIT 187
EXIT 178

WB: Follow IL Hwy 53 thru **WILMINGTON**, and then thru **BRAIDWOOD**, **GODLEY** and **BRACEVILLE**. Curve south into **GARDNER**, and then turn **RIGHT** with **Hwy 53**. Cross the RR tracks, then take the next **LEFT** (before reaching Main St & EXIT 227). Follow the **Frontage Rd** southwest about **6 and 1/2 miles** to **Dwight Rd** (where Bypass 66 curves away), and jog **LEFT** into **DWIGHT**.

On the north side of **WILMINGTON** is a **GIANT ALERT**! One of three huge "brothers" on 66 in Illinois is the **GEMINI GIANT** at the **Launching Pad Drive In**. A great **PHOTO OP** with his space helmet and hand held rocket (great food, too).

SIDE TRIP: West of the **Kankakee River**, we're still using the earlier route, but the later version of '66 comes in from I-55 (EXIT 238) as **Hwy 129**, to parallel **Hwy 53** (with the RR tracks in-between). Unfortunately, the removal of a classic bridge cut this latter-day routing beyond **BRACEVILLE**, where the lower end is reached via **Mitchell St**. Access the upper end of this section from **Hwy 53** via Strip Mine Rd. Back on **HWY 53** in **BRAIDWOOD**, check out the **Polka Dot Drive In** with its '50s décor, then cross the tracks on **Hwy 113** to see the **1939 station** that houses **Lucenta Tire**.

North of **GARDNER** is the **Riviera**, a historic 1928 speakeasy with cool "stalactite" décor over the bar, and a former **streetcar diner** now being restored. **OPTION:** See the map to follow the early route thru **GARDNER**, a rewarding drive that winds its way thru "downtown" via Washington, Center, Depot, Jefferson and Jackson streets (the street signs are hard to read).

EB: From **Dwight Rd**, turn **RIGHT** and follow the **Frontage Rd** northeast. At the **Hwy 53** JCT (near EXIT 227, **BEFORE** Main St) turn **RIGHT** and cross over the RR tracks into **GARDNER**. Follow **Hwy 53** as it turns **LEFT**, and continue thru **BRACEVILLE**, **GODLEY**, **BRAIDWOOD** and **WILMINGTON**.

WB: Take **Dwight Rd** into **DWIGHT**. Curve **RIGHT** to **Hwy 47**, then **LEFT** to continue along the RR on **Macnamara**. After Hwy 47 branches off, curve **RIGHT** onto **Waupansie**, then **LEFT** to Hwy-17(Mazon Ave). Stay **AHEAD** on "**Old Route 66.**" At Bypass **66**, turn **LEFT**. Go about **5 and a half** miles, then jog **LEFT** on **Odell Rd** (becomes **West St**). Curve thru **ODELL**, leaving on **Odell Rd**. Turn **LEFT** at Bypass 66 (**Frontage Rd**). Go about **8 miles** to **Pontiac Rd**. Jog **LEFT** then **RIGHT** along the RR towards **PONTIAC**.

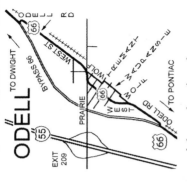

At the junction of Hwy 17 in **DWIGHT** is the old **Becker's Marathon Station** (1933). On the "National Register" as "**Ambler's Texaco,**" an earlier incarnation, its restoration as a visitor center is planned.

South of Hwy 17 (Mazon Ave) is **Smaterjax Grill and Pizzeria**, sited in a former car dealership full of old gas station stuff. **PHOTO OP:** Next door to **Route 66 Tire & Auto** is a charming display of old gas pumps and signs. **Downtown** has a depot museum and other attractions. **Lions Lake Park**, on the south side, is a nice place to stop and rest, with bathrooms and a jogging track. Town INFO: **(815) 584-2091**

ODELL boasts a classic **1932 Standard Station** (also on the Register), restored due to heroic volunteer effort and donations, a great showpiece (815) 998-2133 or (815) 458-6616. **SIDE TRIP:** See the detail map for an older (pre-66) route thru "downtown." South of town, watch for a pullout to view a restored "**Meramec Caverns**" barn sign, and then note the rustic old grain elevator at "**Cayuga.**" **SCAVENGER HUNT:** What tire brand is advertised on **Odell Station**? _____

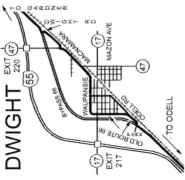

EB: Follow the **Frontage Rd** about **8 miles**, then jog **RIGHT** on **Odell Rd** into **ODELL**. Veer **LEFT** with **West St**. Curve thru town on West St and then along the RR (becomes **Odell Rd** again). Turn **RIGHT** on Bypass 66 (**Frontage Rd**). Go about **5 and a half** miles, and jog **RIGHT** onto "**Old Route 66**" in **DWIGHT**. At the "**Y**" with Odell Rd, veer **LEFT** with "**Old Route 66**" to the JCT with Hwy 17 (Mazon Ave). Stay **AHEAD** on **Waupansie St**, which curves **RIGHT**, then **LEFT** onto **Macnamara**, along the RR. Join Hwy 47 **AHEAD** and follow as it curves **LEFT** towards I-55, but quickly turn **RIGHT** to stay on **Dwight Rd**. At the **Frontage Rd**, turn **RIGHT**.

IL page-10

WB: Take Pontiac Rd into **PONTIAC**. Follow the gradual curve **RIGHT**, then curve **LEFT** onto **Division St**. Cross North Creek, then curve **RIGHT** onto **Ladd St**, and **LEFT** onto **Lincoln**, and **LEFT** onto **Ladd St**. Cross the JCT with Howard (**Hwy 116 joins**). At Reynolds, turn **RIGHT** with Hwy 116. Turn **LEFT** onto **Bypass 66** and follow the **Frontage Rd** thru **CHENOA** and **LEXINGTON** towards **TOWANDA**.

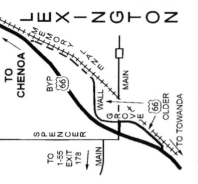

At the **Pontiac Rd** turnoff sits the **Old Log Cabin Restaurant**, another great old-time place dating back to 1926 and the birth of 66. Originally it fronted the old pavement beside the RR tracks, but was turned clear 'round to face the 4-Lane 66 bypass in the 1940s.

Enjoy the feel of old 66 as it zigzags thru **PONTIAC**. Imagine when **ALL** the truck and car traffic had to take these corners. Check out the **North Creek Bridge** on Ladd St. The original **Hwy 4 marker** (pre-dates '66) painted on the concrete rail was saved. **SIDE TRIP:** Be **SURE** to visit the **Route 66 Hall of Fame Museum** downtown at 110 W Howard St for exhibits of memorabilia from '66 Hall of Fame members, and much more. **GIFT SHOP ALERT!** (815) 844-5657.

HISTORIC NOTE: Older 66 took Morehead St thru **CHENOA**; the southern extension was obliterated. **SIDE TRIP:** US 24 will take you east to the historic, picturesque downtown area.

Just north of **LEXINGTON** is an abandoned stretch of 66 called "**Memory Lane**," open for hiking, and to cars during the annual **Taste of Country Fair Festival & Route 66 Reunion**, with vintage billboards and "Burma Shave" signs. **(309) 365-3331**

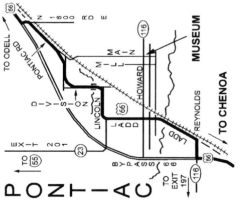

EB: Take the **Frontage Rd** thru **LEXINGTON** and **CHENOA** into **PONTIAC**. At Reynolds St/Hwy 116, turn **RIGHT**, then **LEFT** on Ladd St. Stay **AHEAD** across Howard St (Hwy 116 east). Follow the curve **RIGHT** onto **Lincoln**, then **LEFT** onto **Division**. Take the next curve **RIGHT**, then a gradual curve **LEFT** onto **Pontiac Rd**, along the RR. Curve up to **BYP 66**, and turn **RIGHT** towards **ODELL**.

(see **MAP # 2 on IL page-8**)

IL page-11

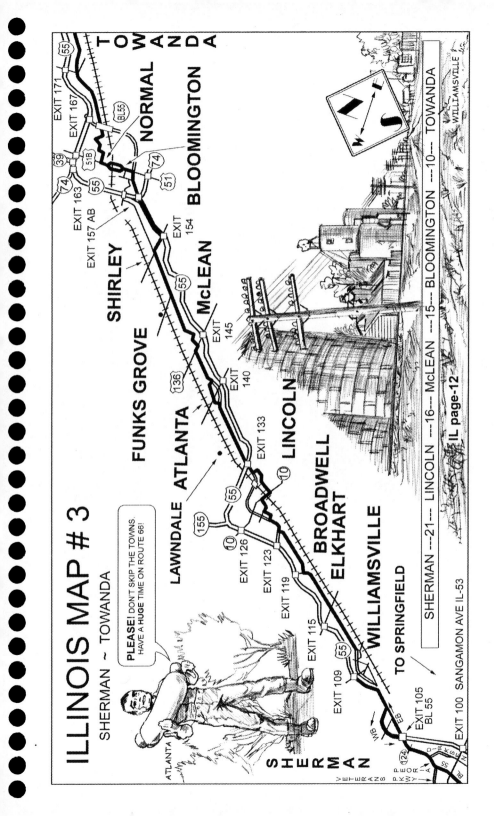

WB: From **LEXINGTON**, follow the **Frontage Rd** thru **TOWANDA**. Cross under Veterans Pkwy. Old 66 is cut ahead, so curve away from the tracks with **Shelbourne Dr**. Stay **AHEAD** across Towanda Dr, then turn **LEFT** on **Henry St**. Follow the curve onto **Pine St**. Cross Beech St, then turn **LEFT** on **Linden**. At the next light, turn **RIGHT** on **Willow**. Turn **LEFT** on **Main St (US 51B)** in **NORMAL**.

Tiny **TOWANDA** is rich in old 66 alignments, including infamous "**Dead Man's Curve**", where **Jackson St** bends sharply onto **Quincy** (see the **detail map** for this **SIDE TRIP** and two more old fragments). The town has made good use out of a portion of the abandoned westbound lanes of former 4-Lane 66, by creating a **Walking Tour** along the defunct roadway. Titled **Historic Rte 66 Illinois** "**A Geographic Journey**," the trail is complete with displays honoring all eight states and "Burma Shave" signs. They even have fliers printed in various languages. The tour begins at **Jefferson St** and ends at **Boyd Wesley Park**, which has toilets and a fishin' hole.

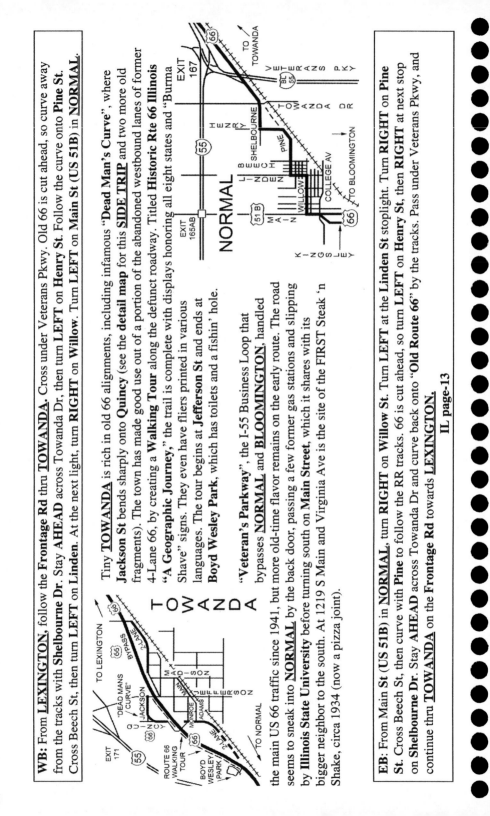

the main US 66 traffic since 1941, but more old-time flavor remains on the early route. The road seems to sneak into **NORMAL** by the back door, passing a few former gas stations and slipping by **Illinois State University** before turning south on **Main Street**, which it shares with its bigger neighbor to the south. At 1219 S Main and Virginia Ave is the site of the FIRST Steak 'n Shake, circa 1934 (now a pizza joint).

"**Veteran's Parkway**", the I-55 Business Loop that bypasses **NORMAL** and **BLOOMINGTON**, handled

EB: From **Main St (US 51B)** in **NORMAL**, turn **RIGHT** on **Willow St**. Turn **LEFT** at the **Linden St** stoplight. Turn **RIGHT** on **Pine St**. Cross Beech St, then curve with **Pine** to follow the RR tracks. 66 is cut ahead, so turn **LEFT** on **Henry St**, then **RIGHT** at next stop on **Shelbourne Dr**. Stay **AHEAD** across Towanda Dr and curve back onto "**Old Route 66**" by the tracks. Pass under Veterans Pkwy, and continue thru **TOWANDA** on the **Frontage Rd** towards **LEXINGTON**.

IL page-13

WB: Follow **Bus US 51** south (One-Way) from Willow St, into **BLOOMINGTON** and past downtown. At the JCT with **Veterans Pkwy** (**BL-55**), turn **RIGHT** and join **BL-55**. At **EXIT 157AB**, join **I-55** westbound. Take **EXIT 154**. From the offramp, turn **RIGHT**, then **LEFT** onto **Old Route 66** (N Frontage Rd) near **SHIRLEY**. Follow the **Frontage Rd** west along the railroad to **FUNKS GROVE**.

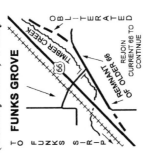

BLOOMINGTON has many claims to fame. It is the hometown of **M*A*S*H***'s "Colonel Blake" (the actor, **McLean Stevenson**, grew up here, as did his kin, **Adlai**). Here is also the world's sole source for "**Beer Nuts**." For those with a sweet tooth, there is the **Nestle** (formerly **Beich**) **Candy Factory**. Fill up on history at the **McLean Co Museum of History** (200 N Main) in the old 1903 courthouse downtown. Or, head to 1000 E Monroe St, for the "**David Davis Mansion State Historic Site**" where you can tour this 1872-era Victorian masterpiece. Visitor Info: (309)-665-0033. http://www.bloomingtonnormalcvb.org

OPTION: An old route south from downtown followed **Oakland** (**One-Way WB**) and **Morris** streets (see detail map). Near the corner of Wood and Morris is **Miller Park** (which dates back to 1887), home to a zoo, war memorials, an 18-acre lake and a restored dance pavilion.

The **SHIRLEY** exit leads to **FUNKS GROVE**. **SIDE TRIP**: The village is across the tracks at the crossroads, but a turn east across **Timber Creek** leads quickly to a short, bypassed strip of older 66 in the woods. South on **current** 66 is the home of **Funks Grove Maple "SIRUP"** (spelled thusly), sold since 1891. **GIFT SHOP ALERT!**

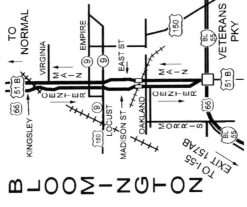

EB: Join **I-55 EB** at **EXIT 154** in **SHIRLEY**. At the **I-55 & I-70 JCT**, follow the signs at **EXIT 157B** to exit onto **Veterans Pkwy** (**BL-55**) into **BLOOMINGTON**. Exit at **Main St** (**Bus 51**) and turn **LEFT**. Follow **Main St** north (becomes One-Way). Stay with **Bus 51** as it veers onto **East St**, then back onto **Main**. Cross College Ave; prepare for the **RIGHT** turn onto **Willow St** in **NORMAL**.

IL page-14

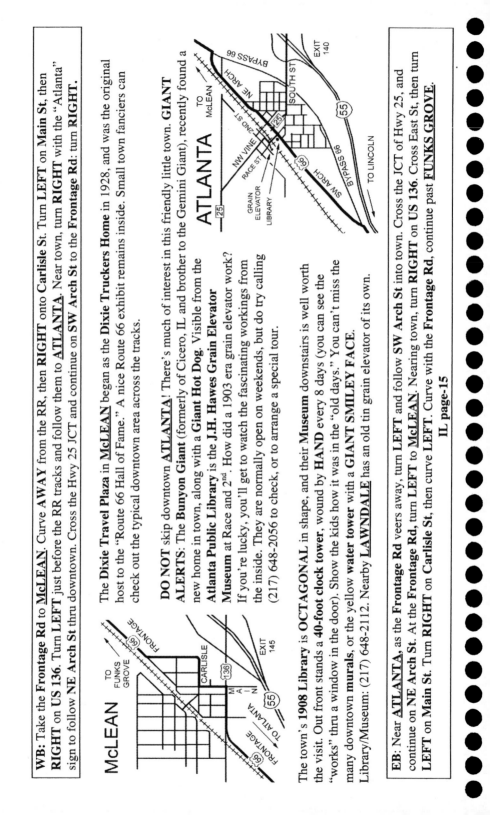

WB: Take the **Frontage Rd** to <u>McLEAN</u>. Curve AWAY from the RR, then RIGHT onto **Carlisle St**. Turn LEFT on **Main St**, then RIGHT on **US 136**. Turn LEFT just before the RR tracks and follow them to <u>ATLANTA</u>. Near town, turn RIGHT with the "Atlanta" sign to follow **NE Arch St** thru downtown. Cross the Hwy 25 JCT and continue on **SW Arch St** to the **Frontage Rd**: turn **RIGHT.**

McLEAN

The **Dixie Travel Plaza** in <u>McLEAN</u> began as the **Dixie Truckers Home** in 1928, and was the original host to the "Route 66 Hall of Fame." A nice Route 66 exhibit remains inside. Small town fanciers can check out the typical downtown area across the tracks.

DO NOT skip downtown <u>ATLANTA</u>! There's much of interest in this friendly little town. **GIANT ALERTS:** The **Bunyon Giant** (formerly of Cicero, IL and brother to the Gemini Giant), recently found a new home in town, along with a **Giant Hot Dog**. Visible from the **Atlanta Public Library** is the **J.H. Hawes Grain Elevator Museum** at Race and 2nd. How did a 1903 era grain elevator work? If you're lucky, you'll get to watch the fascinating workings from the inside. They are normally open on weekends, but do try calling (217) 648-2056 to check, or to arrange a special tour.

ATLANTA

The town's **1908 Library** is OCTAGONAL in shape, and their **Museum** downstairs is well worth the visit. Out front stands a **40-foot clock tower**, wound by **HAND** every 8 days (you can see the "works" thru a window in the door). Show the kids how it was in the "old days." You can't miss the many downtown **murals**, or the yellow **water tower** with a **GIANT SMILEY FACE.** Nearby <u>LAWNDALE</u> has an old tin grain elevator of its own. Library/Museum: (217) 648-2112.

EB: Near <u>ATLANTA</u>, as the **Frontage Rd** veers away, turn LEFT and follow **SW Arch St** into town. Cross the JCT of Hwy 25, and continue on **NE Arch St**. At the **Frontage Rd**, turn LEFT to <u>McLEAN</u>. Nearing town, turn RIGHT on **US 136**. Cross East St, then turn LEFT on **Main St**. Turn RIGHT on **Carlisle St**, then curve LEFT. Curve with the **Frontage Rd**, continue past **FUNKS GROVE.**

WB: Follow the **Frontage Rd** under I-55 at EXIT 133: stay **AHEAD** with **BL 55 (Lincoln Pkwy)** into **LINCOLN**. Turn **LEFT** with the signs and curve with **BL 55** onto **Kickapoo St**. Turn **RIGHT** on **Keokuk**, cross the tracks, then **LEFT** on **Logan** (still **BL 55**). Cross Broadway, then veer **RIGHT** past Clinton onto **5**th **St**. Past Jefferson St, turn **LEFT** on **Washington**. Cross the tracks (now **Stringer St**) and join **BL 55 (Lincoln Pkwy)** south. Before reaching EXIT 123, turn **LEFT** at "**Frontage Rd Entrance**" and head to **BROADWELL**. Approaching EXIT 119, curve to a **STOP**, then **LEFT** on the **Frontage Rd** thru town. Pass thru **ELKHART** to **WILLIAMSVILLE**.

LINCOLN, named for Honest Abe, has plenty of historic sites, plus the **Lincoln College Museum** (300 Keokuk) and the **Heritage in Flight Museum** (Logan County Airport). A replica of the 1841 Postville Courthouse is sited on 5th St (inquire locally).

GIANT ALERT SIDE TRIP! The **GIANT Abe Lincoln** and wagon, formerly of Divernon, Illinois has moved to the corner of Lincoln Pkwy (BYP 66) and IL Hwy 10 (Woodlawn). Hope he sits still a while. Another nearby Lincoln site is the place where he christened the town with watermelon juice (from a cup!) in 1853 (Broadway and Chicago St). Lincoln INFO: www.lincolnillinois.com or (217) 735-2385.

In itty-bitty **BROADWELL**, the **Pig Hip Museum**, honoring the famed café that began in 1937, home of the "Pig Hip Sandwich," burned down. **Ernie Edwards** ("the Old Coot on Route 66") and his wife still welcome visitors next door, where he spins fascinating yarns of his 60 years along Route 66. INFO: (217) 732-2337. Grain elevators dominate the skyline of **ELKHART** (its charming downtown is across the tracks).

LINCOLN

EB: Take the **Frontage Rd** thru **ELKHART** and **BROADWELL**. Before the EXIT 119 overpass, turn **RIGHT** at "**Frontage Rd Entrance**." Near EXIT 123, turn **RIGHT** onto **BL 55 (Lincoln Pkwy)** into **LINCOLN**. Cross Salt Creek and Broadwell Dr, then **ANGLE RIGHT** onto **Stringer St**. Cross the tracks (now **Washington St**), then turn **RIGHT** on **5**th **St** (**BL 55**). Past Union, **ANGLE LEFT** onto **Logan**. Cross Lincoln Ave and turn **RIGHT** on **Keokuk**. Cross the tracks, then turn **LEFT** on **Kickapoo** (still **BL 55**) to the JCT with **Lincoln Pkwy**: turn **RIGHT**. Cross under I-55 at EXIT 133, and stay **AHEAD** to **ATLANTA**.

IL page-16

WB: Enter **WILLIAMSVILLE** on **Oak St** (BYP 66). Turn **LEFT** on **Elm**. Cross Main and curve along the tracks with **Spur 66**. At the end of Elm turn **RIGHT**, then **RIGHT** on Oak. At **Stuttle Rd**, turn **LEFT**. **JOIN I-55**, turn **LEFT**. Take **EXIT 105** and **JOIN BL 55/Sherman Blvd** thru **SHERMAN** (becomes Peoria Rd). Stay with **BL 55** past the JCT of Dirksen Pkwy. Be in the **LEFT LANE** under the RR tracks, and follow **BL 55/Peoria Rd LEFT** from the Veteran's Pkwy stoplight, past Sangamon Ave and onto 9th St in **SPRINGFIELD**.

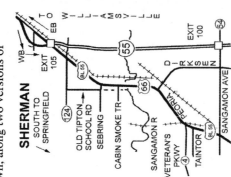

WILLIAMSVILLE is small enough that the guide takes you on a "loop" thru town, along two versions of '66. West on **BYP 66** (Oak) is the **Dream Car Museum**, which houses an admirable collection of nostalgic autos and relics: a must for the car buff (217) 566-3799. **Die Cast Auto Sales**, at 117 N Elm, consists of a 1930's era gas station filled with toy cars and collectibles, plus old gas pumps and signs on view outside. **SCAVENGER HUNT!** What railroad name is painted on the old **boxcar** that houses the **Williamsville Museum** near Elm and Main?

SIDE TRIP: The old route thru **SHERMAN** went west on **Hwy 124** (Andrew) and south on **Old Tipton School Rd** (see detail map).

NOTE: Dirksen Pkwy was a bypass of earlier 66 around **SPRINGFIELD**. Peoria Rd, is **Shea's Historic Route 66 Museum**. Barely contained in this former fuel-outlet is the long-time owner's extensive personal collection of photos and gas station goodies. An even-older station was relocated and restored next door (217) 522-0475. Despite the signs, Taintor Rd was evidently NOT "1926-'30" US 66.

Some motel relics remain, but the road is rough in places. South of the **Illinois State Fairgrounds**, at 2075

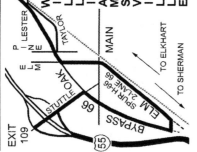

EB: Follow **BL 55/ Peoria Rd** past Sangamon Ave. Turn **RIGHT** with **BL 55** at **Veteran's Pkwy**, cross under the RR. Pass the JCT with Dirksen Pkwy. Across the Sangamon River, Peoria becomes **Sherman Blvd** thru **SHERMAN**. At **EXIT 105**, cross under **I-55**, and stay **AHEAD** along the RR. **Merge onto I-55 EB**. Take **EXIT 109** at **WILLIAMSVILLE**, turn **RIGHT** on Stuttle, then **RIGHT** on Oak (BYP 66). At Oak's end, turn **LEFT**, then **LEFT** onto ELM. Curve up to cross Main. At Oak, turn **RIGHT** onto the Frontage Rd.

(see MAP # 3 on IL page-12)

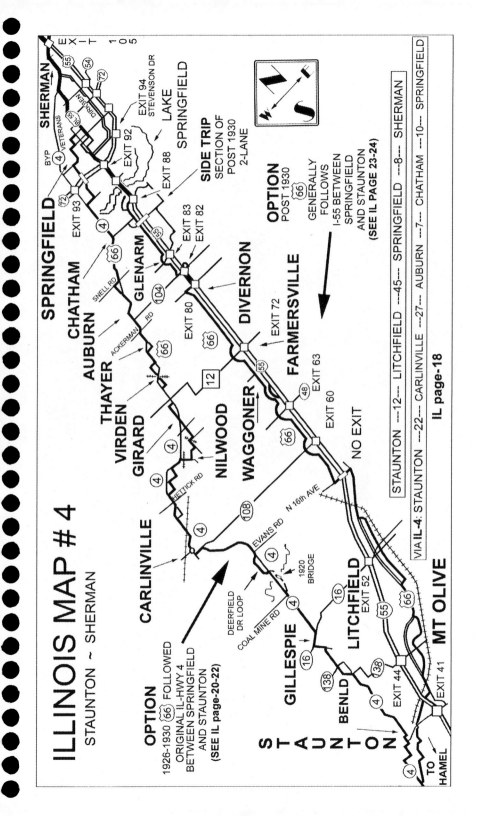

ILLINOIS MAP # 4

STAUNTON ~ SHERMAN

OPTION
1926-1930 66 FOLLOWED
ORIGINAL IL-HWY 4
BETWEEN SPRINGFIELD
AND STAUNTON
(SEE IL page-20-22)

OPTION
POST 1930 66
GENERALLY
FOLLOWS
I-55 BETWEEN
SPRINGFIELD
AND STAUNTON
(SEE IL PAGE 23-24)

SIDE TRIP
SECTION OF
POST 1930 2-LANE

EXIT 105
EXIT 94 STEVENSON DR
EXIT 92
EXIT 93
EXIT 88
EXIT 83
EXIT 82
EXIT 80
EXIT 72
EXIT 63
EXIT 60
EXIT 52
EXIT 44
EXIT 41

SHERMAN
SPRINGFIELD
LAKE SPRINGFIELD
CHATHAM
AUBURN
THAYER
VIRDEN
GIRARD
GLENARM
NILWOOD
WAGGONER
DIVERNON
FARMERSVILLE
CARLINVILLE
GILLESPIE
BENLD
LITCHFIELD
MT OLIVE
STAUNTON
TO HAMEL

SNELL RD
ACKERMAN RD
HETTICK RD
EVANS RD
N 16th AVE
1920 BRIDGE
DEERFIELD DR LOOP
COAL MINE RD
NO EXIT

BYP
VETERANS

| STAUNTON ---12--- LITCHFIELD ---45--- SPRINGFIELD ---8--- SHERMAN |

| VIA IL-4: STAUNTON ---22--- CARLINVILLE ---27--- AUBURN ---7--- CHATHAM ---10--- SPRINGFIELD |

IL page-18

(NOTE: see IL page-20 for the OPTIONAL 1926-1930 Route, or see IL page-23 to continue via the Post 1930 Route)

WB: Follow 9th St /BL 55 south past downtown **SPRINGFIELD**. Cross S Grand. Turn **RIGHT** on **Spruce** (One –Way), then **LEFT** on 5th St (One-Way). Follow **BL 55** south past Stevenson Dr to **EXIT 92** and JOIN **I-55** southbound.

If you want Abe Lincoln sites, then **SPRINGFIELD** has 'em! The **Lincoln Home, Tomb** and **Presidential Library** for starters. Of course, there's a statue of Abe at the Capitol, but at only 10 and a half feet, it's not very exciting. **GIANT ALERT #1:** Thankfully, a **30-foot statue** of a young, skinny Lincoln stands near Gate #1 of the Fair Grounds. Very picturesque is the **OLD State Capitol** at Adams and 6th St, and there's plenty more. City INFO: (217) 525-1173.

OPTION: EB you can follow the **1930-era Route** along 6th St (One-Way) north from Myrtle thru downtown. Then turn right on **Enos St** to rejoin **BL 55**. But don't miss the famed **Cozy Dog Drive-In** (sometimes haunt of Route 66 artist Bob Waldmire) on the **tour route** between Stevenson Dr and the RR overpass, south of town. Off I-72 to the west is the **"Route 66 Drive-In Theatre"** (not on 66 but close to Old Chatham Rd) at **Knights Action Park.**

GIANT ALERT #2 I never get "tired" of the **Lauderbach Giant** at Lauderbach's Tire and Auto Service on the north side of Wabash St (the 1926-'30 route). He's the last of the three giant "brothers' on '66 in Illinois (more giants to come, including a **"Muffler Man"** just west).

WB OPTION: Hwy 4 carried '66 from **1926 to 1930** (IL page-20). This route offers many zigzag turns on old concrete-slab roads (plus some brick road) thru charming towns. The **Post-'30** route, along I-55 thru **LITCHFIELD** and **MT OLIVE**, also has much to offer **(IL page-23)**. If you decide on **Hwy 4**, try to cut over on **Hwy 16** to these two towns, at least.

EB: From I-55, take **EXIT 92** (LEFT EXIT) and follow **BL 55** north into **SPRINGFIELD**. Pass Stevenson Dr, then follow the split onto 6th St north (One-Way). Turn **RIGHT** on Myrtle (One-Way), then **LEFT** on 9th /BL 55 north, past downtown.

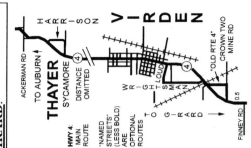

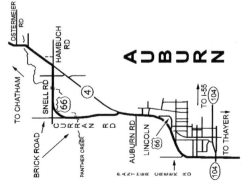

OPTIONAL 1926-'30 ROUTE WB: In <u>SPRINGFIELD</u>, follow Capitol Ave west from 9th St. (map IL page-19). Turn **LEFT** on 2nd at the Capitol. Turn **RIGHT** on S Grand. Turn **LEFT** on Macarthur. Turn **RIGHT** on Wabash. Turn **LEFT** on Old Chatham Rd, and cross I-72 to Woodside Rd: turn **RIGHT**. At Hwy 4, turn **LEFT** and follow Hwy 4 thru <u>CHATHAM</u>. Past Ostermeier Rd, turn **RIGHT** on Snell Rd, then curve left on Curran Rd. Rejoin Hwy 4 south thru <u>AUBURN, THAYER</u> and <u>VIRDEN</u> to <u>GIRARD.</u>

Leaving <u>SPRINGFIELD</u>, wave "Bye" to the Lauderbach Giant on Wabash. <u>**SIDE TRIP**</u>: Off Woodside Rd (0.2 mi west from Chatham Rd) a dead end section of "Old Chatham Rd" runs for under a mile, ending at a swampy area and the closed "**Snake Bridge**" over Lick Creek.

On Snell and Curran Road, between <u>CHATHAM</u> and <u>AUBURN</u>, is a rare 1.4-mile stretch of **BRICK** road (red, not yellow but still a "trip."). **Watch the detail maps** as you travel the **1926-30 Route**. They will point out <u>OPTIONAL</u> sections of **Pre-'30 66** not included in the main tour. Look carefully for two short doglegs (**Planter and Tiller Roads**) at a curve centered on Ackerman Rd (2 miles south of Hwy 104 and <u>AUBURN</u>). Check the map for a dog-leg in <u>THAYER</u>, and the section south from <u>VIRDEN</u>. It's amazing how much this old road hopped around. The <u>VIRDEN</u> town square has the **Battle of Virden Monument**, a series of bronze, bas-relief sculptures memorializing a bloody struggle between coal miners and mine owners back in 1898.

EB: Follow Hwy 4 north thru <u>VIRDEN, THAYER</u> and <u>AUBURN</u>. Past Auburn Rd, turn **LEFT** onto Curran Rd. Curve **RIGHT** on Snell Rd. Rejoin Hwy 4 north thru <u>CHATHAM</u>. About **2** miles north, turn **RIGHT** on Woodside Dr, then **LEFT** on Old Chatham Rd to <u>SPRINGFIELD</u> (see map on IL Page-19). Cross I-72. Turn **RIGHT** on Wabash. Turn **LEFT** on Macarthur. Turn **RIGHT** on South Grand, then **LEFT** on 2nd . At Capitol Ave, turn **RIGHT**. Turn **LEFT** on 9th St/BL-55 to <u>SHERMAN</u>. (see IL page-19).

IL page-20

WB: In <u>GIRARD</u>, turn **RIGHT** on **Madison St**, and **LEFT** on **6**th **St**. Stay **AHEAD** across Hwy 4 on **Cambridge Rd**. Turn **RIGHT** on **Wylder**, then **LEFT**, past the RR underpass. Turn **RIGHT** on **Moream Rd**. Turn **LEFT** on **Pine** and **RIGHT** on **Morean St** in <u>NILWOOD</u>. At Hwy 4 turn **LEFT**, go **1.8 miles**, then **LEFT** on **Donaldson Rd**. Follow the next corner **RIGHT**. Approaching Hwy 4, curve **LEFT** again with **Donaldson Rd**. Turn **RIGHT** at **Allen Rd**, and **LEFT** on Hwy 4 to <u>CARLINVILLE</u>.

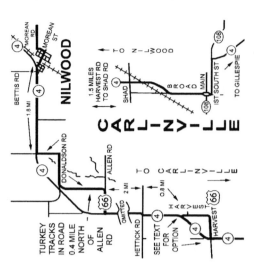

The section from <u>GIRARD</u> to <u>NILWOOD</u> is fantastic, a slice of the 1920s winding tipsy thru the farmland. Frequently a crack, like the snaking course of a river, meanders along the middle of this evocative concrete road.

<u>SCAVENGER HUNT</u>! What's the **DATE** on the small brick and concrete bridge-rail on Cambridge Rd? _____

West of <u>NILWOOD</u>, The **Donaldson Road** zigzags are another great drive. Look for the turkey tracks, highlited in white, in the concrete on Donaldson Rd, 0.4 miles north of Allen Rd.

<u>OPTION</u>: About 0.8 of a mile south of Hettick Rd, **Harvest Rd** performs yet another quaint dogleg.

<u>CARLINVILLE</u>'s brick-lined square defines picturesque, as does their impressive domed **courthouse** from 1870.

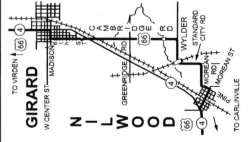

EB: Take Hwy 4 from <u>CARLINVILLE</u>. Cross Hettick Rd. Go **2 miles**, turn **RIGHT** on **Allen Rd**, then **LEFT** on **Donaldson Rd**. Nearing Hwy 4, curve **RIGHT** with **Donaldson Rd**, then curve **LEFT** up to Hwy 4: turn **RIGHT**. In <u>NILWOOD</u>, turn **RIGHT** on **Morean St**, then **LEFT** on Pine. Turn **RIGHT** on **Morean Rd**, then **LEFT** on **Standard City Rd**. Curve **RIGHT** on **Wylder**, under the RR, then **LEFT** on **Cambridge Rd**. Cross Hwy 4, stay **AHEAD** on **6**th St into <u>GIRARD</u>. **RIGHT** on **Madison**, then **LEFT** on Hwy 4.

IL page–21

WB: In <u>CARLINVILLE</u>, follow **Hwy 4** thru the square, then **LEFT** on **1st South St** (Hwy 108). Take **Hwy 4** as it turns **RIGHT** from Hwy 108. **5 miles further** (past Evans Rd), turn **RIGHT** on **Deerfield Dr.** Back at **Hwy 4** turn **RIGHT** towards <u>GILLESPIE</u>. Follow **Hwy 4** as it turns **RIGHT** with **Hwy 16** on **Elm St**, then **LEFT** on **Macoupin**, and **RIGHT** on **Pine** to Staunton Rd. Stay with **Hwy 4** south thru **BENLD** to <u>STAUNTON</u>. In town, jog **RIGHT** on North, then **LEFT** on Hibbard, **RIGHT** on Pearl, and **LEFT** on Hackman. Take **Hwy 4** south (past the JCT with <u>Post-1930 66</u>) to <u>HAMEL</u>. (for **Post-1930 66** see **IL page-24**)

S T A U N T O N

Sleepy? The **Carlin-Villa Motel** (217 854-3201) on the south side gets good reviews. Watch for **abandoned sections** of road along this stretch. About 5 miles south of Hwy 108, be sure to follow the tour along **Deerfield Dr**, as the road curves along a scenic section thru forest and hills. The currently-blocked southern loop crosses a stout (but endangered) little concrete bridge from 1920. After a zig thru **GILLESPIE** and **BENLD**, keep watch on the west for the **Coliseum Ballroom**, a historic structure dating to 1924 that houses a great antique mall. **GIANT ALERT!** The **Coliseum** is now home to a **Giant Surfer Dude** (a prop from the movie "Flatliners"), and a not so big PINK Elephant. **STAUNTON** (also see **IL page-24**) has two glazed-brick former gas stations on Hwy 4.

G I L L E S P I E

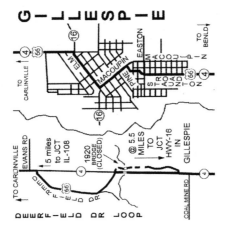

EB: 1926-'30 ROUTE (see **IL page-24** for Post-1930 Route): Follow **Hwy 4** north to <u>STAUNTON</u>. Curve to enter on **Hackman St**, then **RIGHT** on Pearl, and **LEFT** on Hibbard. Jog **RIGHT** on North, and **LEFT** on Edwardsville Rd. Follow **Hwy 4** thru <u>BENLD</u> into <u>GILLESPIE</u>, curving **RIGHT** on Pine, then **LEFT** on Macoupin, and **RIGHT** on Elm with **Hwy 16**. Stay with **Hwy 4** as it turns **LEFT** leaving town. After about **5.5 miles** (past Coal Mine Rd) turn **LEFT** on **Deerfield Dr.** Back at **Hwy 4**: turn **LEFT**. At **Hwy 108** (**1st South St**) turn **LEFT** into <u>CARLINVILLE</u>. Turn **RIGHT** on **Broad St**, pass thru the square, then stay with **Hwy 4** north.

IL page-22

WB: (POST 1930) Take I-55 from Exit 92 to Exit 88. Take the **West Frontage Rd** south thru <u>GLENARM</u>. Rejoin **I-55 SB** at **EXIT 82.** Take **EXIT 80** at <u>DIVERNON</u>. Take the **West Frontage Rd** south past **FARMERSVILLE, WAGGONER** and **EXIT 60**. Next, cross over I-55 at **N 16th Ave** (no exit). Turn **RIGHT** on **"Old Route 66."** Nearing **LITCHFIELD**, cross the RR overpass, then quick-**LEFT** on **"1930-40 66"** into town. Cross Hwy 16, stay **AHEAD** on **"1930-40 66."** At **N 10th Ave**, turn **RIGHT**, then **LEFT** on **"Route 66."**

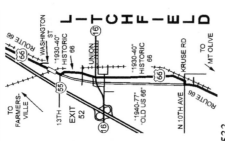

L-I-T-C-H-F-I-E-L-D

ADVISORY: Parts of the **Frontage Rd** south of **EXIT 80** can be bumpy.

SIDE TRIP #1: East of I-55 between **EXIT 88** and **83**, you can drive old **2-Lane 66** (circa 1930) by following the detail map. Or, in **Bridgeview Park** off **EXIT 88** is a dead-end section of **4-Lane 66**, just south of **Lake Springfield** (which cut the route).

SIDE TRIP #2: Follow the signs on **Ponyshoe Lane** and **Pulliam Rd** to **Sugar Creek Covered Bridge**, just over a mile west, to walk this **1880** span.

In **FARMERSVILLE** is the oft-photographed sign of the newly remodeled **Art's Motel**. South from <u>WAGGONER</u> is **"Our Lady of the Highways"** shrine, blessing the road since 1959. A series of signs along a nearby fence recite the **"Hail Mary."**

Linger in <u>LITCHFIELD</u> for the classic **SkyView Drive-in Theatre** (one of few left on 66) and well-preserved and recommended **Ariston Café** from 1931. Or check out the **Route 66 Café** nearby. City INFO: www.litchfieldil.com/chamber/ or (217) 324-2533.

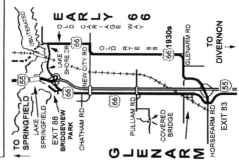

GLENARM

EB: Near <u>LITCHFIELD</u>, turn **RIGHT** at **N 10th Ave** and **LEFT** onto **"1930-40 66."** Stay **AHEAD** past Hwy 16, then **RIGHT** on **Route 66.** Take the **Frontage Rd** for 3 miles, then **LEFT** on **N 16th Ave**, to cross **I-55**. Go **RIGHT** on **"Old Rte 66"** (West Frontage Rd), past **WAGGONER** and **FARMERSVILLE**. At <u>DIVERNON</u>, join **I-55 NB**, via **EXIT 80**. Take **EXIT 82**, curve back to **Hwy 104**, and cross under I-55. At **EXIT 88**, join **I-55 north** to **EXIT 92**. Turn **RIGHT** to rejoin the **W Frontage Rd** thru <u>GLENARM</u>. At **EXIT 88**, join I-55 north to **EXIT 92.**

(See IL page-19 to continue)

IL page-23

WB: Cross St James Rd, then turn **LEFT** on **"Old Rte 66 St"** into **MT OLIVE**. Follow **"Old Rte 66 St"** across the JCT of Hwy 138 and on out of town. At **"US Hwy 66 St"** (BYP 66) turn **LEFT**. Cross under the RR overpass, then turn **RIGHT** on **"Old Rte 66."** Cross I-55 (no exit). At the JCT of Staunton Rd, cross onto **"Historic Old Rte 66 St,"** which curves along the edge of **STAUNTON**. Leave on **Madison St** (becomes **Sievers Rd**), and follow the curve **RIGHT** onto **Williamson Rd**. At Hwy 4, turn **LEFT** towards **HAMEL**.

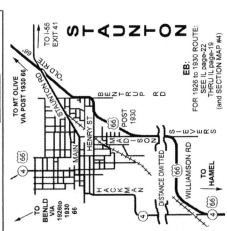

PHOTO OP! The gem of **MT OLIVE** is the restored **Soulsby Station**. Resplendent with its antique red and yellow Shell gas pumps, the station, dating from 1926, sold gas along the road for 65 years. Also, you might visit the **Mother Jones Monument** in the Union Miner's Cemetery on the north side of town.

STAUNTON is where the **PRE and POST-1930** routes of US 66 meet. (**EB:** see **IL page-22** for the **1926-'30 Route**). The **POST-1930** road, which staggers along the edge of town, was in turn bypassed in **1940** by a route thru **LIVINGSTON** along I-55. But Old 66 is really hopping in **STAUNTON**, at **Henry's Rabbit Ranch & Route 66 Emporium**, near Madison St on **POST-'30 66**. Check out the cute critters, and admire the truck and trailers bearing the likeness of **"Snortin' Norton,"** beloved mascot of the defunct **Campbell 66 Express** truck line. **GIFT SHOP ALERT!**

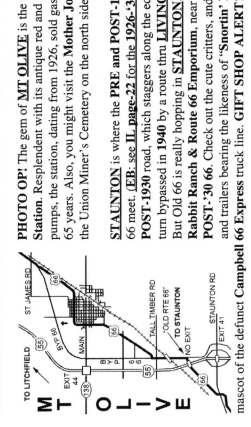

EB: (See **IL page-22** for **1926-'30 Route**). Take **Hwy 4** north. Cross the RR tracks, then turn **RIGHT** 2 miles later onto **Williamson Rd**. At **Sievers Rd**, curve **LEFT** (becomes **Madison**) into **STAUNTON**. At the **"Y"**, follow **"Historic Old Rte 66 St"** as it angles **RIGHT**, curving along the edge of town. Angle to the JCT with Staunton Rd. Cross onto **"Old Rte 66"** and then cross I-55. Turn **LEFT** on **East Frontage Rd**, and pass under the RR Overpass. Prepare for a quick **RIGHT** turn onto **Mt Olive Rd/Old Rte 66**. Enter **MT OLIVE**, cross the JCT with Hwy 138, and curve thru town to the JCT with **"US Hwy 66 St"** (Bypass 66): turn **RIGHT** towards **LITCHFIELD**.

(see **MAP # 4 on IL page-18**)

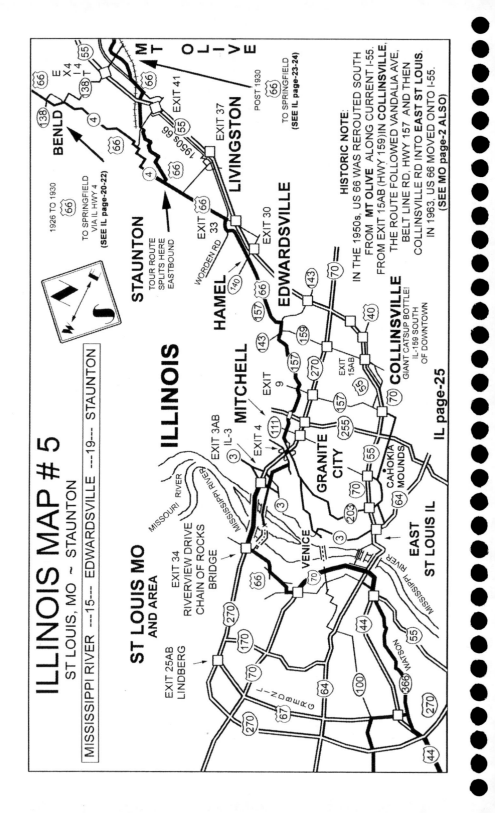

WB: Take **Hwy 4** south from **STAUNTON**. Nearing EXIT 33, turn **RIGHT** with **Worden Rd**, then a quick **LEFT** to continue on the **Frontage Rd** to **HAMEL**. Cross Hwy 140 and join **Hwy 157** ahead to **EDWARDSVILLE**. In town, turn **RIGHT** with **Hwy 157**, past downtown, then follow **Hwy 157 LEFT** at **West St**. When Hwy 157 turns left at S University Dr (near I-270 EXIT 9) stay **AHEAD** thru the stoplight and curve around onto **Chain of Rocks Rd**. Cross over I-255(no exit) and thru the Hwy 111 JCT into **MITCHELL**.

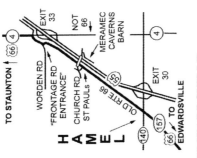

South of **STAUNTON**, you pass **Decamp Junction**, a classic roadhouse from way back. A "roadhouse" of worship is the **St. Paul Lutheran Church** with the **Neon Cross of Route 66**. Over across I-55 is the second of two restored **Meramec Caverns Barns** in Illinois. In the old days, these painted advertisements for the **MISSOURI** cave were everywhere along the road.

Another driver-fuel stop is **Scotty's Route 66 Grille** in **HAMEL**. If you are driving north on **I-55** (for SHAME!) stop at the **Tourist Info Center**, on I-55 north of **HAMEL**, to get the scoop, from the Route 66 display, on what you're missing by taking the freeway!

Watch for remnants of the old interurban right of way along 157 to **EDWARDSVILLE**. The **Stagger Inn** on Vandalia St offers live music for a diverse crowd.

SIDE TRIP: West of town, turn south at **Meridian St**, following the signs for about 2 miles to the **Covered Bridge** (drive it!) and **Yanda Log Cabin** (1853), in neighboring **GLEN CARBON**. Back on '66, look for the **Bel Air Drive-In** sign past **Hwy 111** (if it's still there).

EDWARDSVILLE

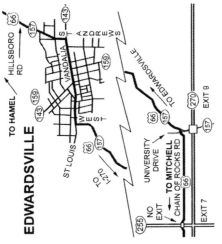

EB: Take **Chain of Rocks Rd** from **MITCHELL**, past the Hwy 111 JCT and over I-255(no exit). At the **Hwy 157 JCT**, stay **AHEAD** and follow **Hwy 157** uphill into **EDWARDSVILLE**. Turn **RIGHT** with **Hwy 157** onto **St Louis St**, and bear **RIGHT** at the "**Y**". Stay with **Hwy 157** thru downtown as **Vandalia St**. Leaving, turn **LEFT** with **Hwy 157**, to the Hwy 140 JCT in **HAMEL**. Stay **AHEAD** onto "**Old Rte 66**," which is the **Frontage Rd**. Nearing EXIT 33, turn **RIGHT** at **Worden Rd**, then **LEFT** onto Hwy 4 to **STAUNTON**.

WB: In <u>MITCHELL</u>, curve left with **Hwy 203**. Before reaching the underpass, get in the left lane, and turn **LEFT** onto the "West I-270" onramp (avoid the off ramp). Immediately after crossing the overpass over the tracks, take the curving ramp down onto **Old Alton Rd**. Turn **RIGHT** and cross under I-270. **AVOID** the on and offramps, then turn **RIGHT** onto the **Frontage Rd** and curve back onto **Chain of Rocks Rd**. At the **Hwy-3 JCT**, turn **RIGHT** and **JOIN I-270 WB** to continue into <u>MISSOURI</u>. (see map on MO page-2)

That '66 feel remains on **Chain of Rocks Rd**, with old motels and signs along the way. The **Luna Café** in <u>MITCHELL</u> (1924) has a great neon sign and quite a history, involving gangsters (Al Capone drove 66!) gambling and "ladies of the night," whose presence was announced by lighting the "cherry" on the neon sign. Its much tamer, now. <u>**SIDE TRIP**</u>: Head west to the <u>ILLINOIS</u> end of the **Chain of Rocks Bridge** for a scenic 4-mile round trip. You can hike across this famous "bent" bridge from the dead end, or from the **MO** side (a bit of a tight turn around for RVs at this end). As always, safeguard your stuff.

Over time, **Route 66** used a bewildering tangle of "main" and "city" routes to cross into <u>MISSOURI</u>, many of which are either under a freeway, or not "tourist friendly" (too complicated, rough, scary, etc). The 1926 route took Nameoki Rd thru <u>GRANITE CITY</u>, then passed thru <u>MADISON</u>, to cross the **Mickinley Bridge** in <u>VENICE</u> (open in 2007). In 1929, US 66 used **Hwy 3** (also **Hwy 203**) south from <u>VENICE</u> to <u>EAST ST LOUIS</u>. Matters are just as complex on the other side of the river, so stick to the "official" **tour route** for now, or use **I-270** (part of the **POST-1936** path of **US 66**) or **I-255 / I-270** to circle past the <u>ST LOUIS</u> area, if time or traffic require. Then double back into <u>ST LOUIS</u> via MO 366.

EB: Take **I-270 EB** across the **Mississippi River** into <u>ILLINOIS</u>. At **EXIT 3A**, join **Hwy 3** south, then **QUICKLY** turn **LEFT** onto **Chain of Rocks Rd**. Follow the curve down to **Old Alton Rd**. Turn **LEFT**, then **LEFT** again onto the "East I-270" onramp (avoid the offramp) before reaching the underpass. Curve up to and over the overpass, then immediately take the next offramp to curve down to **Hwy 203** (Nameoki Rd). Turn **RIGHT**, cross under I-270, and follow the curve back onto **Chain of Rocks Rd** in <u>MITCHELL</u>.

(see Illinois INTRO on IL page-1)   IL page-27   (see MAP # 5 on IL page-25)

SHOW ME MISSOURI!

MISSOURI sure has plenty to show the Route 66 road warrior. From the sprawling city and suburbs of **ST LOUIS**, to the former mining region of **JOPLIN**, with the forested limestone hills of the **Ozarks** in between, **MISSOURI** loves company.

US 66 inherited the path of **State HWY 14**, then was upgraded and finally 4-laned for much of the over 300-mile length in the 1950s. Some of this **4-Lane 66** was later rebuilt to I-44 standards, while other sections, such as near **DEVILS ELBOW**, survive, as do many miles of multi-generation **2-lane road.**

ST LOUIS, gateway to the west, nests in a tangled web of roads and freeways. Over the decades, US 66 used a bewildering variety of streets thru the region: main, city, truck, bypass and optional routes made worse by later road building and One-Way streets. The maps that follow this urban area show **SOME** of those bygone alignments, but **NOT** all the myriad routes. To make it a bit **EZ**-er, the official tour uses a combo of **City 66** (Riverview to Florissant) and **I-70** to connect **Chain of Rocks Bridge** to downtown. If time or traffic conditions require you to cross the area quickly, use I-270 to bypass the city on the north (this was path of **Post 1936 Route 66**), then follow US 67 south from Exit 25AB to Watson Rd. Optionally, I-255 heads south to connect with I-270, then joins I-44. To the west, see **MO page-8** for the **PRE-1932 OPTION** along **MO HWY 100**.

Most of **Route 66** thru the state is more serene, including many scenic wooded drives thru hills and valleys out of sight of the superslab. The people are friendly and history abounds, as do relics of the roadside past. Enjoy what **MISSOURI** has to show. **CAR GAME:** **"Historic 66."** Look for brown and white **"Historic 66"** signs. The **FIRST** to spot one gets a letter. The first to spell **"HISTORIC"** wins!

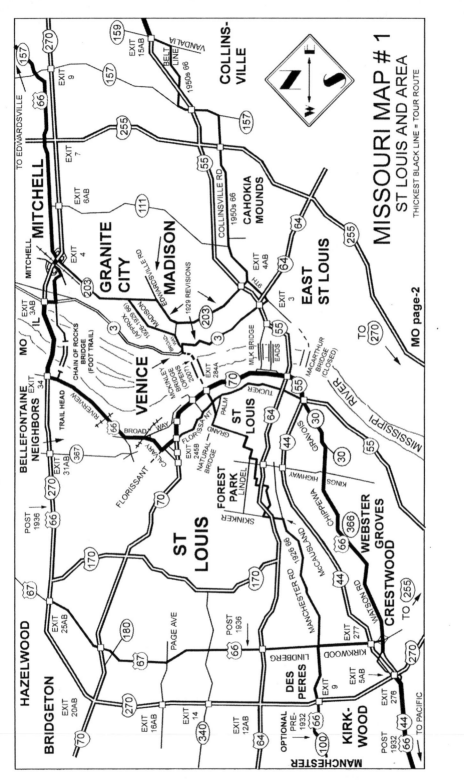

MISSOURI MAP # 1
ST LOUIS AND AREA
THICKEST BLACK LINE = TOUR ROUTE

MO page-2

WB: From **I-270 EXIT 34**, follow **Riverside Dr** south. Turn Left on **Broadway**. Just past the RR overpass turn **RIGHT** at the light, and curve uphill, between the cemeteries, on **Calvary**. At the next light, turn **LEFT** on **Florissant**. At **EXIT 245B**, cross over, then curve around to the right to join **I-70 South** to downtown **ST LOUIS**. (see **MO page-4** for directions to the arch and downtown)

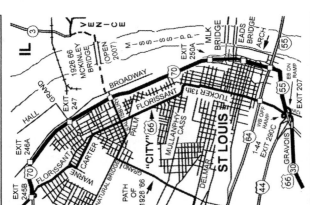

Like all big cities, **ST LOUIS** can dish out the traffic jams, so plan your trip accordingly (and be careful in unfamiliar areas).

The awesome **Chain of Rocks Bridge** (with the 22 degree turn in the middle) was built in 1929 and became part of US 66 in 1936, but was abandoned in 1968. **Trailnet Inc** began refurbishing the bridge in 1997, and it is open to hikers and bikers. INFO: http://www.trailnet.org/trails.html#ocorb There are toilets at the **trailhead** just south of EXIT 34. Riverview Dr was part of "City 66" south to downtown.

South of **I-70 EXIT 245B**, old "**City 66**" narrows as it winds thru a decayed region of empty lots and boarded up row houses, churches and stores, the ghosts of once lively neighborhoods. The many **STOP** signs are annoying, and it is easy to turn wrong (I have). The **Official Tour Route** makes it "**EZ**" for you by skipping ahead to the downtown area (and the Arch) by following **I-70**. It's OK, just this once.

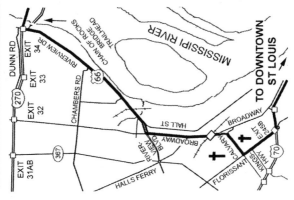

EB: Follow **I-70 north** from downtown **ST LOUIS**. (see **MO page-4** for the Arch). Take **EXIT 254B**, and turn **RIGHT** on **Florissant**. Turn **RIGHT** at the light onto **Calvary** (between cemeteries). Bear **LEFT** at the **Y**, downhill to the stoplight, turn **LEFT** on **Broadway** and cross under the RR tracks. Past Jackson St, turn **RIGHT** on **Riverview** to **I-270 EXIT 34**. Head **EAST** across the river into Illinois.

MO page-3

WB: From **I-70** in downtown **ST LOUIS**, stay AHEAD at the I-64/I-55/I-70 JCT onto **I-55 southbound**. Pass EXIT 208, then **VEER RIGHT** at EXIT 207 towards I-44 West (Tulsa). But stay in the **RIGHT** lane, and **QUICKLY** take **I-44 EXIT 290C** (12th St/Gravois). Curve around onto **Tucker St**, cross the freeways, and stay **AHEAD**, past Russell Blvd, onto **Gravois/HWY 30**. Cross Grand Blvd. At the Chippewa St stoplight, turn **RIGHT** with **Chippewa/HWY 366.**

Curving skyward between the muddy Mississippi River and downtown **ST LOUIS** is the shining **Gateway Arch**, built on the riverfront in **Jefferson National Expansion Memorial** to commemorate the western growth of the US. You can ride an internal tramcar to the tip-top of the 630-foot monument, completed in 1965, for a dizzy panoramic view of the area. Under the arch lies the **Museum of Westward Expansion. GIFT SHOP ALERT!** Two blocks west, the **Old Courthouse** dates to 1839. www.gatewayarch.com www.nps.gov/jeff/mus-tour.htm or city info: (800) 325-7962.

ARCH directions: From the **NORTH**, take I-70 **EXIT 250B** ("Memorial Drive/Downtown"). Follow **Memorial Dr** past Pine St, then turn **LEFT** on **Chestnut** and cross over I-70. Turn **LEFT** on **Memorial Dr** (on the **EAST** side of I-70). Stay in the right lane, and turn **RIGHT** on **Washington**. Park in the garage, or continue to the last street and turn **RIGHT** along the river, to the riverfront parking lot. From the **SOUTH**: From I-55, take **EXIT 209** ("Downtown") and then exit onto **Memorial Drive** (AVOID the lane to ILLINOIS). Afterwards, take **Poplar** back to **Memorial Dr** and **JOIN I-70** north or south, as needed.

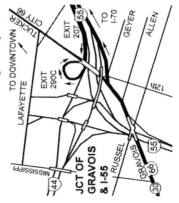

EB: Follow **Chippewa/HWY 366** to the **Gravois** stoplight: turn **LEFT**. Follow **Gravois/HWY 30** to and across I-55. Follow signs **"TO I-55 North"** approaching the next overpass. Past Allen Ave, be in the **"Right-turn ONLY" lane** and **JOIN I-55 North**. At the JCT with I-64 and I-70, stay **AHEAD** onto **I-70** West (going north) past downtown **ST LOUIS**.

WB: Follow Chippewa/HWY 366 west past the **ST LOUIS** city limits (becomes **Watson Rd**) into **SHREWSBURY**. Stay on **Watson Rd**/HWY 366 thru **MARLBOROUGH**, **WEBSTER GROVES** and **CRESTWOOD**, to Kirkwood Rd/US 67, south of I-40 EXIT 277.

FOREST PARK AREA

The route along **Gravois** and **Chippewa** runs thru interesting neighborhoods lined with old businesses and charming houses, with repeated variations of cottage styles, differing in the details. **Ted Drewes Frozen Custard** at 6726 **Chippewa** is the major tourist attraction, selling their thick "concretes" from here since about 1941. http://www.teddrewes.com/

SIDE TRIP: Forest Park is a historic area that early 66 ran thru. Its many attractions include the **Missouri History Museum**. A profusion of short lived "optional," "city," and "truck" routes add to the confusion created by cut streets and a One-Way section as older 66 zigs up to McKinley Bridge thru a decayed neighborhood (**NOT** part of TOUR: shown for historic purposes). A lively neighborhood of old buildings is **DOGTOWN**, on Clayton. Watch for the **GIANT AMOCO SIGN** at Clayton and McCausland. Its ancestor dated back to old 66!

GIANT ALERT! **Giant Farmer and Son** at Sappington Farmers Market in General Grant Center. Nearby in **MARLBOROUGH** was the site of the now-demolished **Coral Court Motel**. It's a shame this "Streamline Moderne" masterpiece was destroyed. To see a preserved example of one of the 1941 bungalows, visit the **Museum of Transportation**, where the reconstructed unit is on "semi-permanent" display, along with many old trains and other transport relics. **Directions:** From I-270 EXIT 8 at Dougherty Ferry Road, head west for a mile to Barrett Station Road, then turn left for one-half mile (see map on MO page-8). **INFO:** http://www.museumoftransport.org/welcome.htm or (314) -965-7998.

EB: From the JCT with **Kirkwood Rd**/US 67, (south of I-44 EXIT 277) follow **Watson Rd**/HWY 366 thru **CRESTWOOD**, **WEBSTER GROVES**, **MARLBOROUGH** and **SHREWSBURY**. Cross into **ST LOUIS** (becomes Chippewa St) and continue with **Chippewa/HWY 366** to the JCT with **HWY 30/Gravois St.**

(see MO MAP # 1 on Mo page-2)

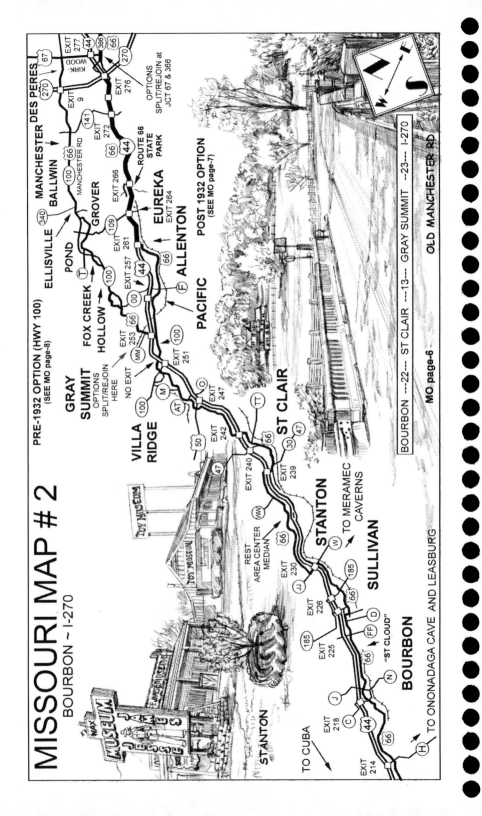

MISSOURI MAP # 2
BOURBON ~ I-270

PRE-1932 OPTION (HWY 100)
(SEE MO page-8)

POST 1932 OPTION
(SEE MO page-7)

DES PERES

EXIT 277

EXIT 276

OPTIONS
SPLIT/REJOIN at
JCT 67 & 366

EXIT 9

KIRKWOOD

270

67

44

66

366

270

MANCHESTER

BALLWIN

ELLISVILLE

340

MANCHESTER RD

100

66

EXIT 272

141

GROVER

POND

EXIT 266

66

44

ROUTE 66
STATE
PARK

EXIT 264

EUREKA

ALLENTON

EXIT 261

109

66

EXIT 257

100

44

EXIT 253

66

00

PACIFIC

FOX CREEK
HOLLOW

T

MM

GRAY
SUMMIT

OPTIONS
SPLIT/REJOIN
HERE

NO EXIT

EXIT 251

100

M

AT

100

O

EXIT 247

VILLA
RIDGE

50

ST CLAIR

TT

66

47

30

EXIT 242

EXIT 240

47

EXIT 239

STANTON

TO MERAMEC
CAVERNS

REST
AREA CENTER
MEDIAN

WM

66

EXIT 230

W

SULLIVAN

JJ

EXIT 226

66

185

185

EXIT 225

FF

D

66

"ST CLOUD"

N

BOURBON

J

C

44

66

EXIT 218

STANTON

TO CUBA

EXIT 214

H

TO ONONDAGA CAVE AND LEASBURG

BOURBON ---22--- ST CLAIR ---13--- GRAY SUMMIT ---23--- I-270

OLD MANCHESTER RD

W N E S

WB: Follow **Watson Rd** past Kirkwood (US 67) to join **I-44 WB** ("Tulsa"). Follow I-44 past the I-270 JCT, then past EXIT 266 (**Route 66 State Park**) and EXIT 264 (**EUREKA**) to **EXIT 261 (ALLENTON)**. Exit, cross under I-44 and follow **BL 44/Osage St** thru **PACIFIC**. Pass the HWY F & "OO" JCT. Stay ahead with **BL 44** past EXIT 257 to **GRAY SUMMIT** at EXIT 253 (JCT HWY 100).

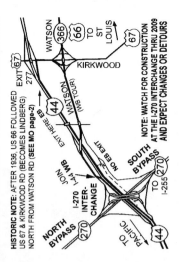

HISTORIC NOTE: AFTER 1936, US 66 FOLLOWED US 67 & KIRKWOOD RD (BECOMES LINDBERG) NORTH FROM WATSON RD (SEE MO page-2)

NOTE: WATCH FOR CONSTRUCTION AT THE I-270 INTERCHANGE THRU 2009 AND EXPECT CHANGES OR DETOURS

WB NOTE: The **PRE-1932 OPTION** via **HWY 100** diverges at **Kirkwood Rd** and **Watson** (see **MO page-8** and choose your route). **THIS** page covers the **POST 1932 ROUTE** along **I-44** west thru **PACIFIC** to **GRAY SUMMIT**. Some I-44 driving is required. **EB NOTE:** If conditions require you to get around **ST LOUIS** quickly, try I-270 around the north of the city, or I-270 south to connect with I-255 (see **MO page-2**)

West of **ST LOUIS**, the route slips thru a region of forested hills, with big cuts and steep grades. **Route 66 State Park**, east of **EUREKA**, is the site of former **Times Beach**, long abandoned and demolished due to dioxin contamination (quite safe now). A nifty **Route 66 Exhibit** is located there in the **Bridgehead Inn**, a former 1935 roadhouse east of the **Meramec River Bridge**. (636) 938-7198.

ALLENTON is home to Six Flags theme park, and is the eastern terminus of a section of **POST-'32 US 66** that winds with the railroad below rugged, scenic limestone bluffs thru **PACIFIC**. The former Red Cedar Inn on the east side of town will reportedly become a Route 66 welcome center. **EB:** see MO page-8 to compare options.

EB: From **EXIT 253** (JCT HWY 100) take the S Outer Rd/BL 44 past EXIT 257, into **PACIFIC** (on Osage St/BL 44). Pass the HWY F & "OO" JCT. Join **I-44 EB** at **ALLENTON** EXIT 261. Pass thru the I-270 interchange, then take **EXIT 277**(Kirkwood /US 67). Turn **RIGHT** on **Kirkwood** and then turn **LEFT** on **Watson Rd** towards **ST LOUIS**.

WB: PRE-1932 OPTION: from Watson Rd, follow Kirkwood/US 67 north to **HWY 100** in **DES PERES**. Turn **LEFT**, and follow **HWY 100/Manchester Rd** across I-270, thru **MANCHESTER, BALLWIN** and **ELLISVILLE**. Cross HWY 340, then Old State Rd. Less than 2 miles west of HWY 340, turn **LEFT** with **Manchester Rd** from off HWY 100. Continue thru **GROVER**. Cross HWY 109. Continue thru **POND** and **FOX CREEK**. Cross HWY 100 on **Booness Rd**, then **QUICK LEFT** onto **Old Manchester Rd**. At the next chance, rejoin **HWY 100 WB**, thru **HOLLOW**. At Fox Creek Rd, turn **RIGHT** on **Old Manchester Rd**, then rejoin **HWY 100** at the JCT of HWY "OO". Continue on **HWY 100** to **GRAY SUMMIT** (EXIT 253), cross I-44, and turn **RIGHT** with HWY 100.

The **PRE-1932 OPTION** shown on this page is a mix of urbanized multi-lane strip east from **ELLISVILLE**, and scenic two-lane stretches thru the hills of the Rockwoods Range west of **ELLISVILLE**. **SUGGESTION**: Use **HWY 109** between **GROVER** and **EUREKA** to combine the scenic western portion of the **Pre-'32 Route** with the **Post-'32 section** (and **Route 66 State Park**) in one trip (you can double back to **PACIFIC** or **MANCHESTER**).

West of **POND** is **B Donovan's Steakhouse**, housed in the main building of the former 1929 Big Chief Cabin Hotel. **SCAVENGER HUNT!** On Old Manchester Rd, east of HWY "OO", what is the **DATE** on **Bridge #364** (west of Basset Rd)?

PRE-1932
OPTION
WESTERN
SECTION

TO ELLISVILLE
MANCHESTER RD
BOONESS
MELROSE
MAN CHESTER
POND
GROVER
FOX CREEK HOLLOW
EUREKA
TO ROUTE 66
STATE PARK
EXIT 266
EXIT 264
109
FOX CREEK RD
ALLENTON
EXIT 261
BL 44
66
POST 1932
EXIT 257
OLD MANCHESTER RD
BASSET
OO
100
PACIFIC
66
100
GRAY SUMMIT
EXIT 253

EB: PRE-1932 OPTION: Follow **HWY 100** across I-44 at **EXIT 253** in **GRAY SUMMIT**. Continue about 5.5 miles, then turn **LEFT** onto Old Manchester Rd (at the JCT with HWY "OO"). Rejoin **HWY 100** at next chance, continue thru **HOLLOW**. After about 2 miles, turn **LEFT** on Melrose, then **QUICK RIGHT** on Manchester Rd. Cross HWY 100 at **Booness Rd**, then curve **LEFT** with **Old Manchester Rd**, thru **FOX CREEK** and **POND**, past HWY 109. Curve down to **HWY 100** (Manchester Rd), turn **RIGHT**, and continue thru **ELLISVILLE, BALLWIN** and **MANCHESTER**. Cross I-270, thru **DES PERES** to Kirkwood Rd/US 67: turn **RIGHT**. Cross I-44, then at the HWY 366 (Watson Rd) JCT, take the off ramp, then turn **LEFT** onto Watson Rd/Hwy 366.
MO page-8

WB: Take HWY 100 west from **GRAY SUMMIT**. **CROSS** I-44 (no exit) and proceed to the stoplight near EXIT 251 (HWY 100 turns). Stay AHEAD to JOIN HWY AT. **CROSS** HWY AT. **CROSS** US 50 to join the **North Outer Road** to **EXIT 242**. **CROSS** I-44, then take the **South Outer Rd** into **ST CLAIR**. Stay AHEAD on Commercial Ave (HWY 47 joins). At the S HWY 47 JCT (HWY 30 joins) stay to the **RIGHT** with Commercial Ave thru the stoplight, then turn **RIGHT** with N HWY 30 to **EXIT 239**. **CROSS** I-44, then **LEFT** with HWY WW. Stay with the North Outer Rd past the HWY WW turnoff, then **CROSS** I-44 at **EXIT 230** (HWY W and JJ) into **STANTON**.

Since 1925, **GRAY SUMMIT** has been home to **Shaw Nature Reserve** (formerly the Shaw Arboretum), with 2,500 acres of natural Ozark landscape and plant collections. The many natural and landscaped settings, including 13 miles of trails, are open year round, 7 am to sunset (the visitor center has its own hours). Their 1879 **Joseph H. Bascom Manor House** contains exhibits titled "People on the Land" covering conservation issues (636) 451-3512.

Nearby on '66, watch for the **Gardenway Motel's** classic neon sign as you drive past. West of EXIT 251, the **Tri County Restaurant** was once home to the old Diamonds Restaurant.
EB: Choose which **OPTION** to take at **GRAY SUMMIT**.

ST CLAIR has the **Lewis Café** on 145 S Main, and a **Museum** at 280 Hibbard St. West of town, '66 briefly continues along the tracks before ending. A few former motels reside on the way to **STANTON**.

EB: In **STANTON**, **CROSS** I-44 at EXIT 230, then **RIGHT** on the **North Outer Rd** (becomes **HWY WW**). At **EXIT 239**, **CROSS** I-44 on HWY 30, then **LEFT** with **HWY 30** on **Commercial Ave** into **ST CLAIR**. Bear **LEFT** with Commercial Ave past the S HWY 30 JCT (HWY 47 joins). Stay AHEAD past N Main (HWY 47 turns here to EXIT 240), and follow the **South Outer Rd** to **EXIT 242**. **CROSS** I-44, and take the North Outer Rd. **CROSS** US 50 to join **HWY AT** ahead, continuing past HWY M. At the **HWY 100** stoplight (near EXIT 251) stay AHEAD onto **EB HWY 100**. **CROSS** I-44 (no exit) then continue to EXIT 253 in **GRAY SUMMIT**.

(see **MO page-8** to follow **PRE-1932 '66**)

(see **MO page-7** to stay on **POST-1932 '66**)   **MO page-9**

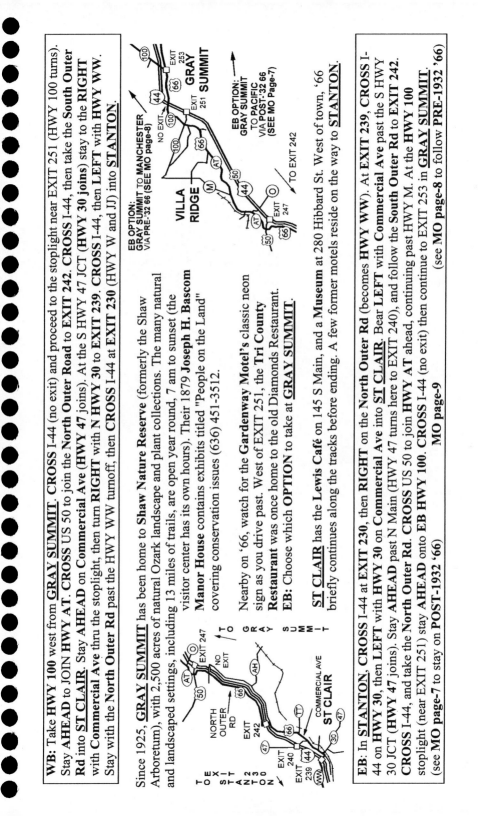

EB OPTION:
GRAY SUMMIT TO MANCHESTER
VIA PRE-'32 66 (SEE MO page-8)

EB OPTION:
GRAY SUMMIT
TO PACIFIC
VIA POST-'32 66
(SEE MO Page-7)

VILLA RIDGE

GRAY SUMMIT

G R A Y S U M M I T

COMMERCIAL AVE
ST CLAIR

NORTH OUTER RD

TO EXIT 247

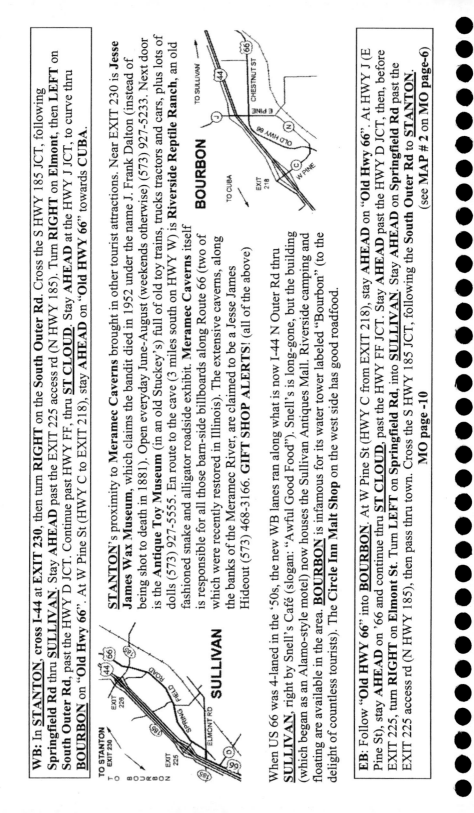

WB: In <u>STANTON</u>, cross I-44 at **EXIT 230**, then turn **RIGHT** on the **South Outer Rd**. Cross the **S HWY 185 JCT**, following **Springfield Rd** thru <u>SULLIVAN</u>. Stay **AHEAD** past the **EXIT 225** access rd (N HWY 185). Turn **RIGHT** on **Elmont**, then **LEFT** on **South Outer Rd**, past the **HWY D JCT**. Continue past HWY FF, thru <u>ST CLOUD</u>. Stay **AHEAD** at the HWY J JCT (HWY C to EXIT 218), to curve thru <u>BOURBON</u> on **"Old Hwy 66"**. At W Pine St (HWY C to EXIT 218), stay **AHEAD** on **"Old HWY 66"** towards CUBA.

<u>STANTON</u>'s proximity to **Meramec Caverns** brought in other tourist attractions. Near EXIT 230 is **Jesse James Wax Museum**, which claims the bandit died in 1952 under the name J. Frank Dalton (instead of being shot to death in 1881). Open everyday June-August (weekends otherwise) (573) 927-5233. Next door is the **Antique Toy Museum** (in an old Stuckey's) full of old toy trains, trucks tractors and cars, plus lots of dolls (573) 927-5555. En route to the cave (3 miles south on HWY W) is **Riverside Reptile Ranch**, an old fashioned snake and alligator roadside exhibit. **Meramec Caverns** itself is responsible for all those barn-side billboards along Route 66 (two of which were recently restored in Illinois). The extensive caverns, along the banks of the Meramec River, are claimed to be a Jesse James Hideout (573) 468-3166. **GIFT SHOP ALERTS!** (all of the above)

When US 66 was 4-laned in the '50s, the new WB lanes ran along what is now I-44 N Outer Rd thru <u>SULLIVAN</u>, right by Snell's Café (slogan: "Awful Good Food"). Snell's is long-gone, but the building (which began as an Alamo-style motel) now houses the Sullivan Antiques Mall. Riverside camping and floating are available in the area. **BOURBON** is infamous for its water tower labeled "Bourbon" (to the delight of countless tourists). The **Circle Inn Malt Shop** on the west side has good roadfood.

EB: Follow **"Old HWY 66"** into <u>BOURBON</u>. At W Pine St (HWY C from EXIT 218), stay **AHEAD** on **"Old Hwy 66"**. At HWY J (E Pine St), stay **AHEAD** on '66, past the HWY FF JCT. Stay **AHEAD** past the HWY D JCT, then, before EXIT 225, turn **RIGHT** on **Elmont St**. Turn **LEFT** on **Springfield Rd**, into <u>SULLIVAN</u>. Stay **AHEAD** on **Springfield Rd** past the EXIT 225 access rd (N HWY 185), then pass thru town. Cross the S HWY 185 JCT, following the **South Outer Rd** to <u>STANTON</u>.

(see MAP # 2 on MO page-6)

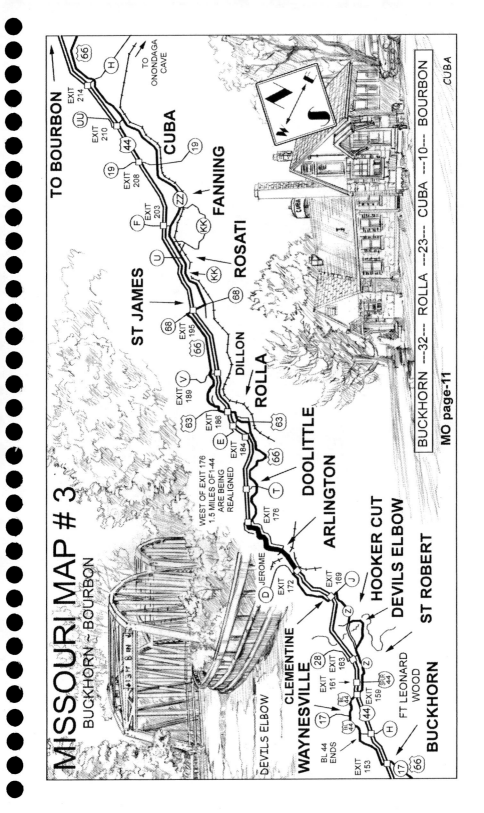

MISSOURI MAP # 3
BUCKHORN ~ BOURBON

TO BOURBON

CUBA

FANNING

ROSATI

ST JAMES

DILLON

ROLLA

DOOLITTLE

ARLINGTON

HOOKER CUT

DEVILS ELBOW

ST ROBERT

BUCKHORN

CLEMENTINE

WAYNESVILLE

DEVILS ELBOW

TO ONONDAGA CAVE

EXIT 214

EXIT 210

EXIT 208

EXIT 203

EXIT 195

EXIT 189

EXIT 186

EXIT 184

WEST OF EXIT 176
1.5 MILES OF I-44
ARE BEING
REALIGNED

EXIT 176

JEROME

EXIT 172

EXIT 169

EXIT 163
EXIT 161

EXIT 159
SPUR 44

FT LEONARD WOOD

BL 44 ENDS

EXIT 153

BUCKHORN ---32--- ROLLA ---23--- CUBA ---10--- BOURBON

MO page-11

CUBA

WB: Take "Old Hwy 66" (becomes the S Outer Rd) from **BOURBON**, past HWY H and HWY UU into **CUBA**, (becomes **Washington St**), to follow **Washington St** (becomes **HWY ZZ**) out of town. Continue on **HWY ZZ** past HWY KK, **FANNING**, and HWY F (EXIT 203). Stay AHEAD when **HWY KK** rejoins at **ROSATI**, continue on **HWY KK** alongside I-44, past HWY U and into **ST JAMES** (becomes James Blvd). Turn **RIGHT** at **Jefferson St** (HWY 68) to **EXIT 195.**

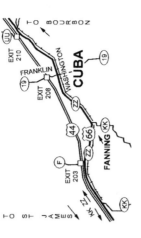

West of **BOURBON** is a nice little drive along the RR thru a green farm scene. HWY H leads to **Onondaga Cave State Park**, which also had some painted barns along '66 (not as many as Meramec Caverns). On the eastern outskirts of **CUBA**, **Missouri Hickory Bar B Q** greets you with their sign of a stereotypical coverall-clad Hillbilly, holding his favorite hog.

CUBA's famous **Wagon Wheel Motel** has a great neon sign and wonderful atmosphere, with cheap, spartan rooms for the more adventurous tourist looking for genuine old time Route 66 experiences (573) 885-3411. Proclaimed the "**Route 66 Mural City**," **CUBA**'s many murals include a depiction of bygone "Al West Motor/Tractor Sales", and another of soldiers going off to war on the "FRISCO." **CUBA** still has a Drive-In Theatre, north on HWY 19. **Route 66 Café** is downtown, along with a restored early gas station. **GIANT ALERT!** Giant ROCKING CHAIR at US 66 Outpost in **FANNING**. It's a nice drive betwixt **CUBA** and **FANNING**.

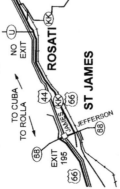

ROSATI, home to Rosati and St James Wineries. Many grape stands are open in season ("Grapes by Bushel, box or pound"). Downtown **ST JAMES** has several antique stores. **NOTE:** The divided, tree-lined alignment of 66 that continues to the west of Jefferson St is soon interrupted by I-44, requiring a jump up onto the N Outer Rd at EXIT 195 on the way to **ROLLA.**

EB: Take **Jefferson St** (HWY 68) south from **EXIT 195** into **ST JAMES**. Turn **LEFT** on **James Blvd/HWY KK** and continue past HWY U thru **ROSATI**. When KK turns south, stay AHEAD, joining **HWY ZZ** past HWY F (EXIT 203) and thru **FANNING**. Stay with **HWY ZZ** past where HWY KK rejoins, and enter **CUBA** (becomes **Washington St**.) Stay AHEAD at the JCT of Franklin St (HWY 19) and follow **Washington St** from town (becomes **S Outer Rd**) past HWY UU and HWY H. Enter **BOURBON** on "**Old Hwy 66.**"

MO page-13

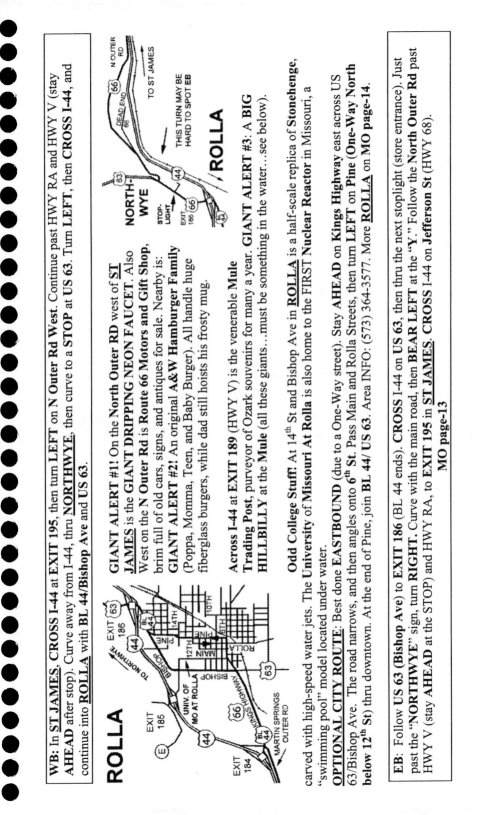

WB: In **ST JAMES**, CROSS I-44 at **EXIT 195**, then turn **LEFT** on N Outer Rd West. Continue past HWY RA and HWY V (stay AHEAD after stop). Curve away from I-44, thru **NORTHWYE**, then curve to a **STOP** at US 63. Turn **LEFT**, then **CROSS I-44**, and continue into **ROLLA** with BL 44/Bishop Ave and US 63.

GIANT ALERT #1! On the North Outer RD west of **ST JAMES** is the **GIANT DRIPPING NEON FAUCET**. Also West on the N Outer Rd is **Route 66 Motors and Gift Shop**, brim full of old cars, signs, and antiques for sale. Nearby is: **GIANT ALERT #2!** An original **A&W Hamburger Family** (Poppa, Momma, Teen, and Baby Burger). All handle huge fiberglass burgers, while dad still hoists his frosty mug.

Across I-44 at EXIT 189 (HWY V) is the venerable **Mule Trading Post**, purveyor of Ozark souvenirs for many a year. **GIANT ALERT #3:** A **BIG HILLBILLY** at the **Mule** (all these giants…must be something in the water…see below).

Odd College Stuff! At 14th St and Bishop Ave in **ROLLA** is a half-scale replica of **Stonehenge**, carved with high-speed water jets. The **University of Missouri At Rolla** is also home to the FIRST **Nuclear Reactor** in Missouri, a "swimming pool" model located under water.

OPTIONAL CITY ROUTE: Best done **EASTBOUND** (due to a One-Way street). Stay **AHEAD** on **Kings Highway** east across US 63/Bishop Ave. The road narrows, and then angles onto 6th St. Pass Main and Rolla Streets, then turn **LEFT** on Pine (One-Way North below 12th St) thru downtown. At the end of Pine, join **BL 44/ US 63**. Area INFO: (573) 364-3577. More **ROLLA** on **MO page-14**.

EB: Follow US 63 (Bishop Ave) to **EXIT 186** (BL 44 ends). **CROSS I-44** on US 63, then thru the next stoplight (store entrance). Just past the "**NORTHWYE**" sign, turn **RIGHT**. Curve with the main road, then **BEAR LEFT** at the "**Y**." Follow the **North Outer Rd** past HWY V (stay **AHEAD** at the STOP) and HWY RA, to **EXIT 195** in **ST JAMES**. CROSS I-44 on Jefferson St (HWY 68).

WB: In <u>ROLLA</u>, turn **RIGHT** with **BL 44** at the JCT of **Kings Highway**. Just before I-44 EXIT 184, turn **LEFT** at the stoplight onto **Martin Springs Drive /Outer Rd**. The road loops south of I-44, then crosses the **HWY T** JCT at **DOOLITTLE** (becomes **Eisenhower St**). At **EXIT 176, JOIN I-44 WB**. Take **EXIT 172**, and turn **LEFT** on **Outer Rd West/ Powellville Outer Rd** (stay **AHEAD** past the crossover). AT **EXIT 169** (HWY J) **CROSS I-44** and QUICK turn **RIGHT** with **HWY Z**.

<u>ADVISORY</u>: The Outer Rd from **EXIT 172** to **EXIT 169** is a bit rough (potholes), so drive with care until it gets fixed! **NOTE**: **A drug sting** is at times operated at **EXIT 176 (EB)** to catch alleged culprits that exit here after a sign warns of an upcoming "checkpoint" on I-44. Route 66 tourists shouldn't worry (just don't carry illegal drugs!).

For a <u>ROLLA</u> map see **MO page-13**. For fast food, try **Maid Rite** on Kings Highway. Along **Martin Springs Dr** is a line of motels and stores, including **Zeno's Motel and Steakhouse**. The **Totem Pole Trading Post** offers antiques and curios.

<u>SIDE TRIP</u>: Stranded on the dead end access road west of **EXIT 176** are the abandoned log rooms of **Johns Modern Cabins** and lonely **Vernelle's Motel**. The realignment of I-44 isolated them further. Cut off by earlier relocations of US 66 and then by I-44 is **ARLINGTON**, on the banks of the **Little Piney River** at the end of the access road. **SIDE TRIP**: West of the river, old 66 once followed **HWY D** east a short way east from **EXIT 172**, the long-gone pathway being lost when the current road curves north to **JEROME**. **FOLK ART ALERT!** Along here at a private residence is an ornate rock arch gateway honoring the **"Trail of Tears"** (the forced migration of the Cherokees). Nearby, a few old cabins are all that remain of the **Stony Dell** resort. Back on the **TOUR ROUTE**: On **Powellville Outer Rd** (named for an old business) is the turnoff to **Onyx Mountain Caverns** (1 Mi) for you cave buffs (573) 762-3341. **CLEMENTINE**, just east of **EXIT 169**, was a community famous for homemade baskets once sold along the road.

EB: Follow **HWY Z** to **HWY J** at **EXIT 169**. **CROSS I-44**, then turn **RIGHT** on **Powellville Outer Rd**. At the **HWY D JCT**, (**EXIT 172**), **JOIN I-44 EB**. Take **EXIT 176** and join **Historic 66** eastbound. Stay **AHEAD** with **Eisenhower St** at **HWY T** in **DOOLITTLE**, and follow the road as it loops south of I-44, then becomes **Martin Springs Outer Rd** (and then **Martin Springs Dr**) towards <u>ROLLA</u>. At the light near EXIT 184 (BL 44), turn **RIGHT** onto **Kings Highway/BL-44**. Turn **LEFT** with **BL-44** onto **US 63 (Bishop Ave)**.

(see MAP #3, MO page-11)

WB: Take **HWY Z** (becomes **4-Lane 66**) thru the **HOOKER CUT**. Turn **LEFT** at first chance onto **Teardrop Rd**. Cross the bridge into **DEVILS ELBOW**. Curve uphill, then turn **LEFT** onto **HWY Z** (becomes 2-lane). At HWY 28 (EXIT 163), stay **AHEAD** on **HWY Z** to **ST ROBERT**. At the "SPUR I-44" JCT, stay **AHEAD** (middle lane) onto **BL 44**. **CROSS I-44** at EXIT 159, stay **AHEAD** with **BL 44** into **WAYNESVILLE** (HWY 17 joins). When BL 44 turns, **stay AHEAD** on **HWY 17** ("Historic 66 West") to **EXIT 153.**

Map: TO EXIT 172 — EXIT — TROUT RD 169 — J — HOOKER — Z — 4 LANE — 66 — TEARDROP RD — DEVILS ELBOW — HOOKER CUT — TO ST ROBERT — 4 LANE — BIG PINEY — 44 — TEARDROP RD — 28 — Z — MORGAN HEIGHTS EXIT 163

This stretch of **4-Lane 66** was the FIRST on '66 in Missouri, built in 1941-45 for wartime traffic to Ft Leonard Wood. At 90 feet, kudzu-covered **HOOKER CUT** was once the deepest road cut in Missouri. 2-Lane 66 went around north of the ridge, then came back down on the east thru **HOOKER** (Trout Rd, north of HWY Z, is a remainder). The 4-Lane bypassed the **1923 Bridge** over the **Big Piney River** that leads to **DEVILS ELBOW**, and the steep slope to the west. **SIDE TRIP**: Double back to drive 4-lane 66 west of Hooker Cut. This relic of 4-lane 66 served until the early '80s.

DEVILS ELBOW, named for a bend in the river that caused logjams, sits below 200-foot tall tree-lined bluffs. The Elbow Inn Bar & BBQ operates from the 1929 Munger Moss Sandwich Shop building. East of the river is the old **Allman's** (now Sheldon's) **Market** and P.O. A rock-walled pullout on old 66 up the hill provides a scenic view of the valley.

SCAVENGER HUNT! What military "vehicle" honors **Ft Leonard Wood** at **George M Reed Roadside Park** (w of Spur 44 in **ST ROBERT**)? _____ **GIANT ALERT!** Just east of **WAYNESVILLE**, a big boulder sticking out of the hill cut is painted like a **GIANT FROG** (or turtle?). Downtown has some neat buildings. The **1923 Rubidoux Creek Bridge** was recently restored. **CLEVER NAME:** "Every Blooming Thing:" a plant store in a renovated gas station.

WAYNESVILLE

Map: 17 — 66 — 44 — EXIT 150 — EXIT 161 — EXIT Y — ST ROBERT — FORT LEONARD WOOD — ROUBIDOUX CREEK — 44 — EXIT 156 — H — EXIT 153 BUCKHORN — T — 17

EB: Take **HWY 17 ACROSS I-44** into **WAYNESVILLE**. **BL 44** joins at Ichord Ave, stay **AHEAD**. When HWY 17 turns, follow **BL 44** east thru **ST ROBERT** and **CROSS I-44** at EXIT 159. At the **SPUR 44 JCT**, stay **AHEAD** (middle lane) onto **HWY Z**. About a mile east of EXIT 163 (HWY 28) **ANGLE RIGHT** onto **Teardrop Rd**. Descend to **DEVILS ELBOW**, and cross the bridge. Turn **RIGHT** on **HWY Z** (4-Lane 66). Pass thru **HOOKER CUT**, and follow **HWY Z** to **EXIT 169.**

(see **MAP #3, MO page-11**)

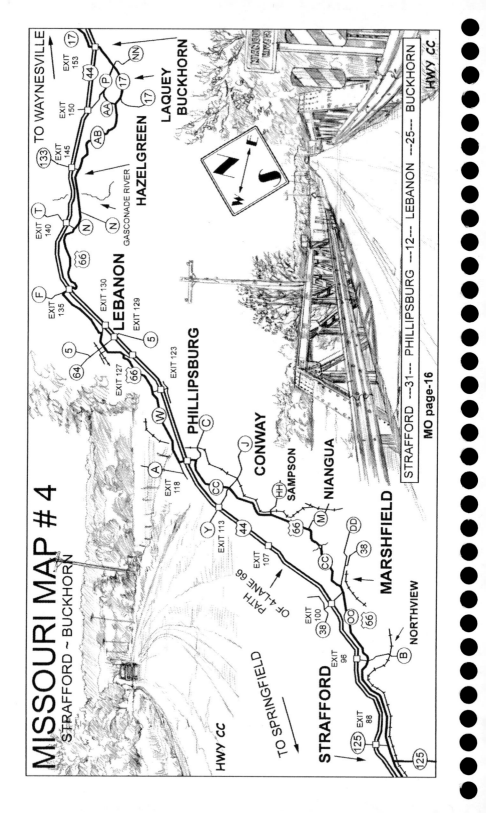

MISSOURI MAP # 4
STRAFFORD ~ BUCKHORN

STRAFFORD ---31--- PHILLIPSBURG ---12--- LEBANON ---25--- BUCKHORN

MO page-16

HWY CC

MO page-17

WB: CROSS I-44 at **EXIT 153** and continue with **HWY 17** thru **BUCKHORN**, past HWY P. At the "Y" where HWY 17 turns, bear **RIGHT** onto **HWY AB**. Pass HWY AA, and continue to the JCT of HWY 133 (EXIT 145): stay **AHEAD** on the **S Outer Rd**, thru **HAZELGREEN**. Cross the **Gasconade River Bridge**, and pass the S HWY N turnoff. At the **HWY T JCT** (EXIT 140) stay **AHEAD** on the **S Outer Rd**. At the **HWY F JCT**, go **ACROSS I-44**, then turn **LEFT** onto the **N Outer Rd West** ("Route 66").

Just east of **EXIT 153** is a **GIANT ALERT**! See the **GIANT BOWLING PIN** (right beside the sign: "Adult SUPER Store" for an interesting juxtaposition).

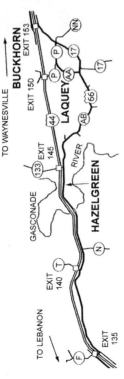

Across I-44, the only things named for little **BUCKHORN** are the Baptist Church and Buckhorn Carpets. But this is a nice drive, taking you away from I-44 for a bit, so savor it.

OPTIONAL ROUTE: Highways P and AA are **EARLY 66** thru **LAQUEY** (site of an old general store, where the roads meet). This scenic drive is nice and twisty, so I suggest looping back to drive it if you've time to do both.

Closer to I-44, you pass the former **Gascozark Trading Post**. Near EXIT 145, a defunct Phillips 66 station serves as a trellis for a clinging kudzu coat. At **HAZELGREEN**, several houses (some on stilts) and a charming Methodist Church perch on the edge of a steep drop. Three thru-truss spans (plus a magnificent **1923 bridge** carries Route 66 over the **Gasconade River**. **SCAVENGER HUNT**! What is the **NAME** of the "**Conservation Area**" south of Route 66 and just east of EXIT 135? _____

TO WAYNESVILLE

BUCKHORN
EXIT 153

EXIT 150

LAQUEY

EXIT 145

133 EXIT

GASCONADE

RIVER

HAZELGREEN

EXIT 140 T

TO LEBANON

EXIT 135

EB: From **EXIT 135** (HWY F) curve down to join the **South Outer Rd EAST**. Pass the HWY T (EXIT 140) and HWY N Junctions. Cross the **Gasconade River Bridge** and continue thru **HAZELGREEN**. At the HWY 133 JCT (EXIT 145) follow **HWY AB** away from I-44. Pass the HWY AA JCT, then stay **AHEAD** at the next **STOP** onto **HWY 17**. Continue past HWY P to **EXIT 153** in **BUCKHORN**.

MO page-17

WB: Follow the **N Outer Rd** ("Route 66") west from EXIT 135 to **LEBANON**. At the JCT of **BL 44**, (near EXIT 130) turn **RIGHT**. Follow **BL 44** as it curves onto **Elm St**. Cross the JCT of HWY 5 (Jefferson Ave); stay **AHEAD** with **BL 44** to EXIT 127. Turn **RIGHT** onto **HWY W** (**BEFORE** reaching on/off ramps at exit). Stay with **HWY W** past EXIT 123 to **EXIT 118. CROSS I-44** with **HWY C**.

Near EXIT 135 is **I-44 Speedway**, a 3/8 mile "high bank clay oval" (they shoulda' named it after Route 66!).

LEBANON is home to one of my "homes away from home," the famous **Munger Moss Motel** from 1946. Bob and Ramona (great supporters of '66) started there in 1971, renovating the units and maintaining the outstanding neon sign (if you can't stay, try the **GIFT SHOP**). They decorated many rooms in **Route 66 themes**, including the "pretty in pink" tribute to the bygone **Coral Court Motel**, with photos by famed Route 66 photographer Shellee Graham. In the TEXAS room, they hung prints of some of my artwork. Hopefully their tradition will continue in the future. (417) 532-3111. www.mungermoss.com. The 'Moss sits on a great Route 66 street, with the **Starlite Lanes** across the road, plus 2 other vintage motels. **Wrinks Market**, a small brick store of long-standing, has reopened after the recent passing of Mr. Wrinkle. On BL 44 near the Old 66 JCT is the **Bell Restaurant**, with good home cooking. **NOTE:** BL 44 thru town may be widened in the future, which could change the directions to access old 66 on each side of town a bit.

LEBANON is justly proud of their new **Route 66 Museum** in the **Laclede County Library**. Inside are memorabilia and recreations of the '66 era, such as an old motel room, 50's diner and soda fountain. Go south from BL 44 to 915 S Jefferson (HWY 5, north of I-44.) (417) 532-2148. There are loads of **"factory outlet"** and antique stores in town.

West of **LEBANON** at EXIT 123, a short bit of old 66 is cut off on the south of I-44, in front of nifty **Route 66 Antiques** and the **Caffeyville Country Store**. Between this exit and a **1926 RR overpass** to the west, is a pair of photogenic **Meramec Caverns Barns**.

EB: From **EXIT 118**, follow **HWY W** (N Outer Rd) east, past EXIT 123. Nearing EXIT 127, curve to the **STOP**, then turn **LEFT** onto BL 44 (Elm St) in **LEBANON**. Cross the HWY 5 (Jefferson St) JCT; stay **AHEAD** with **BL 44/Elm St**, curving back towards EXIT 130. **BEFORE** reaching the off/on ramps, turn **LEFT** onto **"Historic Route 66"** (N Outer Rd), and continue to **EXIT 135. CROSS I-44.**

LEBANON

L
E
B
A
N
O
N

EXIT 130
EXIT 129
EXIT 127
MILLCREEK
ELM
JEFFERSON

WB: Take **HWY C** south from **EXIT 118** in <u>PHILLIPSBURG</u>. Quickly turn **RIGHT** on **HWY CC**. Continue thru **CONWAY** (stay **AHEAD** at HWY J). Continue with **HWY CC** past HWY M, into **MARSHFIELD**. Merge **AHEAD** onto **HWY 38**. When HWY 38 curves right, turn **LEFT** at the light onto **HWY OO**. Stay **AHEAD** past HWY B (EXIT 96) to the HWY 125 JCT in <u>STRAFFORD</u>.

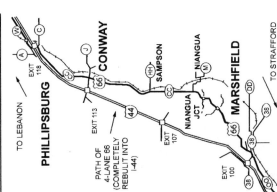

Please note that old 66 on the north side of EXIT 118 ends to the WEST after a short bit. **HWY CC** connects to the continuation of 66 on the south, and offers an **excellent drive** over hills and thru woods and meadows. We can be grateful that **4-lane 66** (and later I-44) ran further west; leaving this section almost untouched (just a light coat of asphalt hides the original curbed concrete). <u>SCAVENGER HUNT</u>! Almost a mile west of the HWY CC JCT at <u>PHILLIPSBURG</u> is the location of a former roadside park (note the line of big trees and the old culvert on the south side). Whose <u>NAME</u> is listed on the small concrete marker as having donated the land for the defunct park? _____

The **Niangua Junction Store** has guarded the **JCT** with HWY M since 1935. Further west, HWY CC crosses a small green-girder bridge over the **Niangua River**. A former cottage-style gas station from 1925 sits just east. <u>MARSHFIELD</u>'s claim to fame is hometown boy **Dr Edwin Hubble**, the noted astronomer and namesake of the **Hubble Space Telescope**, a quarter scale (1,200 lb) model of which is on display in the town square. The town also has some bed and breakfasts, including **The Dickey House** in a 1913 mansion. (417) 468-3000. Out at the JCT of Hwy 38 and I-44, the **RVExpress RV Park** has a nice Route 66 Gift Shop. (417) 859 7839. CITY INFO: 417-468-3943. Along the south side of '66 west of town is the **Exotic Animal Paradise**, a large drive-thru wildlife park (with other attractions). (888) 570-9898. Downtown **STRAFFORD** has some vintage buildings, and **Route 66 Antiques**.

EB: Follow **HWY OO** east from the N HWY 125 JCT in <u>STRAFFORD</u>. Stay **AHEAD** past HWY B (STOP) with **HWY OO** into **MARSHFIELD**. At the JCT, stay **AHEAD** onto **HWY 38**. At the next JCT, be in the left lane and turn **LEFT** onto **HWY CC**. Bear **LEFT** with 'CC at the next "Y". Stay with **HWY CC** past HWY M to <u>CONWAY</u>. Stay **AHEAD** at HWY J, and follow **HWY CC** to the JCT of **HWY C** in <u>PHILLIPSBURG</u>: turn **LEFT** and **CROSS I-44** at **EXIT 118**, then turn **RIGHT** on **HWY W** (N Outer Rd).

(see **MAP # 4, MO page-16**)

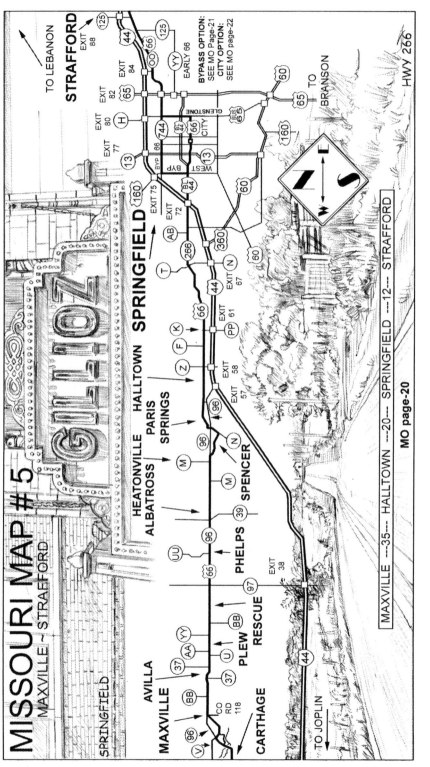

MISSOURI MAP #5
MAXVILLE ~ STRAFFORD

SPRINGFIELD

MAXVILLE

AVILLA

CARTHAGE

PLEW
RESCUE

PHELPS

SPENCER

ALBATROSS
PARIS SPRINGS

HEATONVILLE HALLTOWN

SPRINGFIELD

TO JOPLIN

TO LEBANON

STRAFFORD

EXIT 88

EXIT 84

EXIT 82

EXIT 80

EXIT 77

EXIT 75

EXIT 72

EXIT 67

EXIT 61

EXIT 58

EXIT 57

EXIT 38

EARLY 66

GLENSTONE

CITY

WEST BYP

BYP 66

BYPASS OPTION:
SEE MO Page-21
CITY OPTION:
SEE MO page-22

TO BRANSON

MAXVILLE ---35--- HALLTOWN ---20--- SPRINGFIELD ---12--- STRAFFORD

MO page-20

HWY 266

WB: At the N HWY 125 JCT in **STRAFFORD**, stay AHEAD with **HWY OO** and **HWY 125**. HWY 125 soon turns south, stay AHEAD with **HWY OO**. Merge AHEAD with **HWY 744 (Kearney St)** (near EXIT 84), and **CROSS** US 65 into **SPRINGFIELD**. (See **CITY OPTION, MO page-22**). Stay AHEAD at the Glenstone (BL 44) JCT. Cross the Kansas Expwy. Turn **LEFT** on **West Bypass** (US 160). At the **Chestnut Expwy** (BL 44) JCT, turn **RIGHT**. Cross I-44 at EXIT 72. Stay AHEAD with **MO HWY 266.**

SPRINGFIELD

Map labels: EXIT 77 — EXIT 80AB — EXIT 82AB — EXIT 84 — OO — 744 — 66 — KEARNEY — BYPASS — GLENSTONE — DIVISION — 65 — CHESTNUT EXPWY — CITY 66 — BL 44 — ST LOUIS — BYPASS — EXIT 75 — 744 — EE — BL 44 — 66 — 160 — CHESTNUT EXPWY — WEST BYPASS — KANSAS EXPWY — COLLEGE — 13 — EXIT 72 — 266 — TO CARTHAGE — EARLY 66 — YY — TO HWY 125 — SEE MO page-22 FOR CITY 66 OPTION

Don't miss the majestic neon sign at the **Rest Haven Court** (2000 E Kearney). This classic court is listed in the Federation Dining & Lodging Guide (417) 869-9114. An **EARLY** route took '66 down **HWY 125** From **STRAFFORD**, then west to Glenstone via **HWY YY** (Division St). On the latter street was the headquarters of the late, lamented **Campbell 66 Express**, whose cartoon-camel mascot, "**Snortin Norton**," humped along '66 for years.

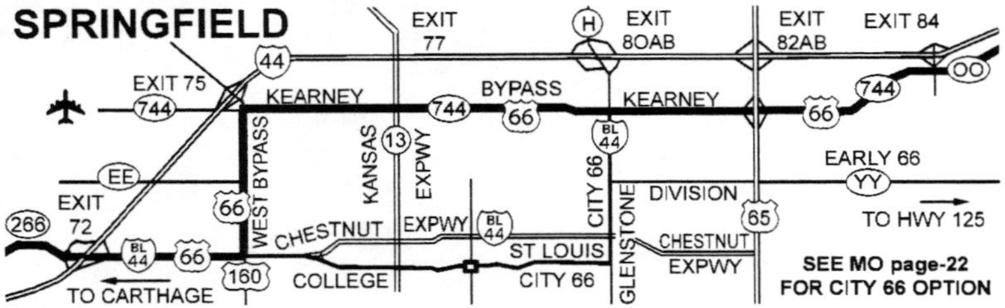

If you're wondering about that "**Branson**" place on all the billboards, why, it's the Musical Mecca of Country Music, about 35 mi south on US 65. INFO: (800) 961-1221. The area around **SPRINGFIELD** is chock-full of attractions, including **Fantastic Caverns** (why walk thru a cave, when you can ride?) and **Bass Pro Shops Outdoor World**. Tourist Info Center: www.springfieldmo.org or (800) 678-8767.

NOTE: THIS page covers the **1936 BYPASS ROUTE** (west from the JCT of Glenstone and Kearney). See **MO page-22** for the earlier **CITY OPTION** thru downtown **Park Central Square**. Serving as the main route since **1936**, the **BYPASS** has many remaining vestiges of old 66 to spot. **GIANT ALERT!** Beware of the **GIANT PISTOL** at a pawnshop near Grant Ave. Just south on **West Bypass**, a classic 1932-era "cottage" houses **Rex Smith Oil Co.** West out of town on **Chestnut Expwy** are more old motels and neon signs. Too bad that **Red's**, the famed burger joint with the "Giant Hamburg" sign and '55 Buick adorned with whirling tinfoil-balls, is long gone.

EB: Follow **BL 44/Chestnut Expwy** into **SPRINGFIELD**. At the JCT of **West Bypass/US 160**, turn **LEFT**. Turn **RIGHT** on **HWY 744 (Kearney St)**. Stay AHEAD at the JCT with BL 44/Glenstone. Continue with **HWY 744 (Kearney)**, across US 65. Join **HWY OO** AHEAD when HWY 744 turns (near EXIT 84). Follow **HWY OO** past S HWY 125 and then past N HWY 125 in **STRAFFORD**.

WB: <u>CITY OPTION</u>: From **Kearney** (HWY 744), turn **LEFT** on **Glenstone** (BL 44). Stay **AHEAD** at the Chestnut Expwy JCT (BL 44 turns). Pass over the RR, then prepare to turn **RIGHT** on **St Louis St**. In downtown, stay **AHEAD** past Jefferson and enter the square on Park Central East. Turn **RIGHT** on **Park**, then **LEFT** along the north side of the square, then **LEFT** again and **RIGHT** on **Park Central West**. Stay **AHEAD** onto **College St**. Cross West St, then curve up to the JCT of **Chestnut Expwy** (BL 44): turn **LEFT**. Stay **AHEAD** past the West Bypass JCT, and cross I-44 at EXIT 72. Stay **AHEAD** with **MO HWY 266.**

RV ALERT! The downtown **Park Central Square** has tight turns: take the **BYPASS (MO Page-21).**

Glenstone Ave still has some 66-era motels. The **Best Western Route 66 Rail Haven** at Glenstone and St Louis is fine, with plenty of history, having opened in 1938. A split rail fence bordered the original cottages, hence the name (417) 866-1963. West on St Louis is a classic **Steak & Shake**, with its slogan-covered exterior ("TAKHOMASAK").

SQUARE DETAIL

Streets enter Downtown's **Park Central Square** in the middle, requiring some tight turns to continue. **Park Central East and West** are now "winding" mall-like streets. **SCAVENGER HUNT!** Who did **"Wild Bill" Hickok** shoot here in the 1860s? _____? Park and look for the marker on the south side of the square. On the east side is the **1926 Gilloz Theatre**. West on **College St** a series of tile mosaics enlivens a retaining wall on the south. Many roadside remnants of former stations and motels await the discerning eye. East of Kansas Expwy the **College St Café** welcomes smokers, while **College St Body Shop** has a big car-shaped sign. The well-kept half-circle of cabins near West St (now apartments) were the **Rock Fountain Court**. **NOTE:** MO 266 was rebuilt at I-44, cutting off a bit of 66. Directions are the same.

EB: CITY OPTION: (see **BYPASS OPTION: MO page-21 & RV ALERT!**) Follow **BL 44/Chestnut Expwy** into **<u>SPRINGFIELD</u>**. Cross the JCT of West Bypass/US 160. Veer **RIGHT** onto **College St** (before the stoplight). Stay **AHEAD** on **College St** at Kansas Expwy (avoid turn lane). Cross Campbell St and stay **AHEAD** onto **Park Central West**. Turn **RIGHT** (One-Way) at the Square, then **LEFT** and **LEFT AGAIN** around the south side. Turn **RIGHT** on **Park Central East**. Stay **AHEAD** at **Jefferson** (careful) onto **St Louis St**. Turn **LEFT** at Glenstone Ave (becomes **BL 44**): stay **AHEAD** to **Kearney St** (HWY 744): turn **RIGHT**.

WB: Take Hwy 266 from EXIT 72. West of **HALLTOWN**, **AVOID** the left "TO HWY 96;" stay **AHEAD** thru **PARIS SPRINGS**. At the HWY 96 JCT, **CROSS** and continue briefly on **HWY N**. Turn **RIGHT** at first chance onto **Farm Rd 2062**: cross the bridge and pass **SPENCER**. Join **HWY 96** thru **HEATONVILLE, ALBATROSS, PHELPS, RESCUE, PLEW** and **AVILLA**, past HWY BB to **MAXVILLE**. Almost **4 miles** past HWY BB, turn **LEFT** on CO RD 118, then QUICK RIGHT onto "Old 66 Blvd."

Route 66 from **SPRINGFIELD** to **CARTHAGE** is a special, I-44-free drive. Reminders of old roadside culture are frequent. The directions are **EZ** so get your head out of the guide and enjoy. **HWY 266** winds thru pastoral settings of rolling wooded hills and green fields, peppered with churches, barns, and roadside remnants. Look for a hillside tableau of an old **Chevy truck, Texaco sign and pumps** just east of HWY T. In **HALLTOWN** one hopes that **Whitehall Mercantile**, long a great spot to find antiques, is still hanging in there.

A newer icon with old-time feel is the **Gay Parita Sinclair Station** at **PARIS SPRINGS**. Gary Turner built this beautiful gas station replica complete with vintage trucks on the site of a long-gone station, named for the builder's wife. He welcomes visitors, so do stop by for a nice long chat and **PHOTO OP**. The winding road west to the remains of little **SPENCER** crosses a **1923 "pony" bridge** over Turnback Creek, and a picturesque **1926 thru-truss** bridge over Johnson Creek.

HWY 96 traffic can be fast and furious, (and farm vehicles go 35 in a 65 mph zone!) so be alert. All the tiny towns strung along '66 have remains of old businesses. Many had been "rocked", like the old garage in **HEATONVILLE**. Skip Curtis' book ID's most of these extinct enterprises. Either side of **PLEW**, one runs a fiery gauntlet of Fundamentalist Burma Shave-style signs and billboards (one with "HELL" writ in big, flaming letters). **AVILLA** has a row of rustic old structures, including the **Route 66 Bar.**

EB: Follow **HWY 96** east from **MAXVILLE**, thru **AVILLA, PLEW, RESCUE, PHELPS, ALBATROSS** and **HEATONVILLE**. Half a mile east of HWY M North, turn **RIGHT** downhill **(across from FR 2059)** on **Farm Rd 2062**, and pass by **SPENCER**. Cross the bridge, then turn **LEFT** on **HWY N**. Stay **AHEAD** across HWY 96 and follow **"Old 66"** thru **PARIS SPRINGS**. At the **STOP**, merge **AHEAD** onto **HWY 266**, thru **HALLTOWN**, to I-44 EXIT 72. Stay AHEAD onto BL 44/Chestnut Expwy into **SPRINGFIELD**.

(see **MAP # 5 MO page-20**)

MO page-23

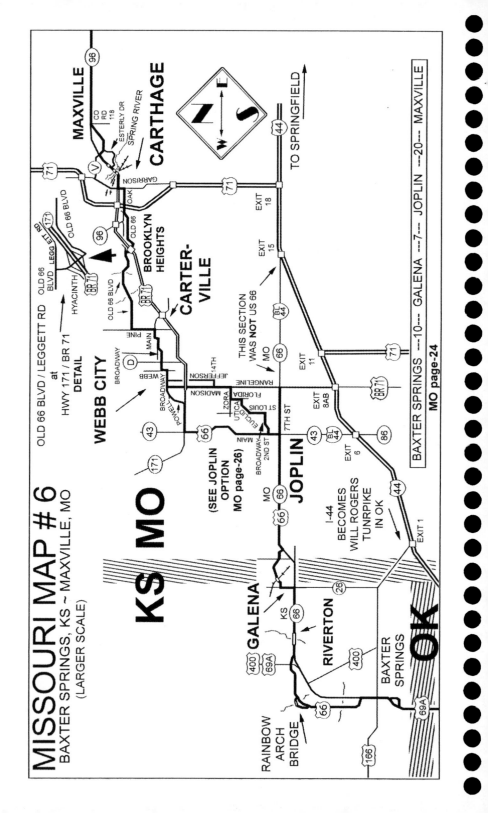

WB: From **MAXVILLE**, follow "**Old 66 Blvd**" to the JCT with **HWY 96** (at **HWY V**) (see **OPTION**). Turn **LEFT** on **HWY 96** to **CARTHAGE** (joins **Central Ave**). At **Garrison**, turn **LEFT** for a couple of blocks, then **RIGHT** on **OAK St.** CROSS over US 71, then **BEAR LEFT** at the "**Y**" and stay with "**Old 66 Blvd**" to the JCT with Bus 71 (HWY 171) in __BROOKLYN HEIGHTS__.

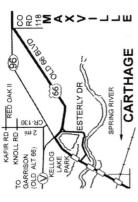

On "**Old 66 Blvd**" west from __MAXVILLE__ is **Carthage Route 66 Tea Room. FOLK ART ALERT!** At **HWY V** and **HWY 96**, the **Flying W Store** has a "flying manure spreader" sculpture by Lowell Davis named the "**Crap Duster.**" Mr. Davis created **Red Oak II**, a site full of relocated and restored old buildings (including a cottage gas station from '66). Now for sale (see map). http://redoakii.com

__OPTION: OLD 66 thru KELLOGG LAKE PARK.__ Follow **Esterly Drive** between **HWY 96** on the west side, and "**Old 66 Blvd**" on the east, for a scenic, peaceful drive along the **Spring River** (which runs barely below the south shoulder at times!). Old 66 dead ends at the west end of the park.

CARTHAGE's classic **Boots Motel**, world famous for its architecture, neon and history, was recently endangered by "development." Now serving as apartments, **HOPEFULLY** some wise soul will restore the Boots to its Route 66 glory. Down Garrison, the **Pancake Hut** has a mechanical "**Chicago Band Box**" that they'll play for you (good food too). The **Civil War Museum** (205 Grant St) has dramatic murals of "**The Battle of Carthage**" and more, near the **Historic Square**. City INFO: (417) 358-2373.

SIDE TRIP: Old 66 continued west on Oak, (across a 1936 RR viaduct) behind the **66 Drive In**, but it dead-ends now. Speaking of the **66 Drive-In**, this roadside theatre, restored after years of being a junkyard, is a **MUST** if you're overnighting in the area. Too precious is **Precious Moments Park**, south of town off US 71, with tours, shopping and **The Chapel.**

EB: Take "**Old 66 Blvd**" from the Bus 71 (HWY 171) JCT, thru __BROOKLYN HEIGHTS__. Curve onto **Oak St** in __CARTHAGE__. CROSS US 71. Turn **LEFT** on **Garrison Ave**, then **RIGHT** on **HWY 96** (Central Ave). Take **HWY 96** to the JCT of **HWY V**, but turn **RIGHT** and JOIN "**Old 66 Blvd**" to **CO RD 118** (see **OPTION**). Turn **LEFT**, then **RIGHT** on **HWY 96** in __MAXVILLE__.

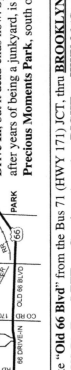

MO page-24

WB: CROSS Bus 71 (HWY 171) and stay AHEAD (NO turns) to the "T" JCT with **"Old 66 Blvd"** (Leggett Rd): turn **LEFT**. Continue to Pine St, turn **LEFT**. Cross the RR into **CARTERVILLE**. At Main St turn **RIGHT** thru downtown, then curve **LEFT** on **Carter**, and **RIGHT** at Lewis. Cross the RR, then **bear LEFT** at the "Y" onto **Broadway** at Main, then **LEFT** on **Webb St**, and quick **RIGHT** back onto **Broadway**. See **JOPLIN OPTION** below or stay **AHEAD** at Madison St.

"Old 66 Blvd" is a pleasant drive on curvy, narrow pavement, across a **1922 bridge** (if not replaced). **CARTERVILLE** offers **"SuperTAM on 66"** Ice Cream Parlor (with a 30-year collection of Superman stuff) plus a **Welcome Center/Gift Shop** in a 1937 Sinclair at 401 W Main. This was a busy mining area; old mining scars mark the way into **WEBB CITY**, where **Bradbury Bishop Deli and Route 66 Diner**, at 201 N Main, has an old-fashioned soda fountain. **GIANT ALERT!** **PRAYING HANDS** off Macarthur/HWY 171 (final US 66 between Carthage and Joplin) in Miner's Park, east of Madison St.

JOPLIN OPTION: (many turns, but very **Recommended**) South from Broadway in Webb City, Early 66 took **Jefferson** to **14th** to **Madison**. Since Macarthur now blocks **Jefferson**, take **Madison** south instead. Follow the detail map along **Zora, Florida, Utica, Euclid, St Louis** and **Broadway**, then veer onto **2nd** to join **Main St** in downtown **JOPLIN**. (EB reverse) This is a surprisingly nice drive thru residential areas, with many reminders of old 66. **Poochies Rib Pit** on Broadway is a colorful reuse of an early gas station, as was **Dale's Old 66 Barbershop** on Utica, which occupied a classic **DX Station** from 1961.

EB: Take **Broadway** past Liberty St, then turn **LEFT** on **Webb St**. **QUICK RIGHT** back on **Broadway**. Cross Main and stay with **Broadway** as it curves towards **CARTERVILLE** (becomes Lewis St). Curve **LEFT** on **Carter** and **RIGHT** on Main. Thru downtown, turn **LEFT** on **Pine St**. Cross the RR, and take the first **RIGHT** on **"Old 66 Blvd."** See detail map: **MO page-24.** Follow "Historic 66" signs **RIGHT** on **"Old 66 Blvd"** (HWY 171), and follow the frontage road curve onto **"Old 66 Blvd"** in **BROOKLYN HEIGHTS**.

MO page-26

MO page-27

WB: Bear LEFT with **Broadway** at College Ave, then **Bear LEFT** at the next "Y" onto **Powell St.** Turn **RIGHT** on **Macarthur Blvd** (HWY 171). At the **HWY 43 (N Main St Rd)** JCT, turn LEFT. Follow **HWY 43/Main** south thru downtown **JOPLIN.** Turn **RIGHT** on **7th St/MO HWY 66.** Pass Malang Rd. After the sign **"Old 66 Next Right"**, turn **RIGHT** and join **"Old 66 Blvd"** into **KANSAS.**

Map labels: BROADWAY, MAIN, WEBB ST, TO CARTHAGE, BR 71, WEBB CITY, 66, BROADWAY, JEFFERSON, 171, JEFFERSON IS EARLY 66 TO 14TH ST (CUT OFF BY McARTHUR), MADISON, 66, BR 71, TO JOPLIN VIA "JOPLIN OPTION" (MO PAGE-26), COLLEGE AVE, McARTHUR DR, BROADWAY, POWELL DR, HATTEN, S COLONIAL DR, N PRAIRIE FLOWER RD, TO JOPLIN VIA MAIN & HWY 43

At Jefferson in **WEBB CITY,** an old gas station now sells Mexican Food. Other former motel units and gas stations line **Broadway** west.

HWY 171 west of **WEBB CITY,** and Main St (HWY 43 S), bypassed the original **"City"** 66 thru **JOPLIN** in the 1930s. Two former gas stations and an **ARMY TANK** (this at Veteran's Way) decorate the route, a more peaceful drive than the **FINAL** route of US 66 along urbanized **Madison** (which becomes **Rangeline**) south to **7th** Ave. Rangeline does have many amenities. There are still a couple of old motels on **7th,** plus a bizarre **FOLK ART** car creation (based on a **VW??**) attracting attention at National Muffler Shop. South on **Rangeline** to I-44 are chain motels and restaurants.

SCAVENGER HUNT! North of downtown on **Main, Bypass 66** crosses a **concrete viaduct** over the RR tracks. What **DATE** was it built? _____ **GIANT ALERTS! Giant Coke Bottle** and **Giant Crayon** on West **7th.** The **Joplin Museum Complex,** off **7th** in **Shifferdecker Park,** contains two historical museums, telling the story of the Tri-State Mining District. City INFO: http://www.joplincc.com or (800)657-2534. West on **MO HWY 66,** you pass **66 Carousel Park,** a local amusement park, on the left. WB, don't miss the turn for Old 66 into **KANSAS,** passing **Paddock Liquors** (2 "visible" gas pumps in front) to the State Line.

Map labels: KS | MO, MALANG RD, MO, 66, TO JOPLIN, OLD 66 BLVD, 66, KS, 66, TO GALENA KS

EB: Take **"Old 66 Blvd"** past **State Line Rd** into **MO.** Curve to the JCT of **MO HWY 66** and turn **LEFT** (becomes **7th** St) to **JOPLIN.** Turn **LEFT** on **Main St (HWY 43)** thru downtown **JOPLIN.** (SEE **JOPLIN OPTION** on **MO page-26,** or stay **AHEAD** on **Main St.**) At the **HWY 171 JCT,** turn **RIGHT** (becomes **McArthur**) and follow **HWY 171** below the airport. Past Hatten St/S Colonial Dr, turn **LEFT** on **Powell Dr.** Curve onto **Broadway,** and continue into **WEBB CITY,** past Madison St (**JOPLIN OPTION** joins).

MO page-27

WB: Stay **AHEAD** past State Line Rd into **KANSAS**. Cross the RR viaduct, then turn **LEFT** on **Main St**, and pass thru downtown **GALENA**. Turn **RIGHT** on **7th St/KS HWY 66**. Continue west across the Spring River thru **RIVERTON**.

CUT the CORNER of KANSAS on ROUTE 66

The **Mother Road** only traverses about 13 miles of the **Sunflower State**, bypassed by an interstate highway. This makes **KANSAS** the sole '66 state thru which it is possible to drive **without** encountering any sign of the superslab. Although short on miles, Route 66 thru **KANSAS** is long on charm and history, so plan to linger and enjoy this small corner of Old 66.

Westbound, your first taste of **KANSAS** is the **State Line Bar**, past which old 66 curves along with the railroad thru a desolate former mining area, and over a vintage (and endangered) concrete-post viaduct above the tracks, to make a quaint 90 degree turn towards downtown **GALENA**. On this corner (119 North Main) is **"4 Women on The Route"** in a beautifully restored Kan-O-Tex gas station, featuring a snack bar and "Tow Tater," inspiration for 'Mater from *CARS*. **GIFT SHOP ALERT!** A Hudson Hornet and a sheriff car are due by the end of summer 2008. Friendly folks! You must stop! (620)783-1366. A Victorian house nearby is planned to become a B&B and tearoom. The town gem is the **Galena Museum** at 319 W 7th St, in the old KATY (M.K.T. RR) depot, housing a fascinating collection of area history. Outside are a restored **ARMY TANK**, switch engine and caboose. Inside are exhibits honoring the history of this mining region, including a room full of ore samples. Admire the ancient horse-drawn hearse, and let the kids try to figger out what all those old contraptions did. Summer hours: Mon-Sat 9-3:30 (closed for lunch). Call (620) 783-2192 off-season. **Howard Litch Park**, downtown, has a **Will Rogers Hwy** marker.

GALENA

EB: Continue with **KS HWY 66** (7th St) to **GALENA**. Turn **LEFT** on **Main St** thru downtown. Cross First St, then turn **RIGHT** on **Front St**. Cross the RR viaduct, then continue past State Line Rd with **Old 66 Blvd** into **MISSOURI** to join **MO 66** toward **JOPLIN**. (see Missouri INTRO on MO page-1)

(see **MO MAP # 6**, MO page-24)

KANSAS

GALENA
RIVERTON
BAXTER SPRINGS 66

WB: West of **RIVERTON**, curve to the **RIGHT** to the US 400 & 69A JCT (KS HWY 66 ENDS): **STOP**, then stay **AHEAD** onto **Beasley Rd.** Continue past the **STOP** at 60th, and cross Brush Creek (see **BRIDGE DETOUR**). Follow the curve south onto 50th St (becomes **Willow St**). Curve **LEFT** to join 3rd **St**, then turn **RIGHT** onto US 69A (Military Ave) thru **BAXTER SPRINGS**. (SEE **OLD 66 OPTION**) Continue south past the US 166 JCT into **OKLAHOMA**.

Check out the famous **Eisler Bros. Grocery and Deli** in **RIVERTON**. **GIFT SHOP ALERT!** Lots of Route 66 stuff. Scope out the original embossed tin ceiling of the 1925 store and an old outhouse in back.

RAINBOW BRIDGE DETOUR: You **MUST** take the short loop across this historic unique bridge, in a lush setting at Brush Creek. This is the **LAST** of three "Marsh Arch" bridges (named for their designer) that once graced US 66 in **KANSAS**. "Progress" claimed the others; preservation saved this one.

In historic **BAXTER SPRINGS**, a 1930s-era **Phillips 66 Station** at 940 Military (on the National Historic Register) has been restored, and now houses a great **Route 66 Visitor Center**. Downtown check out the **Cafe on the Route** and **Little Brick Inn** which occupy a former bank that was robbed by Jesse James in 1876. The cool **Baxter Springs Museum** at 740 East Ave is well worth a stop. http://home.4state.com/~heritagectr (620) 856-2385.
OLD 66 OPTION: Since **KANSAS** has so few '66 miles, be sure to follow the map to drive this short stretch on the south side of **BAXTER SPRINGS**, along Roberts Rd and 30th St, behind the Wal Mart and Mcdonalds.

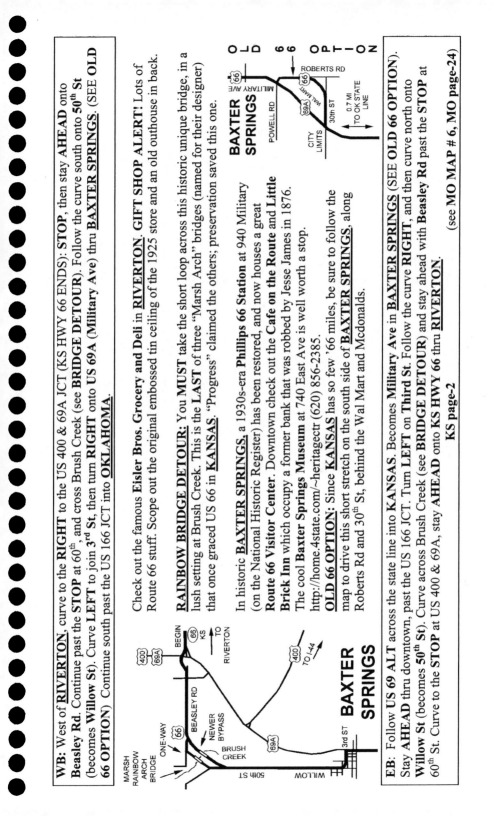

O L D   6 6   O P T I O N

BAXTER SPRINGS

BAXTER SPRINGS

EB: Follow US 69 **ALT** across the state line into **KANSAS**. Becomes Military Ave in **BAXTER SPRINGS** (SEE **OLD 66 OPTION**). Stay **AHEAD** thru downtown, past the US 166 JCT. Turn **LEFT** on **Third St**. Follow the curve **RIGHT**, and then curve north onto **Willow St** (becomes 50th **St**). Curve across Brush Creek (see **BRIDGE DETOUR**) and stay ahead with **Beasley Rd** past the **STOP** at 60th St. Curve to the **STOP** at US 400 & 69A, stay **AHEAD** onto **KS HWY 66** thru **RIVERTON**.

(see **MO MAP # 6, MO page-24**)

ON the ROAD thru OKLAHOMA

OKLAHOMA

Route 66 traces a long jagged path across **The Sooner State**, entering at the very NE corner, and zigzagging its way down to the middle before taking off for **TEXAS**. In **1926**, US 66 was plotted for about 415 miles across **OK**. By 1937 this had been reduced to about 383 miles of first generation paving (including the 9-foot wide "Sidewalk Highway" between **AFTON** and **MIAMI**).

You can **ALMOST** drive across the whole state without hitting an interstate (just a **short** section west of **OKLAHOMA CITY**) but you do drive on upgraded 4-lane sections, especially in the east, where the "free road," bypassed by the turnpikes, still gets plenty of use. West of **SAPULPA**, US 66 was rebuilt in the 1980s (and earlier), so look for miles of old alignment (much undriveable) alongside current OK 66. Fear not, for there are still **PLENTY** of places to see and visit along OK 66. Across the **Western** half of the state are extensive sections of pristine, original **portland concrete**, complete with curbs. You must hop back and forth across I-40 to follow the old pavement, but the "kathumpety-thump" as you roll over the concrete joints is worth the trouble. Western OK is fortunate to have two excellent Route 66 museums, The **OK Route 66 Museum** at **CLINTON**, and the **National Route 66 Museum** in **ELK CITY**. Extremely well done and friendly: see both!

As you motor among red hills, plains, grasslands, woods and rivers keep your eye out for the splendid history of OK, thru small towns connected to the world by a thin ribbon of concrete. **CAR GAME: CREEK CRITTERS: OK HWY 66** crosses many creeks in between **MIAMI** and **LUTHER**, some named after animals. See who is the **FIRST** to spot the following creeks: (WB order) Horse, Bird, Polecat (little and big) Catfish, and Wildhorse Creeks. The one who spots the most on the list wins! (hope the SIGNS are still visible!)

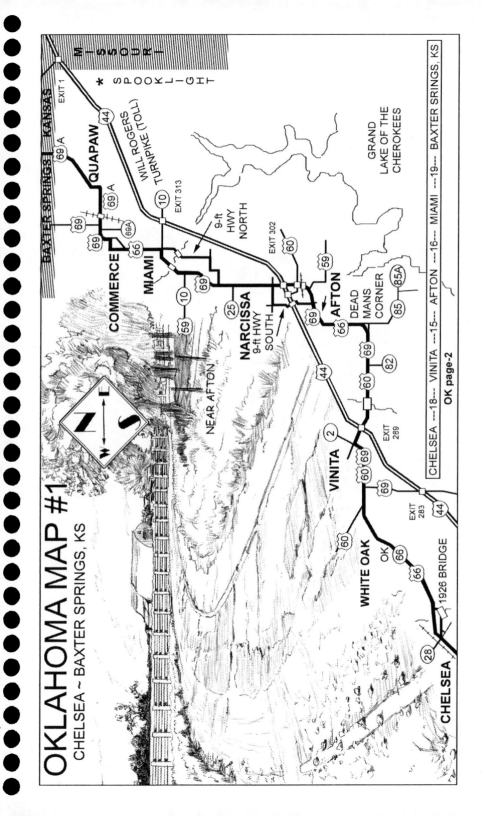

OKLAHOMA MAP #1
CHELSEA ~ BAXTER SPRINGS, KS

MISSOURI

BAXTER SPRINGS KANSAS

* SPOOK-LIGHT

GRAND LAKE OF THE CHEROKEES

EXIT 1

44

69 A

QUAPAW

WILL ROGERS TURNPIKE (TOLL)

69 A

69 A

69

69A

69

66

10

EXIT 313

COMMERCE

MIAMI

9-ft HWY NORTH

EXIT 302

60

59

AFTON

10

69

59

25

NARCISSA

9-ft HWY SOUTH

85A

85

DEAD MANS CORNER

69

66

NEAR AFTON

69

82

44

60

VINITA

EXIT 289

2

60 69

69

WHITE OAK

EXIT 283

44

60

OK 66

1926 BRIDGE

66

28

CHELSEA

CHELSEA ---18--- VINITA ---15--- AFTON ---16--- MIAMI ---19--- BAXTER SRINGS, KS

OK page-2

WB: Follow US 69A south into <u>OKLAHOMA</u>, and curve thru <u>QUAPAW</u>. Stay **AHEAD** onto US 69 at the JCT. Pass the JCT of OK HWY 69A, and continue with **US 69 South** into **COMMERCE**, curving south on **Mickey Mantle Blvd**. Turn **RIGHT** on **Commerce St**, thru downtown, then **LEFT** at the "T" on **Main St**. Stay **AHEAD** at the **STOP** onto **US 69 South** in <u>NORTH MIAMI</u>.

COMMERCE

Over the line, more "chat piles" (old mining tailings) greet you in <u>OKLAHOMA</u>. Several (deteriorating) murals decorate quaint <u>QUAPAW</u>. One honors the coal mining days with a scene of miners and mine works, while others show scenes of a steam engine at the train depot and an old gas station. The **Dallas Dairyette** offers small-town eats. About 12 miles east is the infamous <u>**TRI-STATE SPOOKLIGHT**</u>. Folks have seen "ghostly" lights here since Indian days, but modern sightings are likely to be headlights of cars on Old 66. Paranormal, or "para-headlights," <u>you</u> decide. The viewing site is located just inside <u>OKLAHOMA</u> on **CO RD E50**. You'll need local information to find the spot. Try **Eisler Bros** in <u>**RIVERTON**</u> or the **Galena Museum** in <u>**KANSAS**</u> or **Waylan's Ku-Ku Burger** in <u>**MIAMI**</u> for maps. **NOTE:** The Oklahoma Route 66 Association Guide says: "…local police discourage people from going." So spot the spooks at your own risk!

COMMERCE was **Mickey Mantle's** hometown (his "home" is at 319 S Quincy). North on Main St (from Commerce St) is **Mutt Mantle Field**, named for his dad. Nearby, a small display in a park at 3rd and Main commemorates a local constable slain by **Bonnie and Clyde**. At Commerce and Main, in a 1925-era Marathon station, is the **Dairy King**, a great little small town burger joint. Across the street a former cottage-style gas station, that appears to be "sunken" halfway into a brick wall, houses a gift shop. On later US 66 (Mickey Mantle Blvd) the **Rock Shop** has lots o'rocks and minerals on display.

EB: Follow **US 69 (Main St)** north thru <u>NORTH MIAMI</u>. As US 69 begins to curve right, be in the **LEFT TURN** lane. **AVOID** the first chance to turn, then **CURVE LEFT** at the "Y" and **STOP** in the center median. Cross the WB lanes, then continue north on **Main St** into **COMMERCE**. Turn **RIGHT** on **Commerce St** thru downtown, then **LEFT** on **US 69/ Mickey Mantle Blvd**. At the US 69 North JCT, stay **AHEAD** onto US 69A, and curve thru <u>QUAPAW</u> then on into <u>KANSAS</u>.

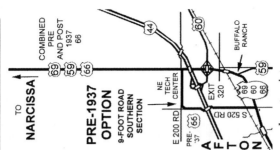

WB: Take US 69 south into **MIAMI**: stay **AHEAD** with Main St thru downtown. At **Steve Owens Blvd** (HWY 10), turn **RIGHT** and follow **US 69** south from town (US 59 S joins ahead) thru **NARCISSA**. Pass under I-44, and under the overpass at the US 60 JCT. Continue with US 69 (US 60 S joins) across the RR overpass, and thru the JCT where US 59 leaves. Stay **AHEAD** on **US 69** to **AFTON**.

On the north side of **MIAMI** (say My-am-uh") is **Waylan's Ku Ku Burger**, and their great 1965 neon sign. **GIANT ALERT!** A **GIANT Ku Ku** is posed as if it just popped out of the building (think coo-coo clock). Downtown at 103 N Main sits the proud **Coleman Theatre Beautiful**, a magnificent 1929 Spanish mission-styled showpiece under restoration, with a Route 66 exhibit and daily tours. **CLEVER NAME:** On south Main is "**On the Corner.**" **MIAMI INFO:** (918) 542-4435.

PRE-1937 OPTION (follow the maps): South from **MIAMI**, remnants of the famous **9-foot Hwy** (AKA: Sidewalk Hwy, Ribbon Rd) zigzag towards **AFTON**. This narrow strip of road, with concrete base and curbs and an asphalt road surface, was paved in 1922, serving US 66 'till 1937. **NOTE:** Some sections are bumpy and gravelly, so go slow. The road is fragile, so **NO heavy rigs! WB:** The **NORTH** section begins as blacktop (past an old "Colonial" style gas station on S Main), then reverts to one-lane road past HWY 125. An old store at **NARCISSA** sits on US 69 between the surviving segments. The **SOUTH** section starts at the NE Technology Center turnoff, and curves south, across I-44 and the RR, ending back at US 69 east of **AFTON**. **EB:** reverse. Between the US 60 and US 59 junctions is **Buffalo Ranch**. A new multi-purpose facility has replaced the original complex, but they **DO** keep some **LIVE BUFFALO** on hand for modern tourists.

EB: Follow **US 69 & 60** north from **AFTON**. After US 59 joins, stay **AHEAD** over the RR overpass. Stay **AHEAD** with US 69 under the overpass at the US 60 JCT, then pass under I-44, and thru **NARCISSA** on **US 69 & 59**. Continue past the US 59 JCT and follow **US 69** into **MIAMI** (becomes Steve Owen Blvd). Turn **LEFT** on **Main St**, thru downtown. Follow **US 69** north from town.

OK page-4

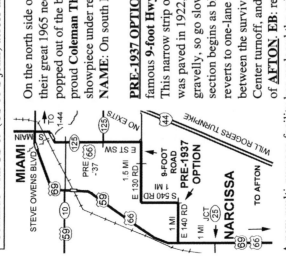

WB: Follow **US 69 & 60** from **AFTON**. Cross under I-44 and enter **VINITA** on Illinois St (**US 69 & 60**). Turn **LEFT** on **Wilson**, and curve out of town, passing the S US 69 JCT. At the US 60 JCT, stay **AHEAD** on **OK HWY 66** thru **WHITE OAK & CHELSEA**.

VINITA

Near **Buffalo Ranch** (JCT US 59) is the charming **Route 66 Motel**, with theme rooms (918) 257 8313. Just east of **AFTON** you'll cross the **Horse Creek Bridge**, with its built-in sidewalks. The **PACKARD** sign downtown marks **Afton Station/Route 66 Packards**, the former **DX gas station** rehabilitated to house Laurel Kane's collection of Route 66 postcards and memorabilia, plus David Kane's 12 antique **Packards**. Limited hours: Call ahead to (918)-382-9465 or (918) 787-8903 for info. **GIANT ALERT! A GIANT PENGUIN statue** from the Tulsa zoo's "Penguins on Parade" promotion lives here. **SIDE TRIP:** South of **AFTON** is **Grand Lake O' the Cherokees**, 1,300 miles of shoreline among the foothills of the Ozarks. At "Monkey Island" near Bernice, **Darryl Starbird's Custom Car Museum** (Hwy 85A) features 40 exotic vehicles, including wild "bubble-top" customs (918) 257-4234.

Between **Dead Man's Corner** (self-explanatory) and I-44 are the pecan groves of **Little Cabin Pecan Co,** with pecans and pottery. **GIFT SHOP ALERT!** 66 has long crossed a narrow, vintage bridge over Little Cabin Creek on the way into **VINITA**. Look for the classic **EAT** sign at **Clantons Café** (owned by the same family since 1927). Downtown offers antiques and the old Vinita Hotel. Old gas station relics abound, while a few Mom and Pop motels are listed in the Federation guide.

GIANT ALERT! The **World's LARGEST McDonalds** (formerly the Glass House) straddles I-44 between Exits 289 and 283. If you want to stand in the middle and watch all the traffic zoom by underneath, sneak south from Illinois St on 7th St (just west of EXIT 289). Mid-September brings the **Worlds LARGEST Calf-Fry Festival** to town (you know what a "calf-fry" is, right?) City INFO: www.vinita.com or (918) 256-7133.

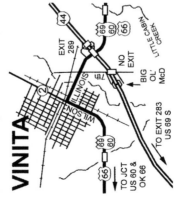

EB: Follow **OK 66** from **CHELSEA**, thru **WHITE OAK**. JOIN **US 60 & US 69** (stay AHEAD) into **VINITA**. Curve north onto **Wilson St,** thru downtown, then turn **RIGHT** with **US 69 & 60** onto **Illinois St**. Cross under I-44, and follow **US 69 & 60** into **AFTON**.

(see **MAP #1 OK page-2**)

OKLAHOMA MAP # 2
RED FORK ~ CHELSEA

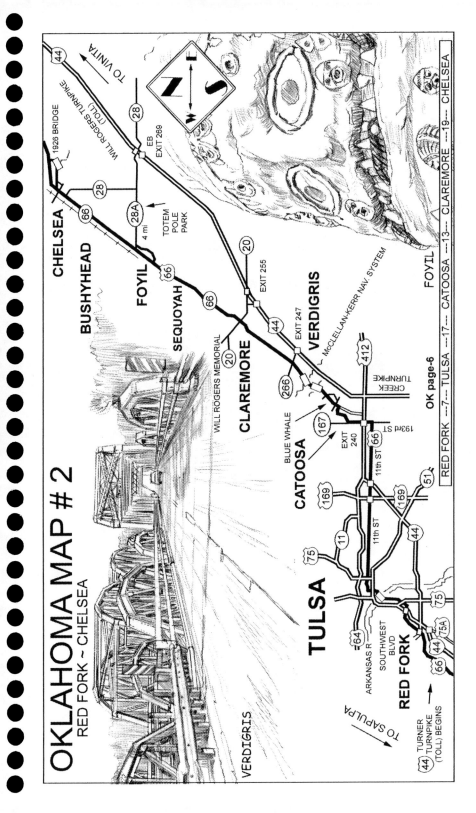

TO VINITA

44

1926 BRIDGE

WILL ROGERS TURNPIKE (TOLL)

28

EB EXIT 269

28A

28

66

28A
4 mi

TOTEM POLE PARK

20
EXIT 255

66

66

44
EXIT 247

266

20

WILL ROGERS MEMORIAL

20

CREEK TURNPIKE

412

McCLELLAN-KERR NAV SYSTEM

BLUE WHALE

167

EXIT 240

193rd ST

66

11th ST

169

169

51

44

11th ST

11

75

64

ARKANSAS R

SOUTHWEST BLVD

75

66 44 75A

TO SAPULPA

44 TURNER TURNPIKE (TOLL) BEGINS

CHELSEA

BUSHYHEAD

FOYIL

SEQUOYAH

CLAREMORE

VERDIGRIS

CATOOSA

TULSA

RED FORK

VERDIGRIS

N
E
S
W

OK page-6

RED FORK ---7--- TULSA ---17--- CATOOSA ---13--- CLAREMORE ---19--- CHELSEA
FOYIL

WB: Follow **OK HWY 66** from **CHELSEA**, thru **BUSHYHEAD**, **FOYIL** and **SEQUOYAH** into **CLAREMORE**.

WHITE OAK consists of an old mill across the tracks, and the Moose Lodge. In **CHELSEA** at 10th and Olive is a vintage house mail-ordered from the Sears Catalog in 1913 (tours by appointment only). Watch for a couple of picturesque old motel signs: the Chelsea Motel sign in town and the Country Court sign east of town. **OPTION:** Follow the detail map to drive across a **1926 iron bridge** over **Pryor Creek** (partly gravel road). Town INFO: (918) 789-2220.

GIANT ALERT! Just 4 miles east of HWY 66 on **HWY 28A**, (northeast of **FOYIL**) is **Totem Pole Park**, site of the **World's LARGEST Totem Pole** (90 feet), created over 11 years by the late Ed Galloway and recently restored. **FOLK ART ALERT!** The property contains a colorful collection of smaller concrete totems, covered in countless critters, plus the 11-sided "Fiddle House" (he hand carved almost 400 violins over the years). Truly a **PHOTO OP!** INFO: (918) 342-9149.

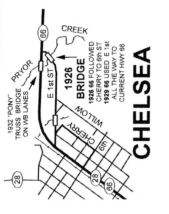

CHELSEA

FOYIL

FOYIL was also home to **Andy Payne**, winner of the 1928 **"Bunion Derby,"** the Transcontinental Foot Race from Los Angeles to New York City that followed all of US 66. **OPTION** (recommended): Drive **Old 66** thru town along Andy Payne Blvd, past the **Bunion Derby Historic Marker**, and the **Andy Payne Statue** (see detail map). Top off your visit at the **Top Hat Dairy Bar** for old-fashioned burgers.

SCAVENGER HUNT! Between **FOYIL** and **CLAREMORE** (south of **SEQUOYAH**) is a store called **Kong's Korner**. What does the "statue" out front depict? _____

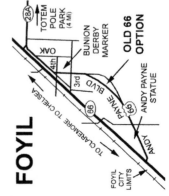

EB: Follow **OK HWY 66** from **CLAREMORE**, thru **SEQUOYAH**, **FOYIL**, **BUSHYHEAD** and **CHELSEA**.

OK page-7

WB: Follow **OK HWY 66** (becomes **Lynn Riggs Blvd**) thru **CLAREMORE** (see **PRE-1958 OPTION**).

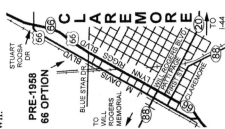

CLAREMORE once was famous for "radium" baths, piped in mineral water discovered in 1903. One dispenser of this "miracle water" was the grand **Will Rogers Hotel**, 6 stories and 78 rooms of opulent Spanish decor (now restored as senior living). **SCAVENGER HUNT!** What **SIGN** is painted at the top of the backside of the former hotel (now the **Will Rogers Center and Apartments**)?

OPTION: PRE-1958 66 followed **J. M. Davis Blvd**, one block west and parallel to current HWY 66. This connects to Lynn Riggs on the north side at the Stuart Roosa stoplight, and on the south, below Claremore St. **PRE-'58 66** features several old road relics, including the **Adobe Village Apts**, which once were the El Sueno Courts, an Alamo-Plaza style motel. Try to loop on both routes thru town.

This town is loaded with memorials (even the street names). The **Will Rogers Memorial and Museum** at 1720 W **Will Rogers Blvd** honors the celebrated movie and stage star and author, who never met a man he didn't like. (800) 324-9455. Another name promoted for Route 66 is **"Will Rogers Hwy,"** as evidenced by many markers, old and new, along the route to California. Also on **Will Rogers Blvd** is a statue of Will sitting on a park bench. **PHOTO OP!**

20,000 guns (and other artifacts) wait at the **J M Davis Arms and Historical Museum**, the Worlds **LARGEST Private Firearm Collection** (plus an **ARMY TANK**) at 333 N Lynn Riggs. Beware those guns that were formerly owned by outlaws and bandits! (918) 341-5707. Less military is the **Lynn Riggs Memorial**, at 121 N Weenonah, honoring the author who inspired the musical *Oklahoma* (the original "Surrey with the fringe on top" from the movie is here) (918) 627-2716. **CLEVER NAME!** "Spirits of 66" liquor store. **GIANT ALERT!** Dottie's Western Wear (south of Patti Page Blvd) has a **Giant PLASTIC BOOT**. For non-plastic food, try **Ron's Hamburgers and Chili**. To rest up, try the **Best Western Will Rogers Inn** (918) 341-4410 or the **Claremore Motor Inn** (800) 828-4540 (both are in the Federation Guide). City INFO: (918) 341-2818 or www.claremore.org

EB: Follow **OK HWY 66** (becomes **Lynn Riggs Blvd**) thru **CLAREMORE** (see **PRE-1958 OPTION**).

WB: Follow OK HWY 66 from **CLAREMORE**. Cross the JCT with HWY 266, and over the large bridges. Past the **Blue Whale**, cross **Spunky Creek**, then turn **RIGHT** on Ford St into **CATOOSA**. Turn **LEFT** on Cherokee, and continue to the HWY 167 (193rd St) JCT.

Near **VERDIGRIS**, **The Nut House** ("Pecans and other nuts") is decorated inside and out with antiques, including a fire truck and vintage wagons (pecan pie…uh-huhuhuh) (918) 266-1604. Since the late '60s, **HWY 66** has crossed over the **McClellan-Kerr Navigation System**, a 445-mile waterway that links Tulsa to the Gulf (check the impressive RR bridge on the north). A photogenic pair of "almost" Twin Bridges crosses the former channel of the Verdigris River (now called Bird Creek). The 1936 span is 24 feet wide, while its 1957 sibling (added for 4-lane 66) is 28 ft wide.

1926-1957 OPTION: Just southwest of the Twin Bridges, an older loop of 66 turns off to the south. Its pavement follows **N 225 E Ave** (**WB:** access from next x-over), cuts the corner of the older Ozark Trail to hit **EW 57**, then rejoins **OK HWY 66**. Along the way, the route passes the front of the former **Arrowood Trading Post** (now a garage). The **Ozark Trail** (Pre-US 66) continues across the 4-Lane on EW 57 (Rice St) to cross a **1913 one lane bridge**, then turns left on Cherokee into **CATOOSA**.

If you drive the **OPTION**, be sure to double back on **4-lane 66**, to visit the **BLUE WHALE**, the grinning, concrete-cetacean star of a former swimming hole, now renovated as a park (no swimming!). **PHOTO OP!** (but not quite a "**giant alert**" considering how big real whales get). On the other side of 4-lane 66 is the picturesque "back" facade of **Arrowood**, with paintings of Indian dancers and its name in huge letters. **CATOOSA** itself has a **Historical Museum** in an old RR depot, with a "Ship it on the Frisco" caboose, on Cherokee St. **SCAVENGER HUNT!** What is the caboose's 4-digit number? _____

Due to the navigation system, the **Port of Catoosa** is billed as the **furthest inland seaport** in the US!

EB: Take Cherokee St thru **CATOOSA**. Past the **Police Dept**, turn **RIGHT** on Ford St. At **OK HWY 66**, turn **LEFT** onto the EB lanes, and continue past the **Blue Whale**, across the large bridges and past HWY 266, into **CLAREMORE** (becomes **Lynn Riggs Blvd**).

OK page-10

WB: Turn **LEFT** on **HWY 167** (193rd E Ave). Stay **AHEAD** under I-44 with **193rd E** Ave, past Admiral Place, then turn **RIGHT** on 11th St. Stay **AHEAD** under I-44 (IGNORE the "OK Hwy 66" sign) and past US 169 (Mingo Expwy) to continue on 11th into **TULSA.**

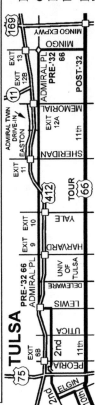

Route 66 runs straight on 11th St to downtown **TULSA.** The east portion is 2-lane country road, but soon grows into a busy artery. Rewarding your stoplight patience are many relics of old 66. **SIDE TRIP: PRE-32 '66** turns up **Mingo Rd** to **Admiral Place**, where it spins "roundabout," a rare **traffic circle. Cyrus Avery**, "The Father of 66" arranged for '66 to pass by his business, the **Old English Inn**, at this point! This route followed **Admiral** west (near the **Admiral Twin Drive-In**) to **Lewis**, then south to **2nd**, but a detour off 2nd and one-way streets now hamper this way into downtown.

Several old motels still exist on 11th, some with classic signs and untapped potential. The **Desert Hills**, east of Yale, has a neat sign and is a possibility for those wanting to stay in an old 66 motel. Examples of old gas stations (now serving other needs) include the former **Sinclair Station** at Jamestown. College-themed street names mark the presence of the **University of Tulsa**. Good eateries include the **Corner Café** at Peoria, **Talley's Café** at Yale and the **Rancho Grande**, with its vintage neon sign of a lasso-twirling vaquero and a cactus, west of Utica St. Also near Yale St is an original **Tastee Freez** from 1954, now remodeled and renamed. From here to Peoria St, the sidewalks are lined with blocks honoring the US 66 shield. **GIANT ALERT**! Well south of 66, but worth a detour for giant fans, is **The Golden Driller**, a 76-foot tribute to **TULSA**'s oil heritage (the former "Oil Capitol of the World"), at 21st St west of Yale. Also well south of 11th is **Route 66 Harley-Davidson Dealership** at the JCT of Broken Arrow Expressway and Memorial Dr. They have a Route 66 exhibit. 918 622 1340. **FUTURE GIANT?**: A **17 story bronze Indian** is proposed for Homes Peak, northwest of town (he **should** be visible from '66)!

EB: Follow 11th St east, under US 169 (Mingo Expy) and then under I-44 (**IGNORE** "East State HWY 66" sign). Follow 11th St past Lynn Lane. A mile later, turn **LEFT** on **193rd E Ave. AVOID** the "turn lanes" at the I-44 JCT: stay **AHEAD** with **HWY 167** (IGNORE the "OK HWY 66" sign). North of I-44, turn **RIGHT** at the light onto **Cherokee St**, and continue into **CATOOSA.**

WB: Stay **AHEAD** with **11th St** under US 75 into downtown. At Elgin St, follow the main curve **RIGHT**, then angle **LEFT** onto **10th St**. West of Boulder St the route rejoins **11th St**. Past Denver Ave, curve to the **LEFT** and cross I-444, then curve **RIGHT** onto **12th St**. Turn **LEFT** at the "T" on **Southwest Blvd** and cross the river. Follow **Southwest Blvd** under US 75, then across I-244 in **RED FORK**.

TULSA is famous for abundant Art Deco architecture. **11th St** has many examples, including the "Streamline" styled **Tulsa Monument Building**, east of Utica. The "ZigZag" tower and terra-cotta details of the 1929 **Warehouse Market Building** bear close examination. The preserved facade, at the Elgin St intersection, houses **Tulsa Treasures** (gifts and collectibles) and **Lyons Indian Store**. Lyon's boasts a huge selection of Indian goodies from over 30 tribes, and OK souvenirs. "Zigzag" style and colorful terra-cotta tiles abound in downtown, including the **Boston Ave Church**. For info check www.tulsaarchitecture.com or call for info on a walking tour: (800) 558-3311.

SIDE TRIP: detour up to **PRE-'32 66** to ogle the 1925 **Blue Dome gas station** (topped by a blue dome, of course) at **2nd** and **Elgin**. One-way streets (and a detour of 2nd St at US 75, via 1st and Norfolk) make the **PRE-32** route via **Admiral Place** harder to follow. Among area attractions are the **Gilcrease Museum** of western art/artifacts and the **Philbrook Museum of Art**. INFO: www.visittulsa.com.

The long-closed Cyrus Avery (**11th St**) **Bridge**, a 1916 Art Deco concrete masterpiece spanning the **Arkansas River**, is being restored. At its east end, **Cyrus Avery Centennial Plaza** will feature a huge bronze statue. Across the river on **Southwest Blvd**, look for the **GIANT Sinclair Dino** on an oil tank, south of Howard Park. In **RED FORK**, the former 66 Motel is gone, but **Ollie's Station Restaurant** has toy trains running along the ceiling! More plans are underway for 66 across the **TULSA** area!

EB: Follow **Southwest Blvd** thru **RED FORK**, and across I-244. Continue on **Southwest Blvd** under US 75, to cross the river into **TULSA**. Turn **RIGHT** on **12th St**. Angle across I-444 (no choice) then curve onto **11th St** EB. Past Cheyenne St, follow the main street as it angles **LEFT** onto **10th** (thru Boulder). Past Detroit Ave, **ANGLE RIGHT** at Elgin onto **11th St**. Follow **11th St** east under US 75.

(see **MAP # 2** OK page-6)

OK page-11

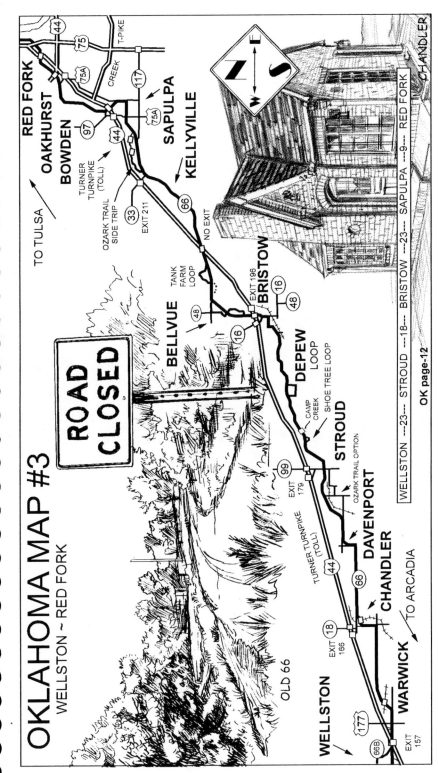

OKLAHOMA MAP #3
WELLSTON ~ RED FORK

ROAD CLOSED

RED FORK
OAKHURST
BOWDEN
44
75
75A
97
44
75A
117
CREEK T-PIKE
TO TULSA
TURNER TURNPIKE (TOLL)
OZARK TRAIL SIDE TRIP
33
EXIT 211
66
NO EXIT
SAPULPA
KELLYVILLE

BELLVUE
TANK FARM LOOP
48
16
EXIT 196
BRISTOW
16
48

DEPEW LOOP
CAMP CREEK
SHOE TREE LOOP
99
EXIT 179
STROUD
OZARK TRAIL OPTION
DAVENPORT

OLD 66
TURNER TURNPIKE (TOLL)
44
66
18
EXIT 166
CHANDLER
TO ARCADIA

WELLSTON
177
66B
EXIT 157
WARWICK

N E S W

CHANDLER

WELLSTON ---23--- STROUD ---18--- BRISTOW ---23--- SAPULPA ---9--- RED FORK

OK page-12

OK page-13

WB: Take Southwest Blvd thru **RED FORK** and along the RR thru **OAKHURST** and **BOWDEN** (becomes **Frankhoma Rd**). At the HWY 166 JCT stay AHEAD with Frankhoma Rd, go under I-44, then turn **RIGHT** on **OK 66 & Alt 75** (Mission St), into **SAPULPA**. Turn **RIGHT** with OK 66 on Dewey Ave, thru downtown.

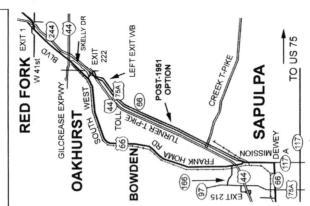

In **RED FORK** at 4070 Southwest Blvd is **Ollie's Station Restaurant**, decorated with a "train" motif. South of the I- 244/I-44 JCT, **Skelly Drive** runs as a service road down to I-44 EXIT 222, past some old motels (one offers a price for "couples"). **Skelly Drive** was the name of the 1959-era US 66 that bypassed **TULSA** (now I-44). South from here, Old 66 ambles along the tracks thru **OAKHURST** and **BOWDEN**, and then past **Frankhoma Pottery**, makers of fine pottery and collectibles since 1933, with a gift shop and outlet store. Currently up for sale, so check locally for status.

OPTION: POST-'51 US 66 (quick, but dull) follows **OK 66 /ALT 75** south to **SAPULPA**. Join I-44 WB at EXIT 222A (S 49th W Ave), then **QUICKLY** get in the far **LEFT** lane to **EXIT LEFT** onto **OK HWY 66/ALT 75** (AVOID the turnpike ahead!). **EB:** Follow **OK 66** north onto I-44, then **QUICKLY** take **EXIT 222A** (S 49th West Ave), cross under I-44 and join **Southwest Blvd** north.

GIANT ALERT! At the **"Tribute to Sapulpa Industry and Workers"** at Frankhoma Rd and OK 66 is a **GIANT COKE BOTTLE** (well, it's pretty big). **Happy Burger** at 215 N Mission is the "oldest hamburger stand in Sapulpa" (since 1957): a great place, with some old photos, too. In front of the offices of the **Tulsa-Sapulpa Union Railway Co** on Dewey (a freight line connecting Sapulpa to Tulsa that began in 1917 as an interurban) is a restored **Trolley Car** and caboose. **SAPULPA** INFO: (918) 224-0170.

EB: Follow **OK HWY 66/Dewey Ave** thru **SAPULPA**. Turn **LEFT** at **Mission St** with OK 66 & Alt 75. Cross the tracks, and turn **LEFT** at the light onto Frankhoma Rd. Pass under I-44, then stay AHEAD with Frankhoma Rd at the W HWY 166 JCT. Continue thru **BOWDEN** (becomes **Southwest Blvd**) and **OAKHURST**. Stay AHEAD with Southwest Blvd into **RED FORK**.

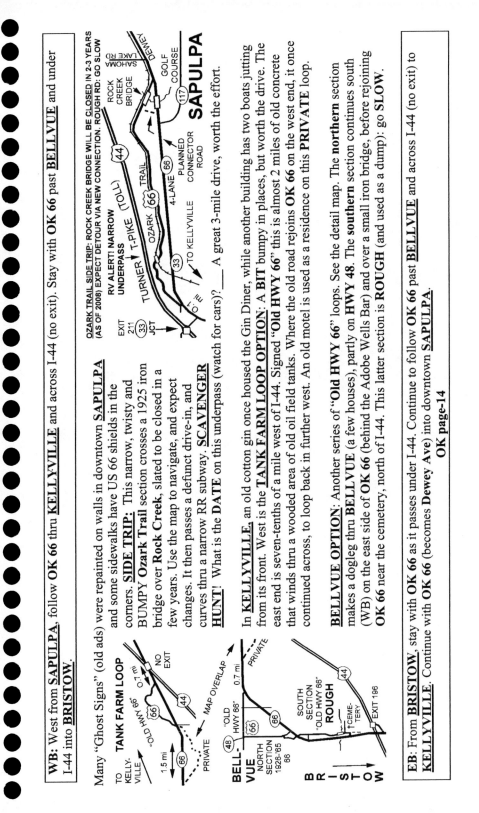

WB: West from **SAPULPA**, follow **OK 66** thru **KELLYVILLE** and across I-44 (no exit). Stay with **OK 66** past **BELLVUE** and under I-44 into **BRISTOW**.

OZARK TRAIL SIDE TRIP: ROCK CREEK BRIDGE WILL BE CLOSED IN 2-3 YEARS (AS OF 2008) EXPECT DETOUR VIA NEW CONNECTION. ROUGH RD: GO SLOW

RV ALERT! NARROW UNDERPASS

SAHOMA LAKE RD

ROCK CREEK BRIDGE

DEWEY

GOLF COURSE

SAPULPA

(44)

OZARK (66) TRAIL

TURNER T-PIKE (TOLL)

4-LANE

PLANNED CONNECTOR ROAD

(117)

TO KELLYVILLE

(33)

EXIT 211 (33) JCT

Many "Ghost Signs" (old ads) were repainted on walls in downtown **SAPULPA** and some sidewalks have US 66 shields in the corners. **SIDE TRIP:** This narrow, twisty and BUMPY **Ozark Trail** section crosses a 1925 iron bridge over **Rock Creek**, slated to be closed in a few years. Use the map to navigate, and expect changes. It then passes a defunct drive-in, and curves thru a narrow RR subway. **SCAVENGER HUNT!** What is the **DATE** on this underpass (watch for cars)? _____ A great 3-mile drive, worth the effort.

In **KELLYVILLE**, an old cotton gin once housed the Gin Diner, while another building has two boats jutting from its front. West is the **TANK FARM LOOP OPTION:** A **BIT** bumpy in places, but worth the drive. The east end is seven-tenths of a mile west of I-44. Signed "**Old HWY 66**" this is almost 2 miles of old concrete that winds thru a wooded area of old oil field tanks. Where the old road rejoins **OK 66** on the west end, it once continued across, to loop back in further west. An old motel is used as a residence on this **PRIVATE** loop.

BELLVUE OPTION: Another series of "**Old HWY 66**" loops. See the detail map. The **northern** section makes a dogleg thru **BELLVUE** (a few houses), partly on **HWY 48**. The **southern** section continues south (WB) on the east side of **OK 66** (behind the Adobe Wells Bar) and over a small iron bridge, before rejoining **OK 66** near the cemetery, north of I-44. This latter section is **ROUGH** (and used as a dump): go **SLOW**.

TO KELLY-VILLE

TANK FARM LOOP

"OLD HWY 66"

0.7 mi

NO EXIT

(66)

1.5 mi

(66)

(44)

PRIVATE

MAP OVERLAP

BELL-VUE

NORTH SECTION 1926-'65 66

(48)

"OLD HWY 66"

(66)

0.7 mi

PRIVATE

SOUTH SECTION "OLD HWY 66" **ROUGH**

(66)

CEME-TERY

EXIT 196

(44)

B R I S T O W

EB: From **BRISTOW**, stay with **OK 66** as it passes under I-44. Continue to follow **OK 66** past **BELLVUE** and across I-44 (no exit) to **KELLYVILLE**. Continue with **OK 66** (becomes Dewey Ave) into downtown **SAPULPA**.

WB: Continue with **OK 66**, south of I-44, into **BRISTOW** (becomes **Main St**). Before reaching the RR, turn **RIGHT** with **OK 66** on 4th St, then follow the curve onto **Roland St** and out of town. Pass by the entrance to **DEPEW** and continue into **STROUD**.

BRISTOW

In downtown **BRISTOW**, look for the old **Bristow Motor Co** building, with plaster sculptures of "spoke wheels" on the facade. **SCAVENGER HUNT!** What is the **DATE** on the building? _____ The **Bristow Museum** is at the Railroad Depot on East 7th St. City INFO: www.bristowok.org. Look for the blue-tile roofed service station near the corner of Main and 4th. Down the road, at 630 S Roland, the **Anchor Inn** has cooked many a burger since 1950. **GIANT ALERT!** Watch for a **GIANT PENGUIN** (from TULSA) at the Chrysler Dealer. NEW in 2005 will be **Route 66 Cottage:** http://route66cottage.visitbristowok.com/

DEPEW LOOP OPTION: From **1926-28**, US 66 made a curious loop thru downtown **DEPEW**, so be sure to drive the original road thru this small town "time capsule," marked by its "Home of the Hornets" water tower. **Coach's Corner Café** comes recommended. While an old gas station is in danger of demolition, a Californian is reportedly buying property to turn the town into an Artist colony. Hope the small town atmosphere remains.

Many cast-off remnants of **US 66** lie alongside current **OK 66** in this area (many bypassed as late as 1984!), some street-signed as "Old Hwy 66." You can drive a few sections for a bit, while landowners block others. One house has a basketball goal set up that uses old 66 as the court. **SHOE TREE LOOP:** On private property, but usually kept open by the enlightened owner (be a good guest). The east entrance to this short stretch of "Old 66 Blvd" is about half a mile west of **Camp Creek** (about 6 miles west of **DEPEW**). Here is the famous **SHOE TREE**; festooned with funky footwear (another shoe tree is way out west near Amboy, CA). Add your own pair of sneakers or heels to this public art collaboration.

EB: Follow **OK 66** east from **STROUD**, past the entrance to **DEPEW**. Continue into **BRISTOW**, entering with **Roland St**, then curving onto 4th St. At the **HWY 48 JCT**, turn **LEFT** onto **Main St** and follow **OK 66** north thru downtown. Pass the **HWY 16 JCT**, cross Sand Creek, then **BEAR LEFT** at the "Y" to **AVOID** the Turnpike entrance (EXIT 196), stay **AHEAD** under I-44 with **OK 66**.

WB: Follow **OK 66** west from **STROUD**, and curve thru **DAVENPORT**. Enter **CHANDLER** on **E 1ˢᵗ St**, then curve with **OK 66** onto **Manvel** at the northside JCT with OK 18 (See **ART ALERT**). Pass thru downtown. Turn **RIGHT** with **OK 66**, and continue thru **WARWICK**, under the RR and past the JCT of US 177 **(STOP)**. Cross under I-44 at EXIT 157, and continue to **WELLSTON**.

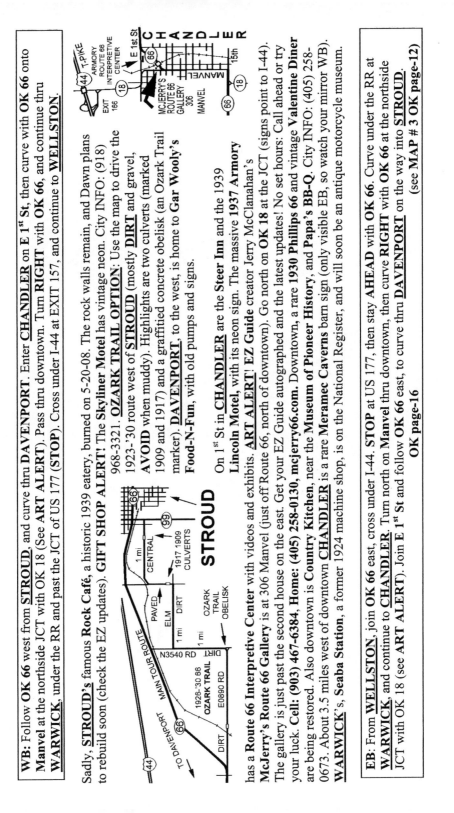

Sadly, **STROUD**'s famous **Rock Café**, a historic 1939 eatery, burned on 5-20-08. The rock walls remain, and Dawn plans to rebuild soon (check the EZ updates). **GIFT SHOP ALERT!** The **Skyliner Motel** has vintage neon. City INFO: (918) 968-3321. **OZARK TRAIL OPTION**: Use the map to drive the 1923-'30 route west of **STROUD** (mostly **DIRT** and gravel, **AVOID** when muddy). Highlights are two culverts (marked 1909 and 1917) and a graffitied concrete obelisk (an Ozark Trail marker). **DAVENPORT**, to the west, is home to **Gar Wooly's Food-N-Fun**, with old pumps and signs.

On 1ˢᵗ St in **CHANDLER** are the **Steer Inn** and the 1939 **Lincoln Motel**, with its neon sign. The massive **1937 Armory** has a **Route 66 Interpretive Center** with videos and exhibits. **ART ALERT! EZ Guide** creator Jerry McClanahan's **McJerry's Route 66 Gallery** is at 306 Manvel (just off Route 66, north of downtown). Go north on **OK 18** at the JCT (signs point to I-44). The gallery is just past the second house on the east. Get your EZ Guide autographed and the latest updates! No set hours: Call ahead or try your luck. **Cell: (903) 467-6384, Home: (405) 258-0130, mcjerry66.com.** Downtown, a rare **1930 Phillips 66** and vintage **Valentine Diner** are being restored. Also downtown is **Country Kitchen**, near the **Museum of Pioneer History**, and **Papa's BB-Q**. City INFO: (405) 258-0673. About 3.5 miles west of downtown **CHANDLER** is a rare **Meramec Caverns** barn sign (only visible EB, so watch your mirror WB). **WARWICK**'s, **Seaba Station**, a former 1924 machine shop, is on the National Register, and will soon be an antique motorcycle museum.

EB: From **WELLSTON**, join **OK 66** east, cross under I-44. **STOP** at US 177, then stay **AHEAD** with **OK 66**. Curve under the RR at **WARWICK**, and continue to **CHANDLER**. Turn north on **Manvel** thru downtown, then curve **RIGHT** with **OK 66** at the northside JCT with OK 18 (see **ART ALERT**). Join **E 1ˢᵗ St** and follow **OK 66** east, to curve thru **DAVENPORT** on the way into **STROUD**.

(see **MAP # 3 OK page-12**)

OK page-16

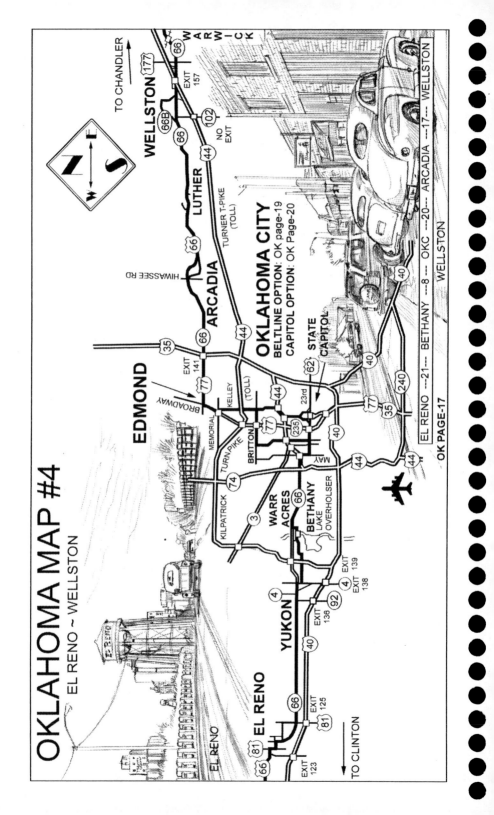

OKLAHOMA MAP #4
EL RENO ~ WELLSTON

WB: Just west of I-44, bear **RIGHT** onto **HWY 66B** thru **WELLSTON**. Rejoin **OK 66** and continue thru **LUTHER** and **ARCADIA**. **OK 66 ENDS** at I-35 **EXIT 141**, stay **AHEAD** onto **2ⁿᵈ St/US 77** into **EDMOND**.

WELLSTON

WELLSTON, bypassed since 1933, has a nice little downtown, plus a **1933 iron bridge** over Captain Creek, west on **66B**. **LUTHER** sits a bit south of 66. On the north side of 66 here are former bridge footings that carried US 66 over a railroad and Deep Fork Creek. **SIDE TRIP:** The western part of this old route, a half-mile **dead end spur**, is reached by turning north onto a road labeled **"Private Historical Site Trucks Prohibited."**

West of **LUTHER** try the great Bar-B-Q at **The Boundary**, housed in an old gas station on the sharp curve east of Indian Meridian Rd. Watch closely on the north for the remains of an old stone service station (west of Choctaw Rd). **FOLK ART ALERT!** On current OK 66 east of **ARCADIA**, watch for John Hargrove's fantastic **"Oklahoma County 66 Auto Trim and Mini Museum."** Look for replicas of the Blue Whale, Twin Arrows, and so much more!

Stop by and visit if the gate is open. **SIDE TRIP:** Just west of Hargrove's, at **Hiwassee Rd**, is the west end of a loop of pristine '66 that heads back east, to rejoin current OK 66 after about a mile. Thanks to preservationist and author Jim Ross, this stretch is on the **National Register of Historic Places**. The east portion is 1928 Portland Concrete, the west section, paved in 1929, is blacktop over concrete, with curbs. **CAUTION:** Be careful leaving and joining OK 66.

The centerpiece of **ARCADIA** is the restored 1898 **Round Barn**. Downstairs is a **Route 66 Exhibit**, while the loft is rented for dances and events. **GIFT SHOP ALERT!** (405) 396-2761. NOTE: **OBEY** the speed limit thru town! **GIANT ALERT! # 1:** After dark, check out the illuminated 66 foot tall **POP BOTTLE** at **POPS**, a great new diner and convenience store, with over 400 kinds of soft drinks! To the west, among large red rocks, look for a small herd of longhorn cattle. **GIANT ALERT! # 2:** At the I-35 JCT is a **GIANT CROSS** (the cross in **GROOM, TX** is taller).

EB: Follow **2ⁿᵈ St/US 77** east from **EDMOND**. Cross I-35 at **EXIT 141**, stay **AHEAD** on **OK HWY 66** thru **ARCADIA** and **LUTHER**. At the JCT of **HWY 66B**, veer **LEFT**, and follow **HWY 66B** thru **WELLSTON**, then rejoin **OK 66** eastbound.

OK page-18

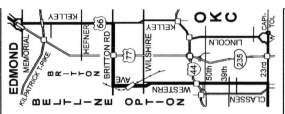

WB: In **EDMOND**, turn **LEFT** on Broadway / US 77. Take the **Memorial Rd/Kelley St EXIT**, turn **LEFT** on the **Frontage Rd** (Kelley), then **LEFT** on Memorial, under US 77. At the light, turn **RIGHT** on **Kelley**. Go just over 2 miles past the Kilpatrick T-pike.
 BELTLINE OPTION (OR: see **OK page-20** for **CAPITOL OPTION**). Turn **RIGHT** on **Britton Rd**, then cross US 77 into **BRITTON**, and **LEFT** on Western Ave. Stay **AHEAD** on Western past I-44. Turn **RIGHT** on **23rd St** (see **OK page-20** to continue).

 NOTE: The JCT at Memorial and Kelley is due to be changed. Kelley will go straight thru at Memorial.
EDMOND outgrew most remnants of old 66. Exhibits honoring what is gone are at the **Edmond Historical Society Museum**, 431 S Boulevard (405) 340-0078. At the corner of 2nd and S Boulevard, the **Sanders Camera Shop** once occupied the first schoolhouse in the OK Territory (1889). The **Historic Downtown Shopping District** is located north of the corner of 2nd and Broadway. **Non-GIANT ALERT!** At this same corner is a replica of the **Statue of Liberty.**

You have a choice of routes thru **OKLAHOMA CITY** (OKC). This page's **BELTLINE OPTION** ("Alt 66") began in 1931 and detoured much of the US 66 traffic around the northwest of the city until 1953 (Western Ave was bypassed in favor of May Ave in 1947). This option misses the Capitol, but offers more route-flavor with numerous old gas stations and other businesses. See **OK page-20** for the **CAPITOL OPTION**: READ AHEAD to decide which option to take.

BRITTON's John Dunning is restoring the **Owl Courts** complex at 742 W Britton Rd. A long-term project, the **1934 gas station** will house a vintage postcard shop and motel office. The café will display a 40-year Route 66 collection. Around the corner at **9100 N Western**, John's **Western Trails Trading Post** is full of vintage collectibles (405) 842-8306. South on **Western Ave**, thru **NICHOLS HILLS**, are more vintage buildings and many restaurants (**Classics Club** has a James Dean mural), plus the **Will Rogers Theatre** near 50th. The Pre-'47 "Beltline" turned west on **39th St**, but **Western Ave** south of 39th thru **Crown Heights** was US 66 from 1930-'33 (see Jim Ross's book for the tangled tale of '66 in **OKC**). At **23rd St** is the glittering **Gold Geodesic Dome** of a former bank, recently saved from demolition.

EB: BELTLINE OPTION: LEFT on Western Ave. Continue north, across I-44, then **RIGHT** on **Britton Rd** in **BRITTON**. Cross US 77, go 1 mile on **Britton Rd**, then **LEFT** on Kelley (**CAPITOL OPTION** joins). Cross the Kilpatrick T-Pike. At Memorial Rd, turn **RIGHT**, then **quick LEFT** and **LEFT** again on the ramp for NB US 77 (**Broadway**) into **EDMOND**. Turn **RIGHT** on **2nd St/US 77**.

WB: CAPITOL OPTION: Continue **SOUTH** on **Kelley** at **Britton Rd**. **JOIN I-44 WB** at **EXIT 128B**, but **QUICKLY** take the ramp for **Lincoln Blvd** at **EXIT 128A**, cross over I-44 and continue south on **Lincoln** towards the **Capitol**. Past 28th St, curve to the **RIGHT** with the **WB NE 23rd St EXIT** (right lane), and **JOIN 23rd St** past Western Ave (**BELTLINE OPTION** joins here **WB**). Follow **23rd St** west to May Ave: turn **RIGHT** towards I-44.

The **CAPITOL OPTION** was "mainline" 66 from 1926 to 1954 (with some changes over the years). Unfortunately, most traces of Old 66 are gone between I-44 and 23rd St, but the view down Lincoln to the new dome atop the Capitol is grand. **NW 23rd** west of Lincoln is full of interest, and worth a detour east if taking the **BELTLINE OPTION (OK page-19)**. Both routes rejoin at **23rd St and Western.**

In 1954, US 66 switched over to the current path of I-35 and I-44, prompting the creation of **Frontier City Theme Park** (NE 122nd ST EXIT). The **National Cowboy and Western Heritage Museum** at 1700 NE 63D (just north of I-44, east of Kelley) honors the real "old west." (405) 478-2250.

Aside from its new dome, the **State Capitol** boasts its own oil derricks. For tour info: (405) 521-3356. South of the Capitol in downtown is the **Oklahoma City National Memorial** at NW 5th and Robinson, which honors the 168 victims of the **Alfred P. Murrah Federal Bldg** bombing of 1995 with memorial grounds and a museum. (405) 235-3313. City INFO: www.visitokc.com or (405) 297-8912.

OKC

The **Tower Theatre** on 23rd has a towering neon sign. **GIANT ALERT! GIANT MILK BOTTLE** on **Classen** (1926-'30 66) just north of 23RD St.) **Chicken in the Rough** (once a widespread early franchise) is now in a new location at Northwest Expressway and Independence.

EB: Take NW 23rd St east to **Western Ave**. See the **BELTLINE OPTION** via Western on **OK page-19**, **OR** take the **CAPITOL OPTION**: Stay **AHEAD** on **NW 23rd**, and cross under US 77/I-235. At the Capitol, pass thru the "subway," then **EXIT RIGHT** on the curving ramp to **Lincoln Blvd NB**. Follow **Lincoln** to **I-44 EXIT 128A**, and **JOIN I-44 EB**, but **EXIT QUICKLY** at Kelley Ave (EXIT 128B). Take **Kelley** north past **Britton Rd** (see the EB directions from **Britton Rd** on **OK page-19** to continue into **EDMOND**).

WB: Follow **May Ave** north. Be in the **left turn lane** crossing I-44, then turn **LEFT** onto the **WB** onramp, and follow the **OK 66** signs (AVOID the HWY 74 ramp) west into **WARR ACRES**. Continue on **OK 66** thru **BETHANY**. Cross the river on the 4-lane, then turn **LEFT** on Countyline Rd. Turn **RIGHT** on **N Overholser Dr**, along the north shore of **Lake Overholser**, then curve **RIGHT** at the "Y" onto **NW 36th**. Pass under Kilpatrick T-Pike (no exit) and continue west to **Mustang Rd**. Turn **RIGHT**, then (because of limited space to join the left turn lane) cross thru the light on **Mustang** and **U-TURN** back to the light, then turn **RIGHT** (west) on **OK 66** to **YUKON**.

<u>**NOTE:**</u> The 1924 **Lake Overholser Bridge** will be closed @ fall of 2010. Until then you may use the MAP to drive across. **RV ALERT!** Stay on 4-Lane 66 going **WB** due to tight turn at Mustang Rd.

39th Expwy west thru **WARR ACRES** is a typical multi-lane urban strip, but a few refugees from old 66 survive. The **Carlyle** and **Nu-Homa** motels, just west of I-44, are listed as business members in the official **Trip Guide of the OK 66 Association**. I've no experience of either, but feel free to check them out. **GIANT ALERT! Giant BOWLING PIN** at **66 Bowl** (and live music acts). **Jacks BBQ** at 4418 NW 39th Expwy has a good neon sign, while **Ann's Chicken Fry House** (at 4106 NW 39th Expwy since 1971) serves up retro décor along with meals. **BETHANY** is home to **Southern Nazarene University**, as well as **Southern Christian University** (**GIANT ALERT!** for their big **METAL GLOBE**). The **Western Motel** on the west side still has a great neon sign to ogle. City INFO: (405) 789-1256. **SIDE TRIP**: South about a mile on W Overholser Rd is a Route 66 themed park, with an 8-state walk, info signs and a statue of Andy Payne, plus a playground for the kids.

EB: Follow **OK 66** from <u>YUKON</u>. Just past the JCT of Mustang Rd, move to the right lane, then turn **RIGHT** and **QUICK LEFT** onto NW 36th St. Pass under the Kilpatrick T-pike (no exit), then curve **LEFT** at the "Y" onto **N Overholser Dr**, curving along the shore of Lake Overholser. Turn **LEFT** on **Countyline Rd**, then **RIGHT** onto **OK 66** (39th Expwy) thru **BETHANY** and **WARR ACRES**. Follow **39th Expwy** as it merges with I-44 towards **OKLAHOMA CITY** (OK 66 ends). Join the right lane, and take I-44 **EXIT 124**. Turn **RIGHT** on May Ave. Turn **LEFT** on NW **23rd St**. (see OK pages 20 & 21 for the two OKC routes.)

OK page-21

OKC

ENDS
EB

44
44
74

66
PORT
LAND

39th

39th
TO
23rd

MAY

BETHANY

66

COUNCIL RD

CANAL RD

OVERHOLSER DR

COUNTYLINE RD

1958 4-LANE 66
39TH EXPWY

N OVERHOLSER DR

OVERHOLSER LAKE PARK

W OVER-
HOLSER DR

W OVERHOLSER DR

LAKE OVERHOLSER

1924 BRIDGE
SEE NOTE

66
PARK

KILPATRICK T-PIKE

NO
EXIT

STOP
SIGN

SARA RD

66

NW 36th ST

Y
U
K
O
N

66

4

MUSTANG RD

WB: GO NORTH ON MUSTANG,
THEN U-TURN BACK DOWN TO
OK 66 & TURN RIGHT
**SEE
RV ALERT!**

EB: GO THRU MUSTANG,
AND TURN HERE

1958 4-LANE 66

WB: Follow OK 66 (Main) thru <u>YUKON</u> and into <u>EL RENO</u>. Cross the JCT of Shepard Ave (US 81 & BL-40 join, OK 66 ends). Continue with **US 81/BL 40** over the RR and into downtown (on **Rock Island St**). Turn **LEFT** on **Wade** for 2 blocks, then **RIGHT** on **Choctaw** for one block and **LEFT** on **Sunset Dr** (US 81 continues north). Follow **BL 40 / Sunset Dr** west from town.

A massive grain elevator emblazoned with the words **Yukon's Best Flour** (in paint and light) dominates the skyline of <u>YUKON</u>. A huge sequentially illuminated sign (bulbs, not neon) shines at the top. Across '66 is **Yukon's Best Railroad Museum**, housed like a hobo in old boxcars. The town is trail-happy, honoring the old cattle-drive days with a **Chisholm Trail Wall Mural** at 4th and Main and the **Chisholm Trail Historic Marker** (at the old watering hole) at 2200 S Holly. Watch for an old **Standard** gasoline sign. INFO: www.yukoncc.com

A few miles west of <u>YUKON</u> (about a mile west of Shell Creek and 2 miles east of Banner Rd near Cimarron Rd) is a rusty metal sign with a leering cowpoke and the message **"Watch Your Curves! Eat More BEEF" SCAVENGER HUNT!** What **organization** is listed on the bottom of this sign?

EL RENO: Pre-1947 OPTION: The early route follows **Shepard Ave** north (WB) from **OK 66**. Past the cemetery, it turns west on **Elm**, and crosses under the RR. Before 1932, the route turned north on **Hoff**, then west on **Wade**. After 1932, US 66 continued west on **Elm** to join **Rock Island**.

CURRENT ROUTE: South of the downtown on BL 40, a rare **twin-engine bomber** from WWII decorates the roadside. It's amazing that US 66 had to endure the tight turns in town up until I-40 came thru. On **Wade**, look for the appliance store that once was a **Chevy dealer** (the "Bow-Tie" above the door gives it away). A Goodyear and two old gas stations (one was a Conoco) round out downtown. For burgers, try **Jobe's** on Sunset or **Johnnie's** on Rock Island. (more <u>EL RENO</u> on **OK page-24**).

E L

RENO

EB: Take **BL 40/ Sunset Dr** to downtown <u>EL RENO</u>. Cross under the RR, then turn **RIGHT** on **Choctaw St** with **BL 40** and US 81. Get in the left lane, and turn **LEFT** at the next block, onto **Wade St**. After 2 blocks, turn **RIGHT** with **BL 40** and **US 81** on **Rock Island**. Cross over the RR, and curve to the JCT of OK 66 and US 81: stay **AHEAD** onto **OK 66** to <u>YUKON</u> (becomes **Main**).

(see **MAP #4 OK page-17**)

OK page-22

OKLAHOMA MAP # 5
CLINTON ~ EL RENO

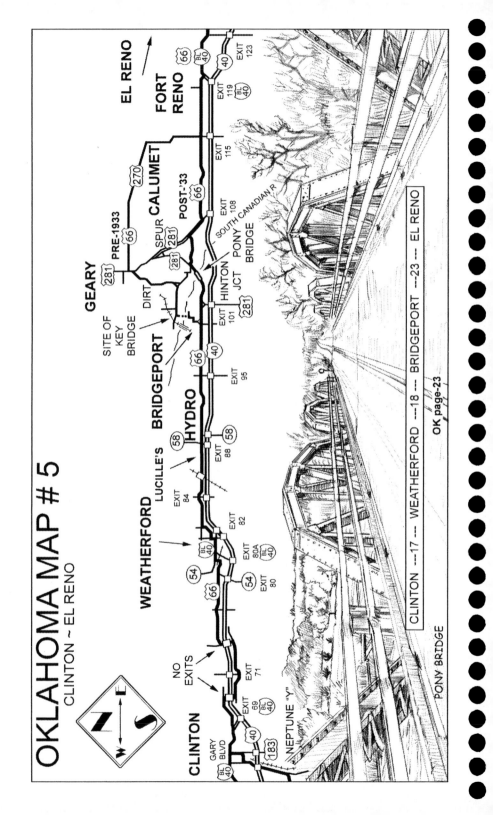

CLINTON ---17--- WEATHERFORD ---18--- BRIDGEPORT ---23--- EL RENO

OK page-23

PONY BRIDGE

WB: Follow **BL 40** west. At the 4-Lane curve, turn **RIGHT** with the "**Ft Reno Next Right**" sign onto **2-Lane 66**. Continue past US 270. At **281 SPUR**, turn **RIGHT**, go about 2 miles, (past the bridge) then turn **LEFT** from the 4-Lane (look for a house). Descend **Bridgeport Hill**, then turn **LEFT** on US 281, cross the **Pony Bridge**, then go past the US 281 turn (**HINTON JCT**) and the **BRIDGEPORT** turnoff.

Before leaving **EL RENO**, check out the **Canadian County Historical Museum and Heritage Park** at Wade and Grand (west of Choctaw) for tickets to the **Heritage Express**, a one-mile loop **trolley** that runs thru downtown from Heritage Park, Wed. thru Sunday. (405) 262-5121. The museum features a replica 1890s town. To the west, '66 passes the entrance to old **Fort Reno** (historic marker).

One of the **BEST** drives on all of '66 is the 1930's concrete west to **HYDRO**. The pristine curbed concrete heads arrow-straight for much of the way, interrupted by charming curves (and ugly SPUR 281) as it crosses fields and woods, and bridges deep gullies on long concrete-post spans (**SLOW** on asphalt patches). Watch for scattered roadside remnants. The long **Pony Bridge** (1933) uses 38 "pony" (small) trusses to cross the **South Canadian River**.

GEARY OPTION: Use **MAP #5** (and this page's detail) to take **PRE-'33 '66** up US 270 thru **CALUMET** (murals downtown and Moberly's Grocery west). Next is **GEARY** (log jail and caboose downtown by the Museum, on Main St north of old 66). Then, go down US 281 (this paved section was **NOT** '66 to join **POST-33 '66** (reverse **EB**).

SIDE TRIP (DIRT RD): **PRE-'33 66** south from **GEARY** is a dead-end on dusty dirt or gravel roads that once led to the 1921 **Key Suspension Bridge** north of **BRIDGEPORT**. Only the anchor piers remain. Use the **detail map** to help navigate to the bridge site, and then retrace your path to pavement. **AVOID** when muddy (or very **HOT**!).

EB: Stay **AHEAD** at **HINTON JCT** (US 281 joins). Cross the **Pony Bridge**, then turn **RIGHT** (first chance) and up **Bridgeport Hill**. Turn **RIGHT** on **281 SPUR** (4-Lane). Nearing EXIT 108, be in the left-turn lane, and turn **LEFT** onto **2-lane 66** (before reaching the truck stop). Continue east, past US 270. Near the Fort Reno turnoff, turn **LEFT** on BL 40 into **EL RENO** (becomes **Sunset Dr**).

WB: Stay **AHEAD** (along I-40) past EXIT 88 (N HWY 58 to **HYDRO**). Dodge EXIT 84, then continue to **WEATHERFORD**. **STOP** and turn **LEFT** at Lyle Rd, onto **E Main** (frontage rd). At the next JCT, turn **LEFT** on **Washington**, then **QUICK RIGHT** onto **Main St** (**BL 40**) thru downtown. **AVOID** the BL 40 curve to EXIT 80A. Stay **AHEAD** on **Main**, then **LEFT** on **4th St** (**HWY 54 S**). Cross the RR. Stay **AHEAD** on the **N Frontage Rd** at the JCT of S HWY 54 (EXIT 80). About 6 miles west, **CROSS** I-40 at the "T" (no exit), then go **RIGHT**. Pass by EXIT 71, go 2 miles and **CROSS** I-40 (near EXIT 69) into **CLINTON**.

SIDE TRIP: BRIDGEPORT PRE-1933

SIDE TRIP: BRIDGEPORT PRE-1933 (see MAP OK page-24): go **NORTH** on Market, **RIGHT** on Broadway and **LEFT** on Main (obliterated ahead, so return). Back on '66 west of the town turnoff; expect vintage bridges and great views on this hilly section. Go **SLOW** at asphalt patches. **HYDRO** is just north of '66, and worth a detour for downtown, with the **Route 66 Soda Fountain**. **Lucille's**, famed home of **Lucille Hamons** (west of HWY 58), has been closed since her passing in 2000, but will be restored to its early appearance by the new owner, who is also building **Lucille's Roadhouse** at EXIT 84.

SCAVENGER HUNT! What **jet fighter** is on display east of **WEATHERFORD**? _____ The jet marks the turn to a **museum** honoring astronaut **Thomas P Stafford** (see a **Russian MIG** and other cool planes and space stuff, including Moon rocks) (580) 772-5871. **Heritage Park** (by City Hall) has his **space-suited statue**. Before 1930, **US 66** followed **E Davis** and **Washington** in a dogleg on the east. In town are a nifty **Sinclair Station** and the **Mark Motor Hotel and Restaurant** (580) 772-3325. Check out the **66 West Twin Drive-In Theatre**, west of town. City INFO: (580) 772-7744. Also west of town and north of EXIT 71 is the **Cherokee Trading Post** (their billboards promise "**Buffalo Burgers**").

WEATHERFORD

EB: Take the **N Frontage Rd** east from BL 40 (near EXIT 69). **CROSS** I-40 at next chance, then **LEFT**. Pass EXIT 71. Next crossroad, **CROSS** I-40, and **RIGHT** on N Frontage Rd. Continue past S HWY 54 (EXIT 80), then curve **LEFT** with HWY 54 on **4th St**, across the RR. Turn **RIGHT** on Main, then join **BL 40 East** thru **WEATHERFORD**. Past Kansas St, join the "middle" left-turn lane to turn **LEFT** on **Washington**, then **QUICK RIGHT** on **E Main** (N Frontage Rd). Turn **RIGHT** at Lyle and continue on the N Frontage Rd, curving past EXIT 84. Stay **AHEAD** past EXIT 88 (N HWY 58 to **HYDRO**). I-40 veers away, continue east past **BRIDGEPORT**.

(see **MAP #5 OK page-23**)

OK page-25

OKLAHOMA MAP # 6
TEXOLA ~ CLINTON

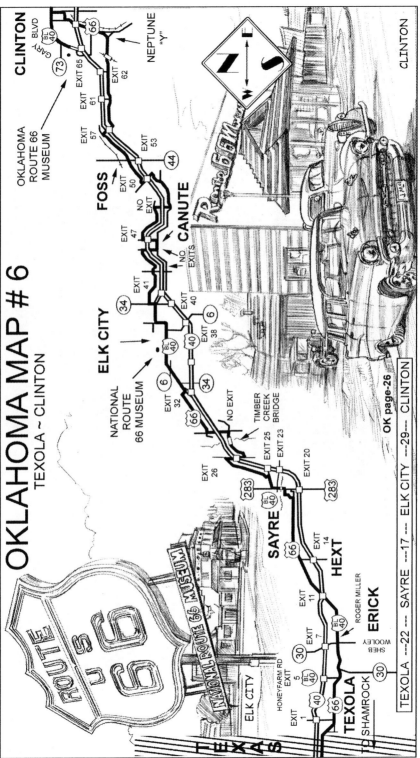

CLINTON

BL 40
GARY BLVD

66

73

EXIT 65

EXIT 62

NEPTUNE "Y"

EXIT 61

OKLAHOMA ROUTE 66 MUSEUM

EXIT 57

EXIT 53

44

FOSS

EXIT 50

NO EXIT

CANUTE

EXIT 47

NO EXITS

EXIT 41

34

EXIT 40

6

ELK CITY

EXIT 38

NATIONAL ROUTE 66 MUSEUM

BL 40

40

6

EXIT 32

34

66

NO EXIT

TIMBER CREEK BRIDGE

EXIT 25

EXIT 23

EXIT 26

EXIT 20

283

283

SAYRE

BL 40

US 40

66

EXIT 14

HEXT

EXIT 11

ERICK

ROGER MILLER

BL 40

SHEB WOOLEY

EXIT 7

30

EXIT 5

BL 40

ELK CITY

HONEYFARM RD EXIT

EXIT 1

40

66

TEXOLA

30

TO SHAMROCK

T E X A S

ROUTE US 66

NATIONAL ROUTE 66 MUSEUM

CLINTON

OK page-26

TEXOLA ---22--- SAYRE ---17--- ELK CITY ---29--- CLINTON

WB: Join **BL 40** (near EXIT 69) east of **CLINTON**, and continue into town (becomes **Gary Blvd**). See **MUSEUM Side Trip**, then turn **SOUTH** on **4th St (US 183)**. Cross Modelle Ave, then curve **RIGHT** onto Opal Ave. Turn **LEFT** on 10th St, and cross under I-40.

CLINTON

A mile east of downtown **CLINTON** is the first trading post in OK, the **Mohawk Lodge Indian Store** (est. 1892, here since 1940). Nearby is the **Cheyenne Cultural Center** (2250 NE Route 66) with crafts and dances (580) 323-6224.

MUSEUM SIDE TRIP: When in **CLINTON**, you **MUST** visit the **Oklahoma Route 66 Museum**, at 2229 W Gary Blvd (between EXIT 65 and HWY 73). Take Gary west, and then return to **Gary** and **4th**. The well-done exhibits feature OK 66, but with a national slant. You'll follow a self-guided narrated tour along the history of 66 from the dirt road days thru the 1960s, incorporating tableaus of antique vehicles, photos and memorabilia, plus a theatre. A restored **Route 66 Diner** sits on the grounds. The museum building itself is an eye-catcher, with glass brick and neon that make for a great night scene. **GIFT SHOP ALERT!** (580) 323-7866. Also on Gary are the **Dairy Best** (Broasted Chicken) at 19th St and the **Trade Winds Motel** (ELVIS stayed here) across from the museum.

GIANT ALERT! Wave to the **Giant INDIAN** at the corner of 4th and Locust. South of downtown, at **10th** and JayCee, watch for the Art Deco neon gateway to **McLain Rogers Park** and the **Route 66 mini-golf** (let the kids blow off some steam). **SIDE TRIP: Early US 66** used 4th, Frisco and 10th thru downtown. On Frisco is the former **Redland Theatre** (now a gift shop) with a classic marquee. In 1959, the route followed Gary Blvd all the way to "4-Lane 66" (now I-40). You can choose among many motels and cafes in town. City INFO: www.clintonok.org or (580) 323-2222.

EB: Pass under I-40 (becomes **10th St**). Just past Jaycee Lane, curve **RIGHT** on **OPAL**. Turn **LEFT** on US 183 (4th St). See **MUSEUM Side Trip**, then follow **Gary Blvd/BL 40** east. Near EXIT 69, turn **LEFT** on Turtle Creek Rd, then jog **RIGHT** on the **N Frontage Rd**.

WB: Stay **AHEAD** under I-40 at **EXIT 65A** (becomes **Neptune Dr**). Continue past Chapman. At the "Y" curve **RIGHT** with Neptune onto **Commerce Rd**. Stay on the **S Frontage Rd** past **EXIT 62** and **61** to **EXIT 57**. Cross under I-40 and turn **LEFT** on the **N Frontage Rd**. Pass HWY 44 (**FOSS**) to **EXIT 50**. **CROSS** I-40, and turn **RIGHT** on the **S Frontage Rd**. **CROSS** I-40 at the **next chance** (no exit) and turn **LEFT** on the **N Frontage Rd** to **EXIT 47**. **CROSS** I-40, and continue on **9th St** south into **CANUTE**. Turn **RIGHT** on "**Hwy 66.**" About one mile further, (past the RR) turn **RIGHT**, go under I-40, then turn **LEFT** on the **N Frontage Rd** towards **ELK CITY**.

On the south side of **CLINTON** at the "Y" is **Neptune Park**, and an ornate old building that once housed a gas station and roadhouse (see map on **OK page-27**).

You cross I-40 **many** times west of **CLINTON**, but the pristine sections of original **portland concrete** are well worth the trouble, especially between **EXIT 57** and **50**, near **FOSS**. At the HWY 44 JCT all that remains are the ruins of **Kobels Place**, but the main town is just north, on a **Pre-1932** dogleg of the Postal Route (not on tour). See **Ross's** book for more info on the early dirt road routes in Western OK.

CANUTE is worth the detour, for all the remains of old businesses, including the former **Cotton Boll** and **Washita Motels, Uniroyal Tires,** and old cafes and stations. East of town, (on the cut-off approach of 2 and 4-Lane 66) is a 1930s-era WPA park, and the **Holy Family Cemetery**, with a **1928 grotto**.

EB: Go past the first crossover, then turn **RIGHT** at the "**T**," go under I-40 and turn **LEFT** on "**Hwy 66**" thru **CANUTE**. At **9th St**, turn **LEFT**, **CROSS** I-40 (**EXIT 47**) then **RIGHT** on the **N Frontage Rd**. Go 2 miles, **CROSS** I-40 (no exit) then **LEFT** on the **S Frontage Rd**. At **EXIT 50**, **CROSS** I-40, then curve **RIGHT** on the **N Frontage Rd**. Stay **AHEAD** at the HWY 44 JCT (**FOSS**) on the **N Frontage Rd**. At **EXIT 57**, go under I-40 and turn **LEFT** on the **S Frontage Rd**. Stay **AHEAD** past **EXIT 61** and **EXIT 62**, into **CLINTON** (becomes **Commerce Rd**). Curve **LEFT** at the "**Y**", then **JOG LEFT** on **Neptune Dr**. Stay **AHEAD** under I-40 at **EXIT 65A**.

WB: Follow the **N Frontage Rd** as it passes north of EXIT 41, then turn **LEFT** on **HWY 34**, and quick **RIGHT** on **BL 40** into **ELK CITY**. Follow **BL 40** as it curves onto **Van Buren** and then **3rd St thru downtown**. Follow **BL 40 west**, past **HWY 6**, towards EXIT 32. Just past the S HWY 34 JCT, and **BEFORE** the exit, turn **RIGHT** and jog **LEFT** onto the N Frontage Rd. 4 Miles further, turn **LEFT** across I-40 (no exit), then **RIGHT** on the **S Frontage Rd**, and cross **Timber Creek Bridge**. Cross I-40 at **EXIT 26** (Cemetery Rd), and turn **LEFT** on the N Frontage Rd towards **SAYRE**.

A **T-33 Jet** guards the airport entrance east of **ELK CITY**. On the east side of downtown is a **179 foot-tall oil derrick** at the **Anadarko Basin Museum of Natural History** (by appt only: call (580) 243-0437). **PHOTO OP!** Take your picture with a statue of an **Elk** at Washington Ave and 3rd St (tell everyone they named the town after him...not).

ELK CITY's **MUST-SEE** attraction is the **National Route 66 Museum**, at 3rd and Pioneer in the **Old Town Museum** complex. **GIANT ALERT!** Huge neon **Route 66 Sign** (plus 2 **Giant Kachinas** from the old Queenan's Trading Post). If you're lucky, you'll get to talk to Wanda Queenan herself. Enjoy the stroll thru the many tableaus of life on Old 66, from auto camping in the desert, thru neon tourist courts, diners and gas stations, all realistically depicted with old vehicles, murals and memorabilia. Recorded narration greets you at each scene. **GIFT SHOP ALERT!** (580) 225-6266. The complex also houses many old buildings, including a one-room school. There are many motels and cafes in town. City INFO: www.elkcity.com or (580) 225-0207.

West of town, be sure to take the short stretch of 66 south of I-40 across photogenic **Timber Creek Bridge**, a thru-truss span built in 1928.

ELK CITY

EB: At **EXIT 26** (Cemetery Rd) cross I-40, then **LEFT** on the **S Frontage Rd**, across **Timber Creek Bridge**, then cross I-40 (no exit) and turn **RIGHT** on the **N Frontage Rd**. Near EXIT 32, curve sharply to a **STOP**, then **LEFT** on **4-Lane 66** into **ELK CITY**, following **BL 40** onto **3rd St thru downtown**. Follow **BL 40** as it curves north onto **Van Buren**, then east to **HWY 34**. Turn **LEFT**, then **quick RIGHT** on the N Frontage Rd.

(see MAP #6 OK page-26)

WB: Follow the N Frontage Rd towards **SAYRE**. Near **EXIT 25**, curve to the JCT of **BL 40** and turn **RIGHT**. Turn **LEFT** with **BL 40** on **4th St (US 283)**. Follow **BL 40** over the river, and take the next **RIGHT** at **Sayre City Park**. Turn **LEFT** at the "**T**," curve **RIGHT** at the "**Y**." Turn **RIGHT** on the N Frontage Rd. Continue past **HEXT** Rd to cross under I-40 at **EXIT 11** (becomes **BL 40**). Stay **AHEAD** thru **ERICK** on 4-Lane 66/Roger Miller. At Honeyfarm Rd (BL 40 turns), stay **AHEAD** on 4-Lane 66, thru **TEXOLA** into **TEXAS**.

On **SAYRE's** east end, watch for the neon cactus at the **Western Motel**, and the mural on the **Route 66 Bar**. The stately **Beckham Co Courthouse** was (briefly) shown in the movie *Grapes of Wrath*. The Art Deco **Post Office** at 201 N 4th St has a 1930s "land run" mural, and **Owl Drugs** has an old-time soda fountain. Train buffs will like the **RS and K RR Museum**, with model trains and track galore, at 411 N 6th, so call (580) 928-3525. From **1926-'58**, US 66 crossed the **North Fork of the Red River** via an abandoned bridge west of US 283, passing by **Sayre City Park's** rock swimming pool. City INFO: www.sayreok.net or (580) 928-3386.

North of **HEXT** the ghostly, abandoned original lanes may become part of a bike trail. **ERICK** birthed much musical talent (mostly in a light-hearted vein). **Roger Miller** (*King of the Road*) was a town native, as was **Sheb Wooley**, infamous for *Purple People Eater*. Nowadays the local musical duo is Harley and Annabelle, the "Mediocre Music Makers" at the **Sand Hills Curiosity Shop**. You'll likely get a redneck serenade here, just south of '66 on **Sheb Wooley Ave** (allow some time). **GIFT SHOP ALERT!** (580) 526-3738. Also in town is the **100th Meridian Museum** at Roger Miller and Sheb Wooley (by appt: (580) 526-3221) and the **Roger Miller Museum** at the SE corner (580)-526-3833. City INFO: www.rogermiller.com or (580) 526-3505.

Tiny **TEXOLA** 'tis the last town before **TEXAS**. On the east side (a block north on the last street east) is the old **Territorial Jail**. West of town are the **Will Rogers Marker** and Welcome to TX or OK signs. **PHOTO OP!**

S A Y R E (vertical label)

Map labels: TO ELK CITY · 66 · 283 · BL 40 · EXIT 25 · EXIT 23 · 40 · BENTON · MAIN · 4th St · BK21 · PARK · TO ERICK · PRE-1958 66 · NO EXIT · EXIT 20 · @1.5 mi · 283

EB: Take 4-Lane 66 thru **TEXOLA**. BL 40 joins at Honeyfarm Rd: stay **AHEAD** past S HWY 30 to **ERICK** (becomes **Roger Miller Blvd**). Stay **AHEAD** thru town, and cross I-40 at **EXIT 11** (becomes 2-Lane). Four mi. past **HEXT** Rd, go under an overpass (no exit). Go 1.5 miles, turn **LEFT**, and jog onto old 66. Curve **north**, by the park, then turn **RIGHT** on **BK-21**. Turn **LEFT** on **BL 40 /US 283** (4th St) thru **SAYRE**. Follow **BL 40 RIGHT** from US 283, towards EXIT 25, but **TURN LEFT** (**BEFORE** the off ramp) onto the N Frontage Rd.

(see **OK INTRO** on **OK page-1**)

TWO LANES ACROSS TEXAS

Map showing Route 66 across the Texas Panhandle, from Glenrio (New Mexico border) through Adrian, Vega, Wildorado, Bushland, Amarillo, Conway, Groom, Jericho, Alanreed, McLean, Lela, to Shamrock (Oklahoma border). US 385, US 60, US 287, US 83, and I-40 are shown.

Ironically, the **largest** of the lower 48 States hosts the **second-shortest** alignment of **Route 66**! Only **KANSAS**, with about 13 miles, owns a shorter length of the Mother Road. The generally accepted figure is that there were 178 miles of old 66 across the narrow **Texas "Panhandle."** Of that, about 150 miles remain, more if you count the drivable dirt road. Much of Old 66 is now frontage road, but still rewarding to drive. Hang your elbow out the window and take it EZ.

The scene thru the windshield shifts from scrubby trees to eroded gullies to cultivated fields to open rangeland as you travel west. Judging by the accounts on the backs of old postcards ("the flattest places I've ever seen") tourists have traditionally felt that the landscape of the **Texas "Panhandle"** is boring, but there's actually much to see. Small towns such as **SHAMROCK, McLEAN** and **ALANREED** still retain their charm, along with numerous roadside remnants. Agricultural icons such as grain elevators and windmills relieve the "flatness" of the terrain, as do water towers and a giant Cross. Views of distant vistas can be had from atop the ridge between **McLEAN** and **GROOM**, or one can commune with nature on **Dirt 66**.

Remnants of another transportation relic, the former **Chicago Rock Island and Pacific Railroad** (also known as the "Cry and Pee" for its initials) cling close to the road across the state, marked by the odd rotting crosstie or bridge timber. **AMARILLO,** Texas 66's big city, is home to a mile of antique stores, plus the **Big Texan** and **Cadillac Ranch.** West of town, the road is hell-bent for **NEW MEXICO,** passing thru **VEGA** and **ADRIAN** along the way. Unfortunately, the last 18 or so miles to **GLENRIO** and the **NM** state line are via I-40, but the view down the sudden drop from the "Caprock" still inspires.

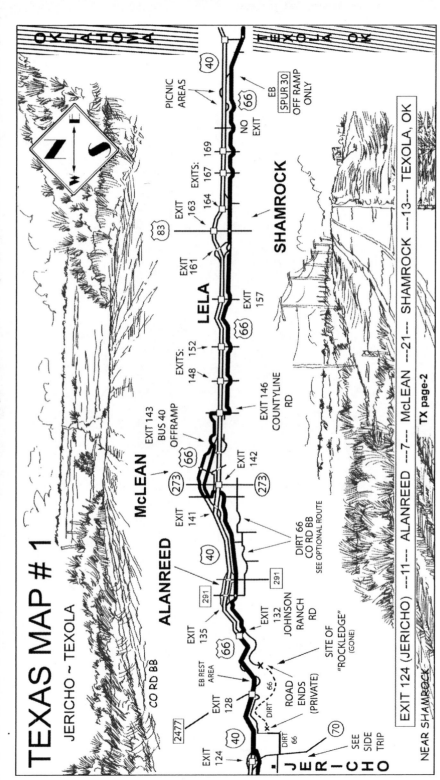

TEXAS MAP # 1
JERICHO ~ TEXOLA

OKLAHOMA

TEXAS OR

N E
W S

PICNIC AREAS

40

66 EB
SPUR 30
OFF RAMP
ONLY

NO EXIT

CO RD BB

EXITS: 167 169

EXIT 164 163

EXIT 161

EXIT 157

SHAMROCK

83

66

LELA

EXITS: 148 152

EXIT 146
COUNTYLINE
RD

McLEAN

EXIT 143
BUS 40
OFFRAMP

66

273

EXIT 142

273

EXIT 141

40

291

291

DIRT 66
CO RD BB
SEE OPTIONAL ROUTE

ALANREED

EXIT 135

EXIT 132
JOHNSON
RANCH RD

66

EB REST AREA

SITE OF
"ROCKLEDGE"
(GONE)

DIRT 66

ROAD
ENDS
(PRIVATE)

2477

EXIT 128

DIRT 66

40

70

SEE
SIDE
TRIP

EXIT 124

J
E
R
I C
H
O

EXIT 124 (JERICHO) ---11--- ALANREED ---7--- McLEAN ---21--- SHAMROCK ---13--- TEXOLA, OK

NEAR SHAMROCK

TX page-2

WB: From **TEXOLA, OK** (south of I-40 EXIT 1) cross into **TEXAS** on **4-Lane 66,** which soon narrows down to become the **South I-40 Frontage Rd.** Continue west past EXIT 164 to the JCT with US 83 in **SHAMROCK** (caution for on-off ramps and STOP signs).

More sections of original circa **1930s concrete pavement** survive (hopefully) east of **SHAMROCK,** rewarding those who shun I-40 here. You'll also see evidence of the oil and gas industry along the way. East of EXIT 169, Old 66 crosses a concrete bridge over the abandoned **CRI&P Railroad.** South from here are visible a few oil wells drilled by the author's Grandpa during WWII.

CAR GAME! The **Texas Panhandle** has been called the place "where the wind pumps the water and the cows chop the wood." It might be hard to spot "cow patties" from the car (settlers burned dried cow dung when they had no wood) but **WINDMILLS** are frequent across **TEXAS.** Divide the landscape up into north and south, and see who can spot the **MOST** windmills between exits (only intact windmills with blades count!).

SHAMROCK offers numerous remnants of old motels, cafes and stations. U-can't miss the recently restored **U-Drop Inn/Tower Conoco** at the US 83 junction: an **Art Deco** masterpiece built in 1936, which now houses offices of the Chamber of Commerce. Drop inn during business hours for a visit, and stick around after dark for the dazzling **NEON** which outlines the building's spires (local motels offer **"FREE GOLF"** at the country club with your room). **SIDE TRIP:** If you've the time, venture south on US 83 to downtown and visit the **Pioneer West Museum** at 204 N Madden (a block east of US 83) and the restored **Magnolia gas station** nearby. The "Irish City" boasts a piece of the original **"Blarney Stone"** (in Elmore Park east of downtown) and hosts an annual **St Patrick's Day Celebration** in March. INFO: www. shamrocktx.net or (877) Irish TX.

EB: From the JCT of US 83 in **SHAMROCK,** pass by EXIT 164 and follow the **South I-40 Frontage Rd** east (caution for off ramps and STOP signs at exits). Past the SPUR 30 off ramp, follow the **S Frontage Road** away from I-40 as it becomes **4-Lane 66,** crossing into **OKLAHOMA** and on into **TEXOLA** (south of I-40 EXIT 1).

WB: From the JCT with US 83 in **SHAMROCK** follow **4-Lane 66** west, which becomes the **South I-40 Frontage Rd** past EXIT 161. Continue past **LELA** to **EXIT 146** (Countyline Rd). **CROSS I-40**, then **TURN LEFT** on the **North Frontage Rd**. At the **EXIT 143 WB** off ramp, **STOP** and **TURN RIGHT** onto **4-Lane 66**. At the "Y" intersection, follow **First St** (One-Way) to Main St in **McLEAN**.

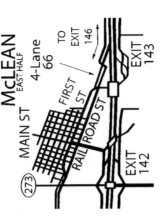

McLEAN
EAST HALF
4-Lane 66
MAIN ST
FIRST ST
RAILROAD ST
273
TO EXIT 146
EXIT 142
EXIT 143

The **South Frontage Road** west of **SHAMROCK** offers another chance to drive original **portland concrete**. West of tiny **LELA** stood the only remnant of a former roadside reptile empire: the "**RATTLESNAKES EXIT NOW**" sign (now relocated to **McLEAN**).

McLEAN was once known as the "**UPLIFT CITY**" for the ladies undergarment factory, which now houses the **Devil's Rope/Old Route 66 Museum.** "Devil's Rope" refers to the museum's huge collection of barbed wire. Also on display is cowboy and ranching history (here's the place to get immersed in western lore). **GIANT ALERT!** The **Route 66 Exhibit** houses a **GIANT COBRA** and a big **BULL** (everything's **BIG** in TEXAS) plus a multitude of memorabilia of the Mother Road. **GIFT SHOP ALERT!** Address: **Kingsley St** between First and Railroad on the east side of town. Check barbwiremuseum.com or 806 779-2225 for seasonal hours of operation.

In 1984, **McLEAN** was the **LAST** town in **TEXAS** bypassed by I-40. Downtown on Main, the **McLean/Alanreed Area Museum** includes info about the WWII prison camp, which housed German POWs nearby. Better housing can be found at the **Cactus Inn Motel** (806 779-2346) which is recommended as a real Mom and Pop. West of Main on First St is a restored **Phillips 66** gas station, the **FIRST** of that brand in **TEXAS**: a great **PHOTO OP.** Other choice roadside remnants abound throughout town. **SCAVENGER HUNT:** What are the **2 huge balls** on display at the **Devil's Rope Museum** made from? _____

EB: From Main St in **McLEAN**, follow **Railroad St** east (One-Way). **AVOID** the right-turn lane for the I-40 EXIT 143 access road: **STOP**, then **STAY AHEAD** with **4-Lane 66**. Approaching the WB off ramp, **CURVE LEFT** to a **STOP**, then cross the WB off ramp lane and **CURVE RIGHT** onto the **North I-40 Frontage Rd**. At **EXIT 146** (Countyline Rd), **CROSS I-40** and **TURN LEFT** on the **South Frontage Rd**, past **LELA** to the JCT with US 83 in **SHAMROCK**.

WB DIRT 66 OPTION: In <u>McLEAN</u>, take **Hwy 273** south to I-40 EXIT 142. Cross I-40 and continue south for **ONE MILE**, then turn **RIGHT** onto **Gray County Rd "BB"**. About 4 miles on, follow the sharp bend south, then turn **RIGHT** (avoid CO 23) to stay with **CO BB** to the JCT of **Hwy 291**. **Stay ahead** on **CO BB**, then turn **RIGHT** with **Main St** into <u>**ALANREED**</u>, and rejoin paved 66 at **Third St**.

TO CONTINUE WB from <u>McLEAN</u> on PAVEMENT (MAIN TOUR) see TX page- 6.

McLEAN

M
A
I
N

FIRST
RAILROAD

(273)

4-LANE
(66)

(40)

EXIT
142

(66)   (273)

CO RD
26

3143

DIRT
(66)

COUNTY
RD BB

EXIT
141

(40)

SOUTH FRONTAGE
IS PART OF 4-LANE 66

2-LANE 66

CRI&P RR (ABANDONED)

66

ROUTE 66 1926 - 1932

DIRT 66 OPTION

ABOUT 8 MILES: ALANREED TO McLEAN

PRE-1932 ROUTE 66

REQUIRES DRIVING ON DIRT, SAND AND GRAVEL SURFACE

AVOID WHEN WET

DRIVE SLOW, USE CAUTION, AND ENJOY THE SCENERY!

CO
23

NO
EXIT

(66)

CO
22

(291) EXIT 135

(291)

CO RD BB

(40)

(66)

ALANREED

CO
23

DASHED LINE = PRIVATE OR OBLITERATED

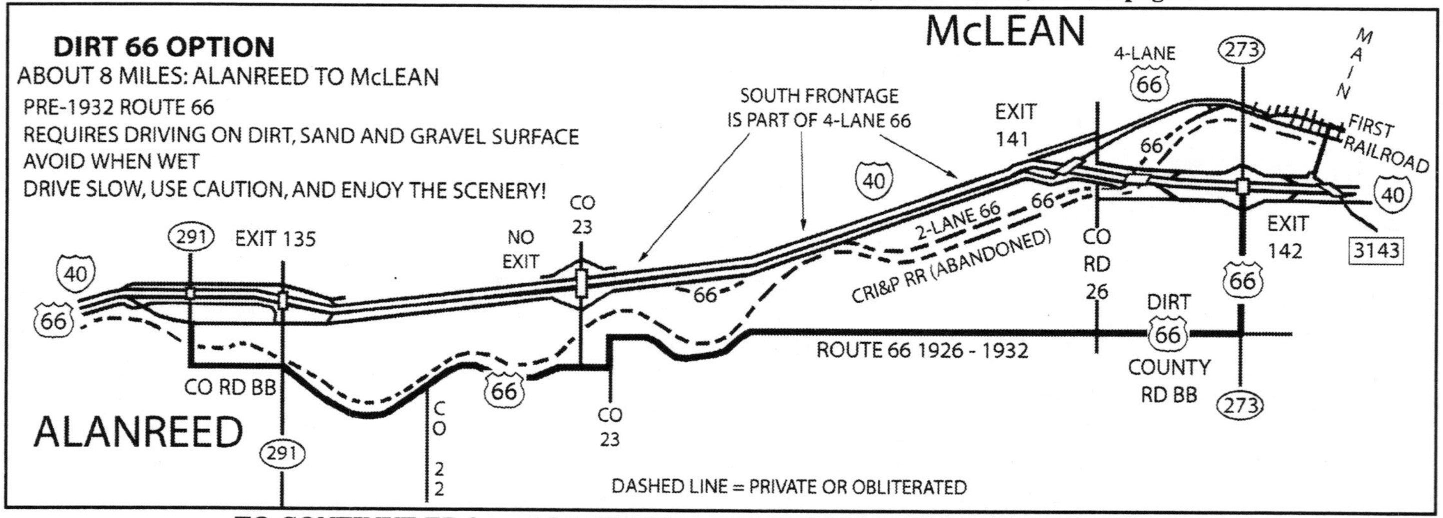

TO CONTINUE EB from <u>ALANREED</u> on PAVEMENT (MAIN TOUR) SEE TX page-6.

EB DIRT 66 OPTION: From **Third St** in <u>ALANREED</u>, turn **RIGHT** on **Main**. Follow the sharp bend **LEFT** onto **Gray County Rd "BB"**. At the JCT with **Hwy 291**, **stay ahead** on **CO BB**. At the "T" junction with **CO 23 SOUTH**, turn **LEFT**, then follow the bend **RIGHT** on **CO BB**. Go about 4 miles to **Hwy 273**. Turn **LEFT**, go one mile, **cross I-40** and rejoin **4-Lane 66** in <u>McLEAN</u>.

TX page-5

WB: From Main St in **McLEAN**, follow **First St** (One-Way WB) as it rejoins the EB lanes, and then cross Hwy 273 on **4-Lane 66**. (**ALSO** See **DIRT 66 OPTION** on **TX page-5**). One mile west, **AVOID** entering I-40 by turning **LEFT** onto **CO RD 26**. Follow the curve **LEFT** onto the **North Frontage Rd** headed back east. At the first opportunity, curve **RIGHT** under I-40, then follow the **South Frontage Rd** west to **ALANREED**, entering on **Third St** (Loop 271) and continuing past Main St.

Just west of Hwy 273 in **McLEAN**, the old 2-lane pavement branches off south and dead ends. This section curved along with the defunct **CRI&P RR**; where their path crosses under I-40, east of Co Rd 26, more of the old pavement is visible. The **south frontage road** west from town was a part of **4-Lane 66**, while the **2-Lane** followed the old RR embankment further south. About 2 miles from the I-40 overpass, the 2-Lane comes back in from the south (**private rd**) and the old RR, festooned with rotten crossties, is clearly visible near the road.

West of **McLEAN** the landscape becomes more arid. Spiky plants and prairie grass cover rolling hills cut by eroded gullies, as the road climbs onto the ridge between the drainage of **McClellan Creek** to the north and the **Salt Fork of the Red River**, a historic transportation corridor.

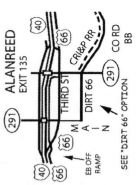

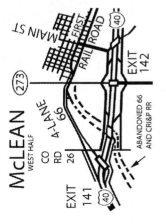

Little **ALANREED** had 3 routings of 66: The original **dirt road** south on **Main**, the paved **2-Lane** on **Third St**, and **4-Lane 66**, which was wiped out by I-40. Along the last route was the **Regal Reptile Ranch**, whose remains were bulldozed in the 1990s. Their **GIANT COBRA** resides now in the Route 66 Exhibit in **McLEAN. PHOTO OP: 66 Super Service Station**, a 1932-era classic restored as a display at Main and Third. **EB Traffic:** See the **DIRT 66 OPTION** to **McLEAN** on **TX page-5**.

EB: From Main St in **ALANREED**, follow **Third St** (Loop 271) across Hwy 291 and onto the **South Frontage Rd**. Near **McLEAN**, at the first chance past EXIT 141 (no connection) turn **LEFT** under I-40 and then turn **LEFT** on the **North Frontage Rd**. Curve **RIGHT** with **CO RD 26**, then turn **RIGHT** and follow **4-Lane 66** past Hwy 273 (becomes **Railroad St** One-way EB) to Main St in **McLEAN**.

TX page-6

WB: From Main St in **ALANREED**, follow **Third St** (Loop 271) west. **AVOID** the EB I-40 off ramp ("**DO NOT ENTER**") and turn **LEFT** onto the **South Frontage Rd**. At the next overpass (**EXIT 132**) join **I-40 WB**. At **EXIT 124** (Hwy 70 South) **CROSS I-40**, then take the **South Frontage Rd** west towards **GROOM**.

West of **ALANREED**, the terrain offers some great long-distance views from the narrow ridgeline. Old 66 loses its pavement shortly past EXIT 132, then encounters **PRIVATE PROPERTY** at a cattle guard. This marks the beginning of the infamous "**Jericho Gap**," the last 18 miles section of 66 paved in this area in the late 1930s. Most of this section is **ABANDONED** or **PRIVATE**.

WB or EB, be sure to stop (whether you need to "go" or not) at the **EB I-40** "**Donley County Texas Route 66 Safety Rest Area.**" The neon signs and Art Deco style honor old 66. Inside are exhibits, travel info and a handy tornado shelter. Outside is a playground and **Route 66-history walk**, the sidewalks of which are mini-highways with center stripes leading past brass brass historic info plaques. **If driving west:** Double back from **EXIT 128** to visit the rest area, then continue.

SIDE TRIPS: From **EXIT 128**: About **2 miles** of pavement heads west on the south side, ending at a dirt road. **Return to EXIT 128** to stay on asphalt. The dirt road joins **Dirt 66** for a short dogleg to **JERICHO** (AVOID if WET).

An easier way to view the few remains of **JERICHO** is to take **Hwy 70** south 1 mi from **EXIT 124**. **JERICHO**, consisting of the ruins of a tourist court and a deserted house or two, is just west on **CO RD B** (sign: "**Jericho Cemetery**." A **historic marker** sits on the east side of Hwy 70). **AVOID when WET!** Farmers made money pulling autos out of the black mud, and this section is still a mudbath after a rain. **Dirt 66** headed west for 6 mi. via CO RD B to Boydston Rd. Instead, **take Hwy 70 back up to EXIT 124.**

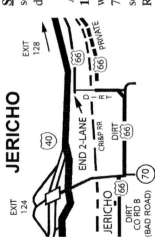

JERICHO

DASHED LINE = PRIVATE OR OBLITERATED

EXIT 124

EXIT 128

EXIT (40)

(66)

(66) PRIVATE

END 2-LANE

D I R T

CR&P RR

DIRT (66)

JERICHO (66)

DIRT CO RD B (BAD ROAD)

(70)

EB: Join **I-40 EB** at **EXIT 124** (Hwy 70 S). Take **EXIT 132** (Johnson Ranch Rd) and turn **RIGHT** from the off ramp, then **LEFT** on the **South Frontage Rd.** Approaching **EXIT 135**, turn **RIGHT** onto **LOOP 271**, which becomes **Third St** into **ALANREED**.

(see MAP # 1 on TX page-2)

TX page-7

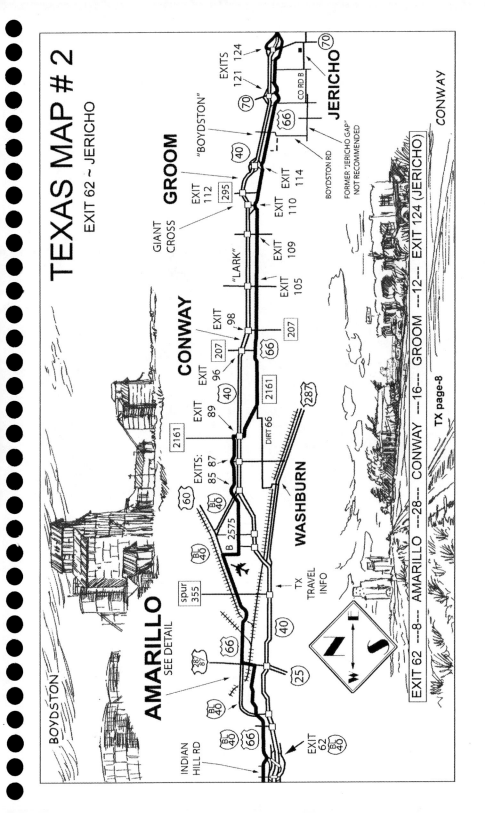

TEXAS MAP #2

EXIT 62 ~ JERICHO

BOYDSTON

AMARILLO
SEE DETAIL

INDIAN
HILL RD

EXIT 62

spur 355

EXITS: 85 87

B 2575

WASHBURN

TX TRAVEL INFO

DIRT 66

EXIT 89

CONWAY

EXIT 96

EXIT 98

"LARK"

EXIT 105

EXIT 109

GIANT CROSS

GROOM

EXIT 110

EXIT 112

EXIT 114

"BOYDSTON"

EXITS 121 124

BOYDSTON RD

FORMER "JERICHO GAP" NOT RECOMMENDED

CO RD B

JERICHO

CONWAY

TX page-8

EXIT 62 ---8--- AMARILLO ---28--- CONWAY ---16--- GROOM ---12--- EXIT 124 (JERICHO)

WB: From **EXIT 124** (HWY 70 S) follow the **South Frontage Rd** west. At **EXIT 121** (HWY 70 N) make a **LEFT** turn **BEFORE** curving onto the overpass to continue on the **South Frontage Rd**. Approaching **GROOM**, curve sharply left and **yield** to the EB I-40 onramp at EXIT 114, then stay **AHEAD** into town with **BL 40**. Continue thru town past the JCT of Hwy 295.

The narrow ridge that '66 follows starts to widen out into flat tableland west of **JERICHO**. Much of this section's terrain is cultivated land: the same rich dirt that made the **"Jericho Gap"** such a muddy terror is great for crops. Many fields are watered by long, wheeled pivoting sprinklers. West of Exit 121 are two lonely tin silos that are the agricultural remnants of **BOYDSTON**.

GROOM marks its presence on the plain in several ways. Concrete silos and the town water tower are typical of the Panhandle. A more unusual water tower marks a former truck stop on the north side of I-40 at EXIT 113. This **"leaning tower of Groom"** was built that way, to attract attention. **GIANT ALERT!** The newest and most spectacular vertical attraction is the **"Cross of Our Lord Jesus Christ"** built in 1995. At 190 foot tall (19 stories) this is billed as the **"Largest Cross in the Western Hemisphere"** (Route 66 also boasts a similar religious monument at Edmond, OK, but that one is "only" 100' tall with a 37' base). The giant cross (illuminated at night) stands just south of I-40 EXIT 112 on HWY 295. The complex also includes statues of the "Stations of the Cross." Town INFO: (806) 248-7929.

GROOM was once home to many gas stations, cafes and motels: their remnants remain to remind of the roadside past. The long-abandoned remains of the **66 Courts** and its classic, often photographed sign were recently demolished. In **1959**, your tour guide stayed here on a trip back east to visit "Gramma." The "McClanahan" suite is now just a memory. For eats, try the **Route 66 Steakhouse** (the old Golden Spread grille). What **government office** is in a small former **gas station** on the west side? _____

EB: Follow BL 40 thru **GROOM**. At EXIT 114, stay **AHEAD** with the **South Frontage Rd**. At EXIT 121 (Hwy 70 N) curve to the **STOP**. Turn **RIGHT** to continue on the **South Frontage Rd** to EXIT 124.

WB: From the JCT of HWY 295 in **GROOM**, stay **AHEAD** with **BL 40** to EXIT 110, then curve to a **STOP**, and join the **South Frontage Rd**. At the JCT with South Hwy 207 (south of EXIT 98), join **HWY 2161** straight **AHEAD** into **CONWAY**. At the JCT of North HWY 207, stay **AHEAD** with **HWY 2161** as it heads west, then angles north back to I-40. At **EXIT 89**, cross I-40 and take the **North Frontage Rd** west to **EXIT 85. AVOID BL 40:** Stay **AHEAD** across all 4 lanes and follow **HWY 2575** west.

West of **GROOM** lies more open land, with far horizons dotted by distant silos and windmills, while faint remnants of the old railroad hug the road on the south. East of EXIT 105 a white painted concrete silo marks the site of "**LARK**."

At **CONWAY** begins the best section of old 66 in **TEXAS**! The little town once lined the north side of the highway, now only a few defunct businesses mark the route's passing. A line of stucco, tile-roofed cabins survive behind a chain-link junkyard-fence. Next door, an old wooden building was once home to **Buddy's Café**. Further on, a pair of tall, white grain elevators guard the silence of the past. Out by EXIT 96 is "**BUG RANCH**," an ironic satire of "Cadillac Ranch," with VWs buried in the dirt instead of "Detroit's finest."

West from town, the speed limit jumps to **70 mph**, (as of this writing: your MPH may vary) the only place in **TEXAS** you can legally drive that fast on old 66! The feel of the old concrete pavement is evident under a thin layer of blacktop, and I-40 is mostly out of sight on the north. No other stretch in **TEXAS** gives you this isolated old-time '66 feel, so savor it while it lasts.

HISTORIC NOTE: During the late 1920s, US 66 went straight west where HWY 2161 angles to the north, then took a zig-zag of dirt roads down to **WASHBURN**. There it joined the early pavement of what became US 287 into **AMARILLO**. Contrary to some accounts, US 66 **NEVER** went thru CLAUDE.

EB: Follow the **North Frontage Rd** to **EXIT 89. CROSS** I-40, and follow **HWY 2161** down to **CONWAY**. At the junctions with North and South HWY 207, stay **AHEAD** and follow the **South Frontage Rd**, to eventually join **BL 40** (from EXIT 110) into **GROOM**. Continue past HWY 295 into downtown.

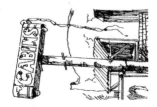

TX page-11

WB: From **EXIT 85**, take **HWY 2575** west along the north side of I-40. At the JCT with HWY 1912, stay **AHEAD** with NE 8th into **AMARILLO**. At the airport fence, turn **RIGHT** onto **AVE B**. Cross under the overpass, and turn **LEFT** onto **Amarillo Blvd** (BL 40/US 60). Cross LOOP 335 and follow **Amarillo Blvd** west. At the signs for the US 287 JCT, get in the **LEFT LANE**. Continue **AHEAD** across Fillmore St and **TURN LEFT** on **Taylor St** (One-Way). Continue south to downtown. **TURN RIGHT** on **SW 6th Ave.**

2-Lane 66 was cut by the airport decades ago (**Triangle Dr** is a remnant). The final route followed **BL 40** up to **US 60** to join **Amarillo Blvd**. Many roadside remnants line this street, but most motels here no longer cater to the tourist trade, although some still have neat signs. The old link to downtown, **Fillmore St**, is now **One-Way** north, requiring **WB** traffic to use **Taylor.** Later, **West Amarillo Blvd** bypassed "**City 66**," which follows 6th Ave west from town.

SIDE TRIP: Drop down **Loop 335** from **BL 40** to that **AMARILLO** icon, the **Big Texan. GIANT ALERT!** The 'Texan's huge Cowboy sign had its beefy beginnings on **Amarillo Blvd** in 1959. He moseyed out to I-40 when 66 was bypassed. Home of the "**Free 72 Oz Steak Dinner**" (if eaten in one hour') of billboard fame, the 'Texan also boasts a motel with a Texas-shaped pool (800-657-7177), and the Cowboy Palace Theatre. The **author's painting** of the former US 66 location (a "Texas-big" 3 by 5 foot canvas) hangs in the lobby.

EB: Follow **Fillmore St** (One-Way) north from **SW 6th Ave** in downtown **AMARILLO**. Pass under the RR overpasses. At Amarillo Blvd (BL 40/US 60) **TURN RIGHT**. Stay **AHEAD** on Amarillo Blvd thru the US 287 JCT and the JCT with LOOP 335. Take the "**Amarillo College East Campus**" EXIT, and follow **Ave B** south. **TURN LEFT** on **NE Eight St**. At the JCT with HWY 1912, stay **AHEAD** onto **HWY 2575**, cross all 4 lanes of BL 40 and join the **North Frontage Rd** eastbound.

WB: From **Taylor St** in downtown **AMARILLO**, follow **SW 6th Ave** west. Stay with **SW 6th** Ave thru the intersections with McMasters St and Georgia St. Follow the wide boulevard as it curves onto **Bushland Blvd** and then onto **9th Ave.** Approaching the JCT of **Amarillo Blvd** and Bell St, **AVOID** the left turn for Bell St, cross under the overpass and **TURN LEFT** onto **West BL 40 (Amarillo Blvd)**. Follow this west past Loop 335 and Helium Rd. When BL 40 curves down to join I-40, **TURN RIGHT** onto **Indian Hill Rd.**

SCAVENGER HUNT! What is the **DATE** on the old **Rock Island Railroad** overpass north of downtown on **Fillmore**? (Sorry, but you **WB** folk will have to double back for this one!) _____

Look for painted **fiberglass ponies** around downtown. With a population of 173,627 souls, **AMARILLO** is **"IT"** as far as big cities go on Route 66 in **TEXAS**! The area's many non-66 attractions, such as **Palo Duro Canyon**, could keep you busy for days. INFO: www.visitamarillotx.com www.amarillo-chamber.org or 806-373-7800.

Make time for **"One Mile Shopping"** in the **Historic Route 66** district along **SW 6th Ave** west of downtown. There are "boo coo" (Texan for "lots") antique stores and cafes between Western and Georgia Streets in the **San Jacinto Neighborhood**, plus many old gas station structures. Look for the **Natatorium**, with its castle-like crenellations, south of the intersection with Georgia. West from town, a few '66-era motels sit across from the hospital, and then the rangeland opens up again.

See TX page-14 for directions to Cadillac Ranch!

AMARILLO WEST DETAIL

EB: Follow **BL 40 (Amarillo Blvd)** east into **AMARILLO**. Stay with **BL 40** past Loop 335 and as it curves north past Coulter St. **AVOID** the Bell St off ramp, then **TURN RIGHT** onto **9th Ave**, and follow the wide blvd as it curves onto **Bushland Blvd** and then onto **SW 6th Ave. AVOID** the **"Turn Only"** lanes at Georgia St and McMasters St. In downtown, cross Taylor, then **TURN LEFT** on **Fillmore St** (One-Way NB).

(see MAP # 2 on TX-page-8)

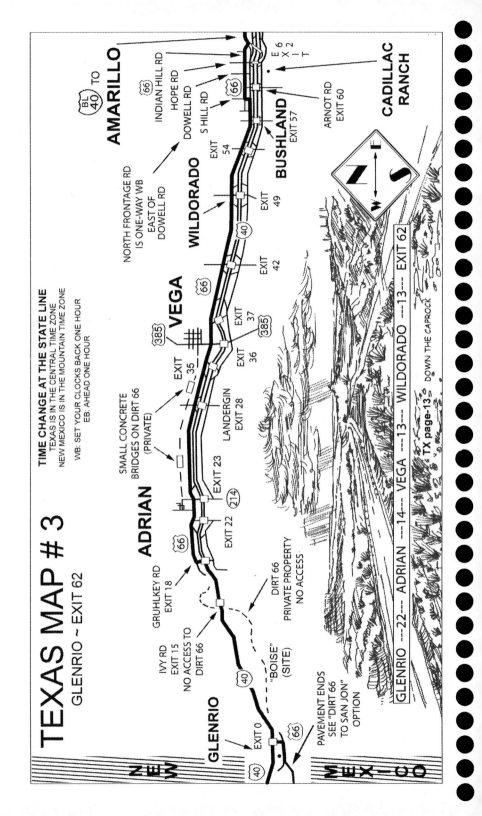

TEXAS MAP # 3
GLENRIO ~ EXIT 62

TIME CHANGE AT THE STATE LINE
TEXAS IS IN THE CENTRAL TIME ZONE
NEW MEXICO IS IN THE MOUNTAIN TIME ZONE

WB: SET YOUR CLOCKS BACK ONE HOUR
EB: AHEAD ONE HOUR

TO AMARILLO
BL 40

EXIT 62

INDIAN HILL RD
HOPE RD
DOWELL RD
S HILL RD

66

BUSHLAND
EXIT 57

ARNOT RD
EXIT 60

CADILLAC RANCH

NORTH FRONTAGE RD
IS ONE-WAY WB
EAST OF
DOWELL RD

WILDORADO
EXIT 54

EXIT 49

EXIT 42

40

VEGA
385

EXIT 37

EXIT 36

385

EXIT 35

EXIT 28
LANDERGIN

EXIT 23

SMALL CONCRETE
BRIDGES ON DIRT 66
(PRIVATE)

66

ADRIAN
EXIT 22

214

GRUHLKEY RD
EXIT 18

IVY RD
EXIT 15
NO ACCESS TO
DIRT 66

DIRT 66
PRIVATE PROPERTY
NO ACCESS.

"BOISE"
(SITE)

40

GLENRIO
EXIT 0

66

PAVEMENT ENDS
SEE "DIRT 66
TO SAN JON"
OPTION

40

NEW MEXICO

N E W

E X I T 6 2

GLENRIO ---22--- ADRIAN ---14--- VEGA ---13--- WILDORADO ---13--- EXIT 62
TX page-13 DOWN THE CAPROCK

WB: Follow **Indian Hill Rd** west past Hope Rd, Dowell Rd and Arnot Rd (EXIT 60) to **S Hill Rd**: **TURN LEFT**, then a quick **RIGHT** onto the North Frontage Rd. Stay **AHEAD** past **BUSHLAND** (EXIT 57) and **WILDORADO** (EXIT 49). Past EXIT 37, join **BL 40** **AHEAD** to **VEGA**.

SIDE TRIP: Despite **MANY** reports, the outdoor artwork titled "**Cadillac Ranch**" was **NEVER** located on Route 66 (even before the cars were uprooted and moved to the current location in 1997)! Still, it is a road icon not to be missed. The 10 luxury-barges, planted nose down in the fertile soil, are located on the **South Frontage Rd** between **Arnot Rd** (EXIT 60) and **Hope Rd**, either of which can be used to rejoin Route 66. Although occasionally repainted for special events, fresh coats of graffiti soon cover the "Caddies." (Also, see "**Bug Ranch**" in **CONWAY**.)

Stanley Marsh 3 (as he prefers), the eccentric millionaire and art patron who commissioned the artist group "**Ant Farm**" to install Cadillac Ranch in 1974, is also responsible for those whacky signs you may have noticed in the area: diamond-shaped signs with puzzling messages such as "**Crock of Gin**" and "**Hot Pink**." In a similar vein (pun intended), keep an eye out for the "**Bates Motel**" sign at the corner of Hope Rd and the N Frontage Rd ("Each room with a shower, knives sharpened").

After the thrill of roadside art, the frontage-road ride past **BUSHLAND**, marked by white concrete silos, is more sedate. Watch for rounded "quonset huts," refugees from old military bases, along the way. About a mile west of EXIT 57, an old RR bell-crossing sign has (hopefully) survived, a remnant of the vanished **CRI&P RR**. **WILDORADO** may be (in)famous for the odiferous cattle feed lot just east of town (roll up the window and hold your nose). Notice that many trees seem to have a perpetual "lean" into the wind. Wind and cattle rule the range, and there are many windmills to count on the way to **VEGA**.

EB: From **VEGA**, follow **BL 40** to EXIT 37, but stay **AHEAD** onto the **North Frontage Rd**. Stay **AHEAD** past **WILDORADO** (EXIT 49) and **BUSHLAND** (EXIT 57). **2 miles east**, **TURN LEFT** on **S Hill Rd**, then a quick **RIGHT** onto **Indian Hill Rd**. Pass by Arnot Rd (EXIT 60) and Dowell Rd. East of Hope Rd, curve right to the **STOP**, then **TURN LEFT** on **BL 40** towards **AMARILLO**.

TX page-14

WB: Follow BL 40 thru **VEGA**, then remain on the **North Frontage Rd** past EXIT 28 (**LANDERGIN**) to **ADRIAN**. Stay with the North Frontage Rd to EXIT 18 (Gruhlkey Rd). **JOIN I-40 WB** for 18 miles to **EXIT 0** in **GLENRIO**. (see **SIDE TRIP**).

VEGA is full of fun and fine folks. Take HWY 385 north a couple of blocks for the restored **1920s Magnolia Gas Station** on older 66 near the courthouse. A few blocks west on dead-end early 66 (W Main at 12th), **Dot's Mini Museum** houses her personal collection of artifacts. For a genuine western event, try the **Oldham Co Roundup** on the 2nd Saturday in August (free BBQ lunch plus a parade, rodeo and music. Ye-Haw!) For an old-fashioned Route 66 stay, try the very-vintage **Vega Motel** (806) 267-2205. A bit newer, the former Sands Motel (now the

Best Western Country Inn) has been in the same family since the1960s (806) 267-2131. INFO: Oldham County C of C: 806 267-2828.

Watch for two small concrete culverts on the north between **VEGA** and **ADRIAN**: remnants of "Dirt 66." Little is left of **LANDERGIN**, where the **Federation** staged the first **John Steinbeck Award Banquet** in a circus tent on October 11, 1997. **ADRIAN**, billed as the geographical midpoint of Route 66, may be small, but has lots to offer at the **Mid Point Café and Gift Shop**. Fran and company always offer fine vittles and friendly faces (you **MUST** try the **"ugly crust pie"** hmmm–hmmm good!). www.midpoint66.com or (806) 538-6379.

A **Stuckeys** has long stuck to the EB off-ramp at **EXIT 18** (Gruhlkey Rd), sticking tourists with pecan logs and rubber tomahawks. Old 66 dead ends to the west, where the remote **Cap Rock Texaco** (long closed) was the last bit o'civilization before the route plunged down the escarpment on its way to secluded **GLENRIO**. Beaten by the bypass, this former bustling road-town, astraddle the **Texas/New Mexico State Line**, is now home to picturesque ruins and barking dogs. The forlorn **Texas Longhorn Motel** once boasted of being both the "First" and **"Last** motel in Texas." After your **SIDE TRIP** here from **EXIT 0**, WB drivers can either join the **"Dirt 66" OPTION** to **SAN JON**, **NM** (see **NM page-3**) or rejoin **I-40** to continue west on pavement. Eastbounders, get ready for the great state of **TEXAS**.

EB: From EXIT 0 in GLENRIO, follow **I-40 EB** for 18 miles to **EXIT 18** (Gruhlkey Rd). **CROSS I-40**, and follow the North Frontage Rd thru **ADRIAN** and past EXIT 28 (**LANDERGIN**) to join **BL 40 AHEAD** thru **VEGA**.
(see Texas INTRO on TX page-1)   TX page-15   (see MAP # 3 on TX page-13)

Navigating New Mexico

Since the days of **Coronado**, <u>NEW MEXICO</u> has been a popular destination for its beauty, history and people. Offering extremes between peaceful isolation to busy city strips, and from small Spanish communities with rustic chapels, to majestic adobe missions, **Route 66** encounters distant peaks, craggy cliffs, multi-hued mesas and tree covered mountain slopes in its nearly 400 mile traverse across the state. That mileage figure is purposely vague, for the mileage you drive depends on which version of 66 you take. **Before 1937**, Route 66 zigged up to <u>SANTA FE</u> before plunging down thru the heart of <u>ALBUQUERQUE</u> to <u>LOS LUNAS</u>, to join the **POST-1937** route at <u>CORREO</u>. Thus, the

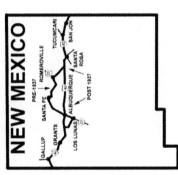

modern tourist must make a choice: **PRE or POST 1937 66**. Both have plusses: Sadly, **Post 37 US 66** from <u>SANTA ROSA</u> to <u>MORIARTY</u> is all I-40, but this does make for a quick drive, and Old 66 west of <u>MORIARTY</u> thru **Tijeras Canyon** and on **Central Ave** into <u>ALBUQUERQUE</u> is rewarding. The **SANTA FE LOOP**, on the other hand, requires much less interstate travel, and offers vistas of magnificent scenery and history. This leg will take much longer but the time is well spent. Let your schedule be your guide (if your trip is bi-directional, do both ways!). See **NM page 23-30** for the **PRE-1937 OPTION**.

Portions of **Route 66**, and its ancestors across the state, have known many names: **El Camino Real, Old Santa Fe Trail, Ozark Trail, National Old Trails** and now the **Route 66 Scenic Byway.** **NEW MEXICO** lays claim to many of the records for **"OLDEST"** in the nation, and much of that history is right on the route, including many **Native American Pueblos**. Inquire at their visitor centers about regulations, especially before photographing, as these are not "theme parks" but people's homes and places of worship. Be a good guest, and you'll find the people of <u>NEW MEXICO</u> to be as warm and friendly as the ever-present Zia "sun symbol" that graces the state.

NEW MEXICO MAP # 1

CUERVO ~ GLENRIO

DASHED LINE = ROUGH, PRIVATE OR IMPASSABLE

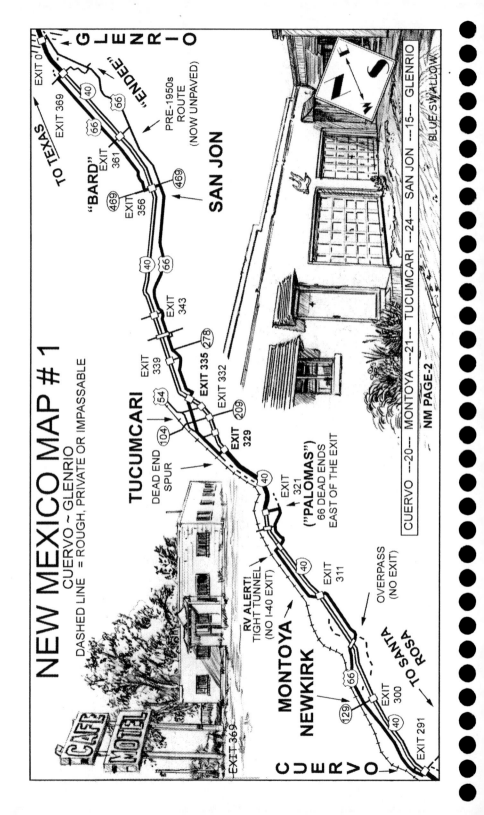

G L E N R I O

TO TEXAS

EXIT 0

EXIT 369

"ENDEE"

40

66

66

PRE-1950s ROUTE (NOW UNPAVED)

"BARD"
EXIT 361

469   EXIT
      356

469

SAN JON

40   66

EXIT 343

278

EXIT 339

EXIT 335

EXIT 332

TUCUMCARI

54

104

209

EXIT 329

DEAD END SPUR

40

EXIT 321

("PALOMAS")
66 DEAD ENDS
EAST OF THE EXIT

RV ALERT!
TIGHT TUNNEL
(NO I-40 EXIT)

40

EXIT 311

OVERPASS
(NO EXIT)

MONTOYA

NEWKIRK

66

TO SANTA ROSA

129

EXIT 300

40

EXIT 291

EXIT 369

C U E R V O

CUERVO ---20--- MONTOYA ---21--- TUCUMCARI ---24--- SAN JON ---15--- GLENRIO

BLUE SWALLOW

NM PAGE-2

WB: From **EXIT 0** at <u>GLENRIO</u>, follow **I-40** across the State Line into NM. Take **EXIT 369**, turn **RIGHT** from the off ramp, then **LEFT** on the **N Frontage Rd**. Pass **EXIT 361** ("**BARD**") and then curve around the Truck Inspection Station. At **EXIT 356**, turn **LEFT** on **Hwy 469**, and cross under I-40 into <u>SAN JON</u>. After about a half-mile, turn **RIGHT** to follow the **South Frontage Rd** west.

OPTIONAL "DIRT 66"
GLENRIO TO SAN JON

If you've made the **SIDE TRIP** from **EXIT 0** into <u>GLENRIO</u>, (or if you're headed **EB** from <u>SAN JON</u>) you have a **CHOICE**. The **tour route** is via the **1950s pavement** north of I-40. **OR:** follow the **"DIRT 66" OPTION:**

TO STAY ON PAVEMENT USE "1950S 66" BETWEEN EXITs 369 AND 356

About **18 scenic miles** of formerly paved '66 (now good dirt and gravel) exist from <u>GLENRIO</u> thru "**ENDEE**" to <u>SAN JON</u>. Enjoy this quiet and peaceful drive away from I-40, across a few quaint wooden-post bridges and beside visible remnants of the abandoned **CRI&P RR**. **WB:** follow the dirt road past where the pavement dead ends west of <u>GLENRIO</u> (the abandoned pavement crosses a long concrete bridge). **EB:** follow 66 thru <u>SAN JON</u>, and then along the south side of I-40 onto the dirt road. Hold the speed to 35 MPH and **AVOID** if muddy. In the middle, lonely <u>ENDEE</u> consists of the ruins of a few old motel cabins and a "two-holer" privy shack, emblazoned with the boast "**MODERN RESTROOMS**" (they DID flush). This is actually the **SECOND** route of US 66 along here. The **FIRST** route ran along the south side of the RR until west of <u>ENDEE</u>, where it rejoined the later route on a tangent to a curve. Little trace of the early path is visible. **EB:** rejoin the main tour at **EXIT 0** (<u>GLENRIO</u>).

NOTE: NM TIME IS ONE HOUR EARLIER THAN TX

GLENRIO
EXIT 0

T
E
X
A
S

P A V E
D

E N D S

NM INFO CENTER
REST AREA
EXIT 392
369

93

"ENDEE"
USE CARE
on DIRT/GRAVEL ROAD
DRIVE 35 MPH MAX
AVOID WHEN MUDDY

1950s 66

DIRT RD

66

EARLIEST 66

TO TUCUMCARI
EXIT 356
469

TRUCK STATION

"BARD"
EXIT 361

PAVE ENDS

SAN JON

40
66

At **EXIT 369** on the **1950s Route** was the demolished **TL2 (Texas Longhorn 2) Motel and Café**. Down the road lie the final ruins of "**BARD**," which had to move a few times to remain on the main road. <u>SAN JON</u> (say "Hone") was devastated by a one-exit bypass. Now mostly ruins of old gas stations and motels (only one still operating) line the broad main drag. Make sure to double back thru town along the town's former stretch of Route 66. A once-famous block long mural is long gone, but the "Free Municipal Camp" remains.

EB: In <u>SAN JON</u>, turn **LEFT** on **Hwy 469**. Pass under I-40 at **EXIT 356**. Turn **RIGHT** on the **N Frontage Rd** (Quay Co Rd 58.5). Pass the Truck Inspection Station. Pass by **EXIT 361** ("**BARD**"). At **EXIT 369**, join **I-40 EB** to **EXIT 0** (<u>GLENRIO</u>) in **TEXAS**.

WB: From <u>SAN JON</u>, follow the **South Frontage Rd** past EXIT 343 and 339. At **EXIT 335**, cross under I-40 and curve with **BL 40 –** Tucumcari Blvd thru <u>TUCUMCARI</u>. On the west side, rejoin **I-40 WB** at **EXIT 329**. (see SIDE TRIP NM page-5)

TUCUMCARI

West of <u>SAN JON</u>, '66 briefly cuts away from I-40 as it drops down thru red hills. An old gas station ruin below the ridge (private) once had a canopy roofed with flattened oilcans. Flat-topped **Tucumcari Mountain** looms ahead.

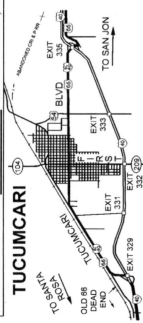

Old and picturesque motels remain in <u>TUCUMCARI</u>, but many have lost their neon (some due to a 2007 storm)! Hopefully the neon at the **Blue Swallow Motel**, including a large neon swallow atop the sign arching over the driveway and the little neon swallows perched on newly repainted blue stucco walls, will survive. Long home to the late Lillian Redman, proud new owners are keeping up the tradition. (505) 461-9849 during tourist season. Also recommended is the **Pow Wow Inn** (505) 461-0500. The **Tucumcari Historical Museum** on Adams Street (a few blocks north of Route 66) has a Route 66 exhibit with vintage images. CITY INFO: (505) 461-1694.

Curious for curios? Then enter **Tee Pee Curios** thru their big teepee. Their noctilucent neon sign was recently restored with Federal grant money, as many signs in New Mexico have been, thanks to work by the NM Association. For fine food, try **Del's Restaurant** (with the bovine-topped sign). The sombrero-topped **La Cita** has reopened. For an educational experience, visit the **Mesalands Community College Dinosaur Museum**, at 211 E Laughlin St (north of 66 on First St, right on Laughlin) for the "Largest collection of life sized bronze skeletons in the world" (505) 461 DINO. Look for the **Route 66 Sculpture** near the Convention Center, on the west side of town. The "twin sixes" ride a chromed tailfin; complete with three blazing teardrop taillights.

EB: Take **EXIT 329**, and follow **BL 40/Tucumcari Blvd** thru <u>TUCUMCARI</u>. On the east side, cross under I-40 at EXIT 335 (AVOID the EB onramp) and turn **LEFT** onto the **South Frontage Rd**. Stay ahead past EXIT 339 and 343 to <u>SAN JON</u>.

WB: Join I-40 WB at **EXIT 329**. Take **EXIT 321** ("**PALOMAS**") across I-40. (See **ALERT first…especially RVs and bikers!**) Go south to the **Frontage Rd**, and turn **RIGHT**. Continue ahead on the **S Frontage Rd** past the next overpass (no exit). **SLOW** to curve sharply thru a narrow tunnel under I-40, then continue on the **N Frontage Rd** thru **MONTOYA**. At **EXIT 311**, cross I-40, and follow the **S Frontage Rd**. Cross I-40 again (no exit) and continue along the RR thru **NEWKIRK** to **CUERVO**. Join **I-40 WB** at **EXIT 291**.

ALERT! The tunnel under I-40 between **EXIT 321** and **EXIT 311** is narrow, with a tight approach. Don't use when flooded **OR** muddy! RVs stay on I-40 here. Many "dips" (**low water xings**) exist on these sections. **DO NOT** drive into running water! (if raining, stay on I-40).

SIDE TRIP: Where **Tucumcari Blvd** turns towards **EXIT 329**, a **dead end** spur of 66 turns off **RIGHT**, and can be followed a short ways along the tracks. South of the big RR trestle is an older approach to a long gone bridge. Nearby, a hand-painted TEXACO advertisement fades on west-facing boulders. The squat towers that dot the area are pump houses. A side road under I-40 leads to old **5 Mile Park**, where the historic pool house is being restored.

There are several short, concrete bridges east of **MONTOYA**. **SCAVENGER HUNT!** What is the **DATE** on these bridges? (they're all the same… watch for cars!) _____ Road and railroad here travel a wide-open valley, rimmed with steep bluffs of various hues. On the mesa to the south, light colored streaks of mining tailings give evidence to something desirable hidden in one layer of strata.

NEWKIRK has decaying remnants of an old motel and stations, including Wilkerson's Gulf. There are extensive stretches of an earlier 66 east of town, but all are inaccessible. If you happen to be at the **EB Rest Area** (shame for not being on 66!) you can see the old road and a couple of old houses to the south. **NOTE:** The frontage road to **CUERVO** becomes a **bit rough**. I-40 chopped this town in two. The single line of mostly empty businesses hint at past commerce, while to the south, an attractive stone chapel, and a boxcar turned abode, abut the ruddy slopes of **Cuervo Mesa**.

EB: From **EXIT 291**, take the **N Frontage Rd** thru **CUERVO** and **NEWKIRK**. Cross over I-40 (no exit) and follow the **S Frontage Rd** to **EXIT 311**. Cross I-40. (See **ALERT first!**) and follow the **N Frontage Rd** past **MONTOYA**. At the tunnel, cross under I-40, and follow the **S Frontage Rd** to **EXIT 321**. Turn **LEFT** to the exit, and join **I-40 EB**. At **EXIT 329**, follow **BL 40** into **TUCUMCARI**.

(see **MAP # 1** NM page-2)

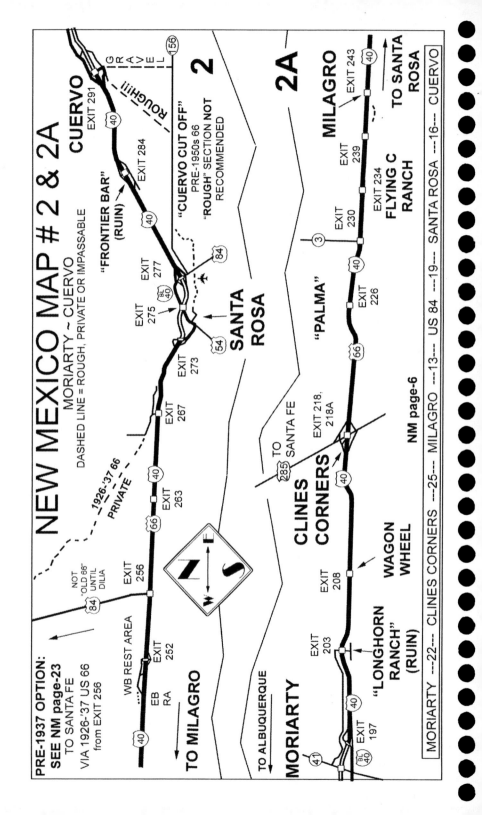

NEW MEXICO MAP # 2 & 2A

MORIARTY ~ CUERVO
DASHED LINE = ROUGH, PRIVATE OR IMPASSABLE

PRE-1937 OPTION:
SEE NM page-23
TO SANTA FE
VIA 1926-'37 US 66
from EXIT 256

CUERVO — EXIT 291

iiiROUGH!!!

GRAVEL

156

2

2A

"CUERVO CUT OFF"
PRE-1950s 66
"ROUGH" SECTION NOT
RECOMMENDED

MILAGRO — EXIT 243

TO SANTA ROSA

EXIT 239

EXIT 234

FLYING C RANCH

EXIT 230

3

EXIT 226

"PALMA"

EXIT 218, 218A

TO SANTA FE — 285

CLINES CORNERS

40

WAGON WHEEL

EXIT 208

MORIARTY

EXIT 203

"LONGHORN RANCH" (RUIN)

EXIT 197

41

BL 40

40

TO ALBUQUERQUE

40

"FRONTIER BAR" (RUIN)

EXIT 284

EXIT 277

EXIT 275

BL 40

84

54

EXIT 273

SANTA ROSA

66

EXIT 267

EXIT 263

66

40

1926-'37 66
PRIVATE

NOT "OLD 66" UNTIL DILIA

84

EXIT 256

WB REST AREA

EB RA

EXIT 252

40

66

TO MILAGRO

NM page-6

MORIARTY ---22--- CLINES CORNERS ---25--- MILAGRO ---13--- US 84 ---19--- SANTA ROSA ---16--- CUERVO

Before the early 1950s, US 66 west of <u>CUERVO</u> followed the "**CUERVO CUT OFF**" (which cut the corner on the old gravel "dog leg"). This road today is in **VERY BAD** shape, with many washouts and plenty of potholes and bumps. Even though the biggest washout was filled in with dirt, I do **NOT** recommend this road to the casual vacationer (it shows up with no warnings on some tourist maps)! The paved section, along Hwy 156 from **EXIT 277**, is a nice drive. Near US 84, oldest 66 dropped from the mesa and thru the airport toward <u>SANTA ROSA</u>.

SANTA ROSA DETAIL

I-40 overlays the final route of '66, passing the ruins of the **Frontier Bar and Museum** at EXIT 284. Perched on a long downhill slope leading to the Pecos River, this defunct business began its downhill slide years ago, and now is little more than a bathroom for truckers. A crude mural of Indians, Spaniards and Frontiersmen pays homage to the past.

On the east side of <u>SANTA ROSA</u> is the **Route 66 Auto Museum** where, for a small fee, you can see a collection of customs, hot rods and restored vintage cars (some for sale). You can't miss the yellow street rod on the tall pole in front! **GIFT SHOP ALERT**! A few motels in town still cling to their neon tubes, as does the **Comet II Restaurant** on Parker. Less fortunate was the famous **Club Café**, closed for years. Their "Fat Man's" friendly face still grins from **Joseph's Bar & Grill**. Old storefronts line 4th St Downtown, where the original route joins Parker Ave. INFO: (800) 450-7084.

SIDE TRIP: Follow **4th St** from Parker. Turn **LEFT** on **La Pradira**, then angle **RIGHT** at 6th St, before Lake Dr, to the **Blue Hole**, a deep, clear blue sinkhole favored by landlocked divers. Old 66 enters private property as it runs east towards the airport.

WB: From downtown **SANTA ROSA,** follow **BL 40** across the **Pecos River,** then curve **RIGHT** with **BL 40** at the US 53 JCT, under the RR tracks to **EXIT 273.** Join **I-40 WB.** Pass the JCT with **US 84,** and then US 285. At **EXIT 197,** take **BL 40** into **MORIARTY.**

On the way west from **SANTA ROSA,** 66 crosses the **Pecos River,** then curves under the railroad. You won't see the iron rails for many a mile. **Riverside Drive,** which curves along under the west side of the RR bridge close to the river, is a bit of older 66. One last section of old businesses line '66 before the evil necessity of superslab travel rears its limited access head.

US 66 to **MORIARTY** is almost totally buried under I-40. The good news is this makes for fast driving (your chance to make up time) but watch the weather closely when **snow** is predicted! EXIT 267 marks the point where **Pre-1937 "Dirt 66"** headed towards **DILIA** (impassable today). **US 84 (EXIT 256)** is the **WB** starting point for the **SANTA FE LOOP OPTION** (see **NM page-23** if you chose to drive this option).

A rare fragment of **Post-1937** 66 survives at the **WB Rest Area** (EXIT 252), running a short distance west past the WB I-40 on ramp (undriveable). An old blacktop curve is visible on the south side, just west of **MILAGRO,** one of the few outposts of civilization along this long, empty stretch. They have a long Route 66 pedigree, as does **FLYING C RANCH** (their **"Running Indian"** mascot still pauses to catch his breath on their billboards). Watch for slow trucks crawling up steep **Palma Hill.**

If you've been wondering if it's really **"Worth Waiting For,"** then check out **CLINES CORNERS.** Begun in 1934 (before 66 came this way), Cline's is the biggest gift shop in this area (someone had a sense of humor in these land-locked plains, naming the street in front of the store "Yacht Club Dr"). Next stop is little **"WAGON WHEEL,"** a name harking back to the old west, as do the ruins of **LONGHORN RANCH,** which lie scattered across old 66 from a topless joint and the Longhorn Motel at EXIT 203. **HISTORIC NOTE:** Going **WB,** watch closely along the north side of I-40 for a glimpse of a rundown complex a few miles west of EXIT 203. Claar's **Hitchin Post** reposes here in empty quietude, a far cry from the noisy days when the trading post offered a free museum, roadside zoo, and the **"Den of Death."**

EB: From **MORIARTY,** join **I-40 EB** at EXIT 197. Pass US 285, and go past EXIT 256/US 84 (the **EB Pre-'37 OPTION** ends here). At **EXIT 273,** take **BL 40** into **SANTA ROSA.** Cross under the RR, then curve **LEFT** at the US 54 JCT onto **Parker Ave** thru downtown.

(see **MAP # 2/2A** NM page-6)

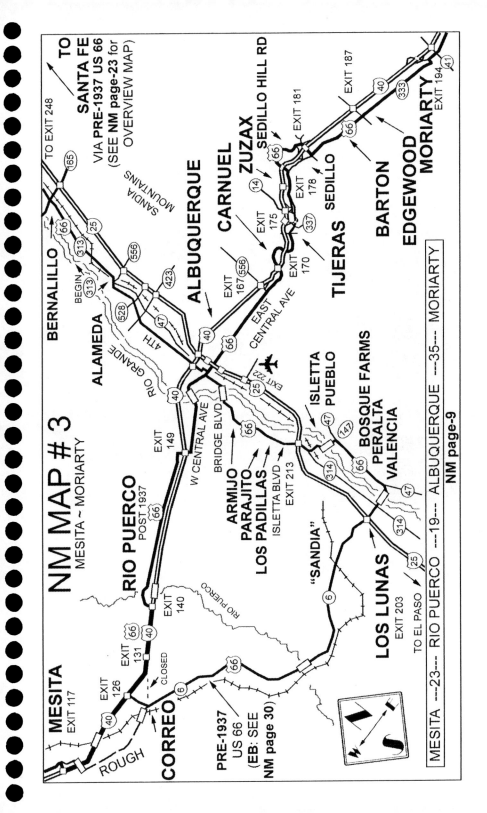

WB: Follow **BL 40/Hwy 333** thru **MORIARTY**. About a mile past the HWY 41 JCT, **AVOID** entering I-40 at EXIT 194 by turning **LEFT** just before the exit ramps, then immediately **RIGHT** with **HWY 333**. Continue thru **EDGEWOOD** and **BARTON** to **EXIT 181**. Cross over I-40 and curve **LEFT** with **Sedillo Hill Rd** (AVOID the WB I-40 on ramp). At Meadow Dr stay with **Sedillo Hill Rd** as it curves back to cross under I-40. Turn **RIGHT** on **Hwy 333**, and continue past **ZUZAX** to the HWY 14 JCT in **TIJERAS**.

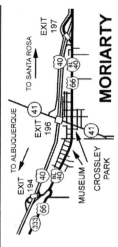

TO SANTA ROSA

TO ALBUQUERQUE

EXIT 194

EXIT 41 196

CROSSLEY PARK

MUSEUM

EXIT 197

MORIARTY

MORIARTY maintains memories of the Mother Road. Here is the last remaining **Whiting Bros** gas station still open under the yellow and red "WB" signs. **Whiting Bros** began in 1917, and established a chain of cut-price stations across 66 from Shamrock, TX to west of Barstow, CA. On Route 66 is the **Moriarty Historical Museum**. You can t miss the **El Comedor de Anayas**, the restaurant with the last surviving "**neon rotosphere**" on 66. Its rotating neon spikes perform a brilliant show every night. Just west of HWY 41, **Crossley Park** has four statues depicting area history, including the surveying of US 66. INFO: (505) 832 4087.

The route gradually climbs as it passes thru **EDGEWOOD**, and then **BARTON** (marked only by some old gas pumps). Next comes the long steep drop thru **Tijeras Canyon**. Near the top is **Sedillo Hill Rd** (1937-1949 era 66). Although not currently marked as Historic 66, it is definitely the route of choice. One mile longer (but miles better) than staying on HWY 333, this is an enchanting descent (or climb) along a twisty but well maintained road thru verdant forest, with awesome vistas of a valley rimmed by surrounding peaks. There are few places to pull off (and drive carefully on the narrow **2-lane**) but the drive is satisfying (**WB** drivers, IGNORE the "Mountainous Unimproved Road" sign, which refers to a side road). Back on HWY 333, **ZUZAX** has a strange name (and once had a small aerial tram), but now is not much more than a station and RV Park.

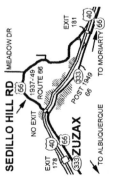

SEDILLO HILL RD | MEADOW DR

NO EXIT

1937-49 ROUTE 66

ZUZAX

EXIT 178

TO ALBUQUERQUE

POST 333 66 1949

TO MORIARTY 66

EXIT 181

EB: From the HWY 14 JCT in **TIJERAS**, follow **HWY 333** uphill. About a mile past EXIT 178 (**ZUZAX**), turn **LEFT**, and cross under I-40 on **Sedillo Hill Rd**. After about 3 1/2 miles, turn **RIGHT** to cross I-40 (first, **AVOID** the I-40 on ramp), then turn **LEFT** on **HWY 333**, thru **BARTON** and **EDGEWOOD**. Nearing **MORIARTY** (EXIT 194), curve **LEFT**, then **RIGHT** on **BL 40** thru town.

NM page-10

WB: At the HWY 14 JCT stoplight, turn **LEFT** with **HWY 333**, along the south side of I-40 thru **TIJERAS** (AVOID all "turn ONLY" lanes and on ramps). Pass under the next overpass (no access), then **STOP** at the **HWY 337** JCT. Stay **AHEAD** with **HWY 333**. Curve under I-40, and continue thru **CARNUEL**. At **EXIT 170**, join the **LEFT** lane. Cross OVER I-40 and stay **AHEAD** with **HWY 333**. Cross Four Hills Rd and Tramway Blvd (near EXIT 167), stay **AHEAD** onto **Central Ave**, toward downtown **ALBUQUERQUE**.

TIJERAS

NM **HWY 14**, the "**Turquoise Trail Scenic Byway**," gives access to several attractions, including **HWY 536**, the road that climbs thru the **Sandia Mountains** to 10,678 foot **Sandia Crest**. On the way, **Sandia Crest Rd** passes **Tinkertown Museum** (**FOLK ART ALERT!**) a 40-year collection of carved figures, animated scenes, and odd collections, housed in a 22-room museum (some walls are built from 50,000 bottles) (505) 281-5233. Up HWY 14 towards **SANTA FE** are the former ghost towns of **Madrid** and **Cerrillos**, now cultural extensions of the capitol city. Another way to reach the mountaintop is via the **Sandia Peak Tramway** (the "worlds longest"), from off Tramway Blvd, north of EXIT 167.

Back on 66, the mountains tightly confine the path thru **Tijeras Canyon**. East of **CARNUEL**, a road cut for older 66 scars the hillside above. Watch for the **Mountain Lodge** neon sign, a stereotypical "se_or" astride a burro. Finally, the road escapes the boulder-strewn slopes to continue its downhill dash into **ALBUQUERQUE**. East Central Ave once traversed a mostly empty land, now packed to the foothills with homes and commerce. Many old motels (mostly of the mission/pueblo style) and businesses remain (some on the National Register) along with a colorful variety of neon signs. There's almost TOO much to absorb amongst the hustle and bustle (there's also a lot of transients at times). Stay in the inside lane to avoid turns.

ALBUQUERQUE

EB: Follow **Central Ave** east from **ALBUQUERQUE**. Stay **AHEAD**, thru the intersections with Tramway and Four Hills Rd (near EXIT 167), onto **HWY 333**. (AVOID all "turn ONLY" lanes and on ramps). At **EXIT 170**, follow **HWY 333** OVER I-40 to **CARNUEL**. Curve under I-40, then climb with **HWY 333** into **TIJERAS**. **STOP** at the **HWY 337** JCT: stay **AHEAD** with **HWY 333**. When HWY 14 branches off left, stay in the **RIGHT** lane, and curve **RIGHT** with **HWY 333**, staying on the south side of I-40 thru **ZUZAX**.

GIANT ALERT! Another "lumberjack" style axe-man perches on the **May Café** sign just south of '66 at Louisiana Blvd. Nearby, Central Ave passes the **State Fair Grounds**. NOTE: If you're in town during the September Fair, you'll have trouble getting a room (unless you've reserved ahead!). Same deal with the annual **International Balloon Festival** in October. These are "plan ahead" events. www.NMStateFair.com   www.balloonfiesta.com

At 3821 Central is the 1931 **Aztec Motel** with its "funkydelic" decorated exterior and great neon sign, devoted to affordable short or long-term lodging. Visitors are welcome to enjoy the eclectic atmosphere. Nearby **Nob Hill** is an early strip-mall from 1947, with stylish "streamline modern" architecture punctuated by stepped towers. A mile east is **Hiland Theatre** and **Shopping Center**, dating to 1952. More "streamline" style, complete with stubby tower, is found at **Kelley's Pub and Restaurant**, housed at 3222 Central in a 1939-era Ford Dealer. More towers sprout from former gas stations along Central. Across '66 is the 1936 **Monte Vista Fire Station**, a "Pueblo Revival" structure where only appetites are extinguished today.

Another great "pit stop" is the neon draped **Route 66 Diner** at 1405 Central NE, with excellent food and vintage "roadside Americana" décor (including the front of an old car "stuck" into a dining room). Across from the **University Of NM** campus, at 2106 Central, is a building that once housed a **Pig Stand** (an early fast food chain). Look for the outlines of a pig and calf on its wall.

West of the colorful "Santa Fe" RR underpass is colorful downtown. The city center can be busy and congested, but there's much to enjoy along Central. The old Hotel Alvarado is gone (a replica serves as a transport center) but the **La Posada De Albuquerque** (a former Hilton Hotel and the first modern multi-story hotel in town) offers old-fashioned opulence at 125 2ⁿᵈ St. Park and walk the downtown streets (see **NM page-13**). City INFO: (505) 842-9918 (also see **NM page-29** for **PRE-1937 66**).

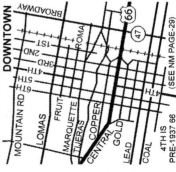

EB: Follow **Central Ave** from downtown **ALBUQUERQUE**, under I-25, towards the Tramway Blvd intersection (near EXIT 167).

NM page-12

(see NM page-29 for Pre-1937 66)

WB: From downtown **ALBUQUERQUE**, stay on **West Central Ave**, across the Rio Grande.

While downtown, be sure to see the restored **KiMo Theatre** at 423 Central. Built in 1927, this showplace embodies **"Pueblo Deco"** style, a mix of Southwestern and Art Deco style with Indian motifs, plus cow skulls, murals and even "Swastikas" (they pre-dated WW II). Self-guided tours of the fantastic interior are available on weekdays, guided tours by appt. Check at http://www.cabq.gov/kimo/ for a virtual tour and info on performances, or call (505) 768-3522. **SCAVENGER HUNT!** What is the **NAME** on the **KiMo** Building plaque out front? _____

Across from the **KiMo** in the next block is **Maisel's Indian Jewelry** (circa 1939), a most authentic place to shop for turquoise and silver goodies. Down the street, a rope-twirling neon cowpoke leans languidly on the **Avalon Restaurant** sign. Headed west, another rope-wielding cowboy spurs his neon stallion from atop the recently restored El Don Motel sign. *"Route 66 New Mexico"* (Fall, 2003) gave them a good review. Yet more neon action is at the **Dog House**, where an animated wiener dog happily wags his neon tail while scarfing hot dogs.

Old Town (north on Rio Grande Blvd) is the site of **"Villa De Albuquerque,"** founded in 1706 and grown into a classic Spanish plaza with over 130 shops and restaurants, plus several museums, including the **American International Rattlesnake Museum. GIFT SHOP ALERT:** "skins and fangs!"(www.rattlesnakes.com). Nearby is a tribute to recent history, the **National Atomic Museum**, for the "Story of the Atomic Age" from Madam Curie thru the Cold War. **GIFT SHOP ALERT!** "Up ?N? Atom," the museum store, offers mushroom cloud t-shirts! A new facility will open in 2006 near I-25 (www.atomicmuseum.com). The **Federation Dining and Lodging Guide** lists many motels in town, but the only one I have had recent (repeated) experience of is the **Monterey Non Smokers Motel** at 2402 Central (near Old Town), for its clean, quiet and reasonable rooms. This vintage motel has a nifty neon sign, too! (505) 243-3554. Closer to the Rio, the 1937 **El Vado Motel** is likely the most authentic looking old motel, with a beautiful neon sign (unfortunately, its future is in question).

EB: Cross the river on **Central Ave**. Stay in the right lane to **AVOID** Lomas. Join the **LEFT** lane past 10th St, and follow the **"Central Ave Left Lane ONLY"** sign (**AVOID** the curve onto Gold) to downtown **ALBUQUERQUE**. (see NM page-29 for Pre-1937 66)

(Map)

UNIVERSITY · 25 · BROADWAY · 2ND 3RD · 4TH ST 5TH ST · LOMAS · MOUNTAIN RD · CENTRAL

40 · EXIT 157 · RIO GRANDE BLVD · OLD TOWN · LOMAS BLVD · 66 · RIO · CENTRAL · GOLD LEAD COAL · GRANDE · 47

EB AVOID

POST 1937
ALBUQUERQUE

WB: Follow **Central Ave** from the Rio Grande in **ALBUQUERQUE**, up "Nine Mile Hill" to **EXIT 149**. Turn **RIGHT** with the sign "East Santa Rosa" but **AVOID** the on ramp: stay **AHEAD** across I-40 ("To Frontage Rd"). Turn **LEFT** on the **N Frontage Rd**, and go to **EXIT 140 (RIO PUERCO)**. Join **I-40 WB** past EXIT 126 to **MESITA** at **EXIT 117**. Turn **RIGHT** from the off ramp, then **LEFT**.

EXIT 149

PASEO DEL VOLCAN

TO RIO PUERCO

66 · 40

CENTRAL AVE

66

TO ALBUQUERQUE

Across the river, **ALBUQUERQUE** struggles westward for a ways, finally petering out on the sandy slope of "**Nine Mile Hill.**" Many old motels on this faded section of Central Ave lost the struggle and were demolished, but a few soldier on. Most notable is the **Westward Ho Motel** at 7500 Central, with its brilliant green **Saguaro Cactus** neon sign (recently the beneficiary of restoration funds). I stayed here as a kid, and will always have a soft spot for this place. The current owners have been working to improve the vintage units, and two movies filmed scenes here

recently. **Mac's La Sierra Coffee Shop** has a cute sign depicting a bull sitting in a basket of French fries and biscuits, hawking their specialty "Steak in the Rough." Race fans, look south past Unser Blvd for the old **Unser Garage** (now "Auto Glass"). Past the Grandview Motel, the high ground west of town indeed offers a grand view, as twilight fades to night and the sparkling city lights fill the valley below, with the **Sandia Mountains** forming a glowing backdrop.

At **RIO PUERCO**, stop and walk across the preserved **1933 Rio Puerco Bridge. SCAVENGER HUNT!** Who ERECTED this "Parker Through-truss bridge?" _____ Multiple **GIANT ALERT!** Across I-40 waits Laguna Pueblo's Giant **Route 66 Casino**, behind the huge "**neon gas pump sign**" and the **giant arrows** in the parking lot. Inside, the '66 theme continues, with **Johnny Rockets Diner** (that evokes **TEXAS**' U Drop Inn), **Kicks Café**, and much more! Also inside (where he's safe from giant arrowheads) is **BIG TEX**, in front of the **Hungry Cowboy Café.**

Old 66 crossed the RR in **CORREO**, where **HWY 6**, the **Pre-1937 OPTION**, connects to **LOS LUNAS** (**EB**: DECIDE NOW!) The old road continues west across **Laguna Pueblo** lands to **MESITA** (crossing over I-40 east of EXIT 117) but is **rough** and partly unpaved (respect Pueblo rules, and don't trespass when driving across their land). The tour follows **I-40** along the path of the **1950s 4-lane 66**.

EB: From **MESITA**, join **I-40 EB** past EXIT 126 (see **Pre-1937 OPTION NM page-30**). Take **EXIT 140 (RIO PUERCO)**, and join the **N Frontage Rd** to **EXIT 149**. Cross I-40, then turn **LEFT** onto **Central Ave**, towards the Rio Grande and downtown **ALBUQUERQUE**.

(see MAP # 3 NM page-9)

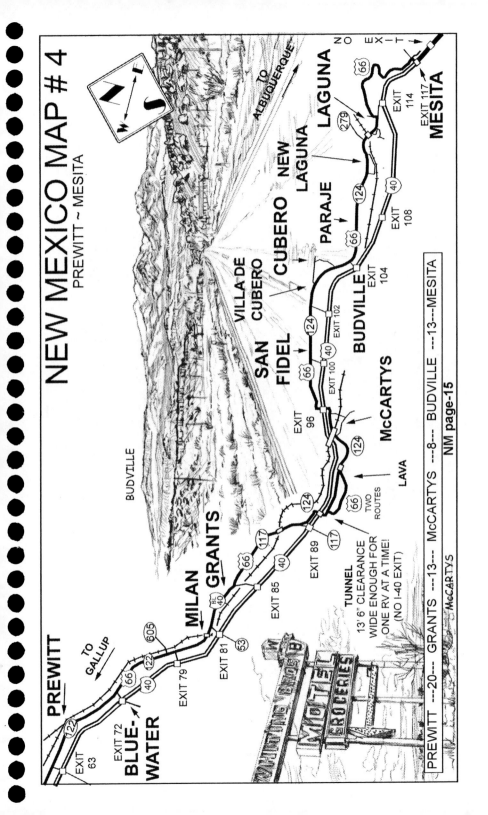

NEW MEXICO MAP #4
PREWITT ~ MESITA

PREWITT ---20--- GRANTS ---13--- McCARTYS ---13--- BUDVILLE ---8--- BUDVILLE ---13---MESITA

NM page-15

WB: From **EXIT 117** (**MESITA**), take the **East-side Frontage Rd** towards **LAGUNA**. Follow the curves away from I-40, and around "Dead Man's Curve." Approaching town, follow the sharp **LEFT** turn, then turn **RIGHT** onto **HWY 124**, thru **LAGUNA**. Stay with **HWY 124** across the RR, past **NEW LAGUNA**, **PARAJE**, and **BUDVILLE** (near EXIT 104), then thru **VILLA CUBERO**.

From **MESITA**, the route still traverses **Laguna Pueblo Land**, so be a good guest and obey posted rules about cameras, trespassing, etc. This quality drive takes you away from I-40 for quite a while. **Westbound**, the road curves past a mesa that I-40 (and 4-lane 66) blasted thru. **GIANT ALERT!** Suddenly, up looms the large lava outcrop known as **"Owl Rock."** Next is notorious **'Dead Man's Curve,"** a looong tight loop around a narrow point of rock that SURELY deserved the name.

More curves await uphill **WB**, before the drop into old **LAGUNA**. Topping the picturesque village is **San Jose Mission**; built in 1699 (a pullout from I-40 south of town offers an excellent view). "DIRT" 66 followed an abandoned **AT&SF RR** grade around the base of the hill (now a paved street), while the paved 2-lane ran above town. For info on annual events: (505) 552-6654. Santa Fe Blvd ("L 50") carried earlier 66 along RR tracks thru neighboring **NEW LAGUNA**. Current **HWY 124** is a nice, peaceful drive thru the rocky hills, among rock buildings scattered around the Pueblo. Just west of Encinal Rd, an ancient concrete bridge is visible to the north, in the deep gully.

Outside the Pueblo is **BUDVILLE**, home of the **Budville Trading Co** (since 1928). Beyond the boulder-strewn hills, mighty **Mt Taylor** dominates the horizon. US 66 bypassed the small village of **CUBERO** in 1937, while the current road curves past **Villa Cubero Trading Post**, a 1937 "Mediterranean Revival" structure still selling groceries and gas (listen to the "ding-ding" of the driveway bell). **Hemingway** wrote part of **"The Old Man and the Sea"** in the cafe here.

LAGUNA TO MESITA

EB: From **VILLA CUBERO**. follow **HWY 124** past **BUDVILLE** (near EXIT 104), **PARAJE** and **NEW LAGUNA**, then across the RR and thru **LAGUNA**. Cross the **Rio San Jose**, join the **LEFT** lane, then turn **LEFT** (signs: "Laguna School/Historic 66"): **AVOID** joining I-40. Follow the road as it curves along north of I-40 and around "Dead Man's Curve" to join **I-40 EB** at **EXIT 117** in **MESITA**.

WB: Take **HWY 124** thru **SAN FIDEL**. Cross **OVER** I-40 at **EXIT 96**: stay with **HWY 124** on the south side, past **McCARTYS** and under the RR. Curve sharply **UNDER** I-40 (narrow tunnel) then sharply out on the north. Turn **RIGHT** onto **HWY 117** (at **EXIT 89**).

RV ADVISORY: the **HWY 124** tunnel under I-40 is a bit narrow and the curve out is tight: **USE CARE**.

Many local drivers give friendly waves here on the **Acoma Reservation**. This is a quiet stretch of lonely road, past the remains of the **Mt Taylor Motel** (now a stable) towards **SAN FIDEL**. Quite charming is **St Josephs' Church**, a small stucco chapel with two blue, horn-tooting cherubs flanking the door. **Rte 66 Gallery** occupies one of the old buildings, while **Ray's** Bar and the ramshackle **White Arrow Garage** round things out. West of town, near EXIT 96, the ruins of a former **Whiting Bros** continues to decay, while some of its old signs still beckon uselessly.

At **McCARTYS**, "Route 38" runs south to **Acoma Mesa** and "**Sky City**," termed the oldest continuously inhabited city in the country, perched hundreds of feet above the valley floor and site of the **San Esteban Del Rey Mission**, built between 1629-1640. Also accessed south from EXIT 102 or EXIT 108. Call (800) 747-0181 for tour info (including a one hour guided walking-tour). Back in **McCARTYS**, the stone **Santa Maria de Acoma Church**, perched on the hillside above the RR tracks, resembles Acoma's mission. HWY 124 gives a good view from afar. **NOTE: DO NOT** take photos on the Acoma Reservation (approximately EXIT 96 to Exit 89). **DO NOT trespass.** The rough lava flows along here (called "**malpais**") hindered early travel thru this narrow valley. **SIDE TRIP**: **Early 66** skirted the south side of the lava beds, running alongside a small working aquaduct on **Anzac Rd** (not a water park, so don't trespass). This road veers southwest from just west of the **small girder bridge** over **Rio San Jose**, then reconnects just east of the I-40 tunnel. See the map for details.

EB: From **HWY 117**, turn **LEFT**, just **BEFORE** EXIT 89, onto **HWY 124**, and continue along the north side of I-40. Curve sharply **UNDER** I-40 (narrow tunnel) and curve **LEFT** on the south side. Stay with **HWY 124**, under the RR and past **McCARTYS**. At **EXIT 96**, cross **OVER** I-40, and stay with **HWY 124** thru **SAN FIDEL** and **VILLA CUBERO**.

NM page-17

see MAP 4 NM page-15)

WB: From **EXIT 89**, follow **HWY 117** across the RR to <u>GRANTS</u>. Merge **AHEAD** onto **BL 40/HWY 122** on the east side, and continue thru town, past EXIT 81. Follow **HWY 122** thru <u>MILAN</u> (past EXIT 79) and **BLUEWATER** to **PREWITT** (EXIT 63).

<u>GRANTS</u> offers you the chance to "Go Underground," at the **New Mexico Mining Museum**. Cold war era uranium mining was big in the region, and this facility recreates a typical mine (one story underground) plus fossil and Route 66 exhibits 800-748 2142. On the other extreme, the railroad tracks run **higher** than most of the motel roofs along '66. Radioactive lore was honored in the name of the (closed as of this writing) **Uranium Café**, whose **giant, mutated pancakes** (called "**yellowcakes**" after the name of processed Uranium ore) were more than mortal could master. Try the **Grants Café**. There's still some good neon in town, and while some are now dark, others, like the recently restored **Grants Café** sign, shine on. Among the signs to look for (bright or busted): Franciscan Lodge, the West and Lux Theatres, and Pat's Bar. The **Sands Motel** gets some good reports, and is further from the trains.

South of EXIT 85 is the **Dinosaur Discovery Museum**, home of robotic dinosaurs and hands on exhibits. The nearby **Northwest New Mexico Visitor Center** provides info on area attractions. **SIDE TRIP:** 28 miles southwest of EXIT 81 on HWY 53 is **Bandera Volcano and Ice cave**, where blue-green ice survives year round in a lava cave. (888) ICE-CAVE

<u>MILAN</u> is usually a good place to fill up your tank. Numerous remnants of old motels, garages and trading posts line the west side of old 66 (4-lane for much of the way) thru **BLUEWATER** to **PREWITT**. Faded murals of Indian life still decorate the former Bowlins "Old Crater" Trading Post (their "Running Indian" mascot barely clings to cracked stucco).

GRANTS

MILAN

TO PREWITT

EXIT 79

EXIT 81

EXIT 85

RIO SAN JOSE

TO McCARTYS

TO HWY 124 AT EXIT 89

BL 40 RR OVERPASS

EB: Take **HWY 122** thru **PREWITT**, **BLUEWATER** and **MILAN** into <u>GRANTS</u> (past EXIT 81). On the east side, just **BEFORE** reaching the BL 40 railroad overpass, turn **LEFT** to curve onto **HWY 117**(Historic 66). Follow **HWY 117** towards EXIT 89.

see MAP 4 NM page-15)

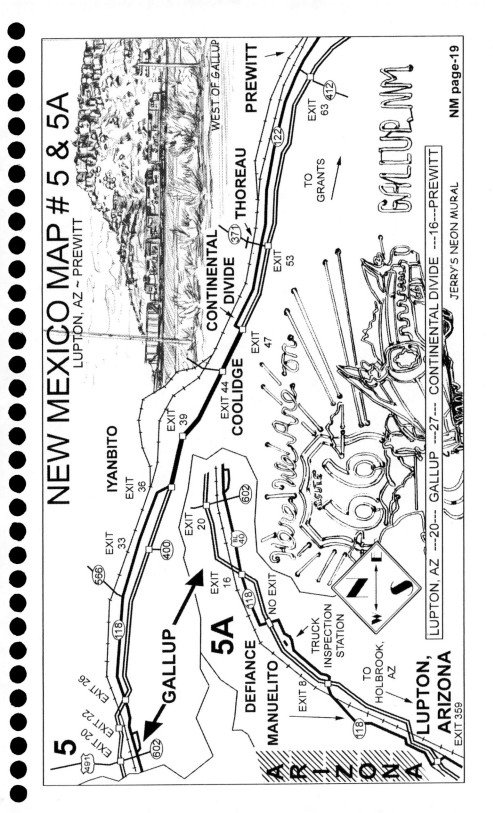

NEW MEXICO MAP # 5 & 5A

LUPTON, AZ ~ PREWITT

WEST OF GALLUP

PREWITT

THOREAU

CONTINENTAL
DIVIDE

EXIT 63 412

122

TO
GRANTS

EXIT 53

EXIT 47

COOLIDGE

EXIT 44

EXIT 39

IYANBITO

EXIT 36

EXIT 33

566

118

GALLUP

EXIT 26

EXIT 22

EXIT 20

191

602

5

400

EXIT 20

602

BL 40

EXIT 16

118

NO EXIT

5A

DEFIANCE

MANUELITO

TRUCK
INSPECTION
STATION

EXIT 8

TO
HOLBROOK,
AZ

118

LUPTON,
ARIZONA

EXIT 359

A R I Z O N A

N
W   E
S

JERRY'S NEON MURAL

GALLUP NM

LUPTON, AZ ---20--- GALLUP ---27--- CONTINENTAL DIVIDE ---16---PREWITT

NM page-19

WB: Continue with **HWY 122** from **PREWITT**, past **THOREAU** to **CONTINENTAL DIVIDE**. Here, join **I-40 WB** at **EXIT 47**. Take **EXIT 36 (IYANBITO)** and follow **HWY 118** along the north side of I-40, then under **EXIT 26** into **GALLUP** with **BL 40**.

East of **PREWITT**, a small building covered in hubcaps is home to **"Swap Meet 66"** (if you catch it open). On the other end of town, near EXIT 63 is the hot pink facade of the Quonset hut that is **Tomahawk Bar**. To the west, peek carefully thru each railroad trestle for several glimpses of old bridges along abandoned **"Dirt 66"** north of the tracks (don't trespass). Along here is where Route 66 begins to parallel a long row of pink-tinged cliffs and hills. These provide a majestic backdrop all the way thru **LUPTON, ARIZONA.**

At the side road to **THOREAU** (HWY 371), sits the **Red Mountain Market and Deli**. Just west is **Herman's Garage**, a pre-fab steel service station (now stuck to a stucco garage) first erected in 1931 in **GALLUP** and moved to **THOREAU** in the 1930s. A mile west are the remains of an old trading post, notable for its mural of a flying hawk and pink cliffs. Next up is the **Thunderbird Bar**, then comes confusing **CONTINENTAL DIVIDE**. Confusing, because the elevation is variously given from 7263 to 7,275 feet, and because it is often claimed to be the highest point on 66. Points in AZ and NM are higher! Anyway, a marker here (**PHOTO OP!**) marks the divide separating the water drainage to the **Pacific** from that which drains into the **Gulf of Mexico**. Trading posts have long balanced here on the backbone of the land, to divide tourists from their wampum (you've been seeing the classic billboards for miles). A "Historic 66" sign atop a **"DEAD END"** marker makes a poignant juxtaposition. Along this spur is an abandoned **Whiting Bros Motel** and station.

An old dirt route existed between the RR tracks from **COOLIDGE** to **IYANBITO** (continuing the early road from **PREWITT**). Stick to I-40 past the huge travel center to EXIT 36. The final run into **GALLUP** provides a nice panorama of colorful rock cliffs and spires, including **Church Rock**, and **Red Rock State Park and Museum**, north on HWY 566 and host to the **Inter Tribal Indian Ceremonial**, an annual celebration of Native Americans. www.ceremonial.org.

EB: On **GALLUP**'s east side, follow **HWY 118** under I-40 at **EXIT 26**, and continue to **EXIT 36 (IYANBITO)**. Here, join **I-40 EB** to **EXIT 47 (CONTINENTAL DIVIDE)**. Cross over, and join **HWY 122** east, past **THOREAU** to **PREWITT** (near EXIT 63).

FORMER US 666 · EXIT 22 · FORD · EXIT 26 · TO EXIT · 491 · 66 · 118 · 40 · VISITOR CENTER AND CHAMBER OF COMMERCE · FIRST · 2ND · 66 · EXIT 20 · TO EXIT 16 · 80 40 66 · COAL · MUNOZ · ARNOLD · 602

GALLUP DOWNTOWN

The sharp, slanted ridge of the **Hogback** slashes across east **GALLUP**. This barrier, breached naturally at this point, made the city a target for nukes during the heat of the **Cold War** (one bomb could take out US 66, the RR, pipelines and communications).

Despite the cold war's passing, there remains much evidence of old 66, including many old motels (some with nice neon) like the Blue Spruce and Lariat. Many hotel and café signs also survive. An oldie but goodie is historic 1937 **El Rancho Hotel** with its impressive lobby and rooms named after movie star guests (800) 543-6351.

GALLUP has a profusion of trading posts and galleries and public art, including the **neon mural** designed by the author: "**Here We are On Route 66, Gallup NM**" depicting a pink '59 Caddy headed into a Route 66 neon sunset, atop the **Chamber of Commerce Bldg** on **BL 40** downtown. Nearby is the **Gallup Cultural Center** in the Amtrak station, with a "Welcome" Hogan (Navajo house) and FREE parking (convenient for a stroll downtown). The rail action at the train yard is still visible, but the scene is framed and screened by decorative red fences. On the west side of downtown, the **Rex Museum** (great neon sign) offers local history, including the coal mining days, the WWII saga of the Navajo code talkers, and Rte 66 of course. City INFO: (800) 242-4282. www.GallupNM.org

SIDE TRIP Old 66 turned south on **First St,** then followed **Coal St** thru downtown (see the map). This narrow street later carried "one way" traffic WB, but is 2-way again, past cafes, shops and the **El Morrow Theatre**. Double back and drive both sections thru downtown.

GIANT ALERTS! Days past, postcards promoted the town with images of a **GIANT KACHINA** on the east side (a smaller one said "Hurry Back", on the west). A similar (if not identical) giant now stands north of I-40 at EXIT 22. Also, at Coal and 5th St, a **GIANT MUFFLER-MAN COWBOY** stands proud at John's Used Cars.

EB: Follow **HWY 118/Route 66** under I-40 at EXIT 16, joining **BL 40** into **GALLUP**. On the east side, stay **AHEAD** with **HWY 118**.
NM page-21

WB: Follow Hwy 118 for 3.5 miles from **EXIT 16**. Turn LEFT at **DEFIANCE** (with the **HWY 118** sign). Cross under I-40 (narrow tunnel) and turn **RIGHT** with **HWY 118**. Continue past the inspection station. Cross under I-40 at **EXIT 8** (AVOID on ramps), and stay with **HWY 118** thru **MANUELITO**, to the **ARIZONA** state line and **EXIT 359** at **LUPTON**. (see **AZ page-1 to continue WB**)

RV ADVISORY: the HWY 118 "tunnel" at **DEFIANCE** is a bit narrow, so use care.

Route 66 makes one last scenic break from I-40 before hitting the state line, passing thru **MANUELITO**, which is marked by the ruins of **Mike Kirks Trading Post**. Headed west, the road climbs and clings to the sheer side of **Devil's Cliff**, beneath boulders balanced precariously above (a mesh fence offers protection). Ahead is a grand view of '66, the RR and the Rio Puerco as they squeeze between rugged mesas into **ARIZONA**.

TO MANUELITO AND
LUPTON AZ

DEFIANCE
RIO PUERCO

TO GALLUP

TRUCK
STATION

NARROW "TUNNEL"
NO EXIT

EXIT 8

Near milepost 4 are faded remnants of various old-time advertisements painted on the rock walls by canny businessmen, including "**Rocky Point Trading Post Navajo Rugs Homemade Jewelry**," one of the many old enterprises that formerly lined this stretch (no new graffiti, please). Another, the **Cliff Dwelling Trading Post** (as it was last known), was located a bit further west, in front of a big hollow in the rock face. Fake cliff dwellings were an attraction, and a movie, "*Ace in the Hole*" starring Kirk Douglas, was filmed here.

The true path of old 66 is lost before reaching **ARIZONA**, buried where **HWY 118** curves to avoid I-40, but the faux fort at **Chief Yellowhorse's** is the latest in a long line of tourist enterprises at what has been variously called "**Cave of the Seven Devils**" or "**Millers Cave**." Yet another "cliff dwelling" waits within the cave-like opening in the ruddy cliff. Excited signs hawk **WILD BUFFALO**, along with blankets and sand paintings. A line painted down the middle of the floor reportedly marks the state line. **NOTE: ARIZONA** doesn't follow Daylight Savings Time (check your watches). **TO CONTINUE WB**: see **AZ page-1** (SKIP the **Pre-1937 "Santa Fe Loop"** section that follows).

EB: From **EXIT 359** at **LUPTON, ARIZONA**, follow **HWY 118** thru **MANUELITO**. Cross under I-40 at **EXIT 8** (AVOID onramps), and continue with **HWY 118** past the truck inspection station. At **Salt Water Wash Rd**, turn **LEFT**. Cross under I-40 (narrow tunnel), then turn **RIGHT** with **HWY 118**, to **EXIT 16** on the west side of **GALLUP**.
(see **NM INTRO NM page-1**.) **NM page-22**

(see **MAP 5&5A NM page-19**)

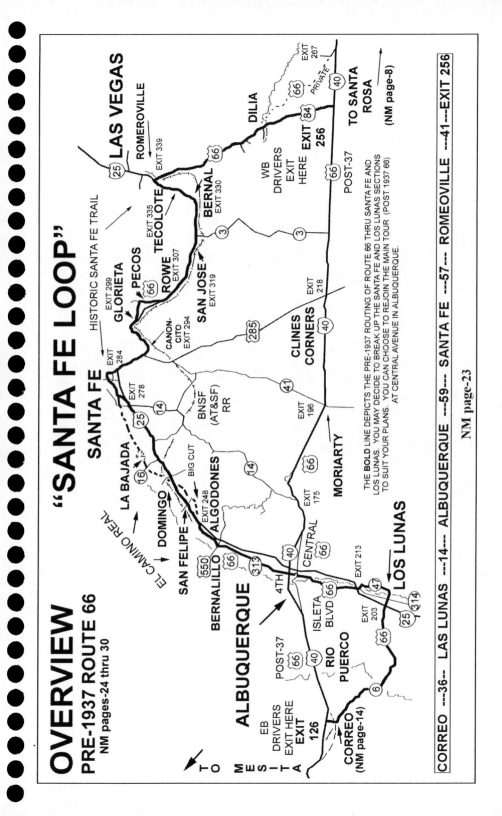

OVERVIEW
PRE-1937 ROUTE 66
NM pages-24 thru 30

"SANTA FE LOOP"

THE **BOLD** LINE DEPICTS THE PRE-1937 ROUTING OF ROUTE 66 THRU SANTA FE AND LOS LUNAS. YOU MAY DECIDE TO BREAK UP THE SANTA FE AND LOS LUNAS SECTIONS TO SUIT YOUR PLANS. YOU CAN CHOOSE TO REJOIN THE MAIN TOUR (POST 1937 66) AT CENTRAL AVENUE IN ALBUQUERQUE.

NM page-23

CORREO ---36-- LAS LUNAS ---14--- ALBUQUERQUE ---59--- SANTA FE ---57-- ROMEOVILLE ---41--EXIT 256

PRE-1937 WB: Follow **I-40 WB** from **SANTA ROSA**. Take **EXIT 256**, and follow **US 84** north thru **DILIA**. At **I-25 EXIT 339** (**ROMEROVILLE**) join the **North Frontage Rd**, past **TECOLOTE**, **BERNAL**, and **SAN JOSE**. Cross I-25 at **EXIT 319**.

Old **"Dirt 66"** lies stranded east of the current route along **US 84** between I-40 and **DILIA**. Here is the first of a series of picturesque old churches. North of town, **US 84** overlays old 66 as a peaceful scenic drive. At I-25 **EXIT 339**, old **HWY 85** (the frontage road) takes over. **SIDE TRIP 1:** Just before reaching I-25, a dirt road (avoid if muddy) veers right (before the hill cut): this is "Dirt 66" down to **ROMEROVILLE**, which crosses the RR at grade, then continues west to EXIT 339. **SIDE TRIP 2:** The old road (now blacktop) continues west, from the south side of EXIT 339, as **Sheridan Rd** (some potholes). From the **KOA** (a nice setting for camping), a rough dirt road heads west a short way, to end at a charming **concrete post bridge** in a quiet canyon (if in doubt, ask at the **KOA** beforehand).

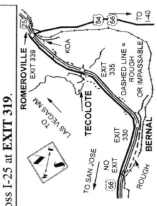

There's a trace or two of old 66 on the way to **TECOLOTE** (EXIT 335). **SIDE TRIP:** '66 curves thru the plaza, past a tin-roofed adobe church and **Santa Fe Trail Marker**, to END at a defunct bridge, whose supports can be seen from the 1940-era US 85 Bridge west of town. Old 66 consists mostly of abandoned fragments west to **BERNAL**. **SIDE TRIP 1:** Here, south from **EXIT 330**, a short, dead end paved section heads east, past an old store and a 1916-era church. **Starvation Peak**, a tragic Santa Fe Trail landmark, haunts the background. **SIDE TRIP 2:** West from **EXIT 330**, on the **south** side, the pavement turns to **ROUGH** dirt along the RR for about 4 miles, then squeezes thru a tunnel under I-25 to rejoin the **N Frontage Rd** (for Route-Buffs only).

SAN JOSE SIDE TRIP: EAST of **EXIT 319**, **WEST** of **HWY 3** (EXIT 323). On the west side of the **Pecos River**, turn south on **Entrada de San Jose**, and pass under I-25 (mixed dirt/pave). Curve thru town, past the 1826 plaza church, to the closed **1921 thru-truss bridge**, then retrace your path.

EB: From **EXIT 319**, cross I-25, and follow the **N Frontage Road** east, past **SAN JOSE**, **BERNAL**, and **TECOLOTE**. At **EXIT 339** (**ROMEROVILLE**) cross I-25, and follow **US 84** south, thru **DILIA**, to I-40 **EXIT 256**. Join **I-40 EB** to **SANTA ROSA**.

NM page-24   (END of **PRE-1937 OPTION**: to continue EB see NM **page-8**)

WB: From **EXIT 319**, continue on the **South Frontage Rd** ("Ilfield Frontage"), past **SANDS** and **ILFIELD** to **ROWE**. At **EXIT 307**, cross under I-25, and follow **HWY 63** north to **PECOS**. Turn **LEFT** to follow **HWY 50** to **GLORIETA**. Join **I-25 WB** at **EXIT 299**. Take **EXIT 294** (**CANONCITO**), and follow the **N Frontage Road** (**Old Las Vegas Hwy**), past the JCT of US 285, to **SANTA FE**.

This is another scenic stretch, backstopped by long, tree-covered **Glorieta Mesa**. There's not much to the quiet towns here. **ILFIELD** has just a gas/grocery; while in **ROWE** is long shuttered **E.T. Padilla's Grocery and Victory Bar**, mainly notable for the faded painting of a beer bottle and foaming glass. South of **PECOS** is Pecos National Historic Park, home to the ruins of a pueblo and mission church. This area saw some heavy Civil War action. On **Hwy 50**, about a mile east of **GLORIETA**, the **Pigeon Ranch** ruins crowd the east side of the road. Inside (peek but don't enter) are old brands written on walls of this former stage stop, site of a battle between Union and Confederate troops in 1862.

CANONCITO

Northwest of **GLORIETA** (famous for the Baptist Conference) is Glorieta Pass, at over 7,500 feet, **the highest point on '66** (Pre-1937). From **EXIT 297**, old 66 heads briefly east (private) and west on "Sabino Gonzales Rd" (dead ends after a mile). For **EB travelers:** just east of milepost 295, a wide spot on the south shoulder (**NOT** an official pull off) is home to "**Glorieta, Gettysburg of the West.**" **FOLK ART ALERT!** This sincere assemblage pays homage to the victims of the battle of March 26, 1862, when Union forces wiped out a Confederate supply train. Included are a mock burial (with feet sticking out) and an improvised canon, plus many, many signs. The road and railroad squeeze thru Apache Canyon to **CANONCITO**, site of another classic chapel (on the dead end east). **SCAVENGER HUNT!** At the turn to **EXIT 294** is a small **Santa Fe Trail Marker**. What **YEAR** was the marker dedicated? _____ The drive up towards **SANTA FE** parallels I-25, past **Bobcat Bite** and **Harry's Roadhouse**, longtime popular roadside stops.

EB: From **SANTA FE**, follow **Old Las Vegas Hwy** (the Northeast Frontage Rd) past US 285. At **CANONCITO**, join **I-25 EB** at **EXIT 294**. Take **EXIT 299** (**GLORIETA**), cross I-25 to follow **HWY 50** to **PECOS**. Turn **RIGHT** on **HWY 63**, and head to I-25 at **EXIT 307**. Cross under I-25, and turn **LEFT** on the **S Frontage Rd** ("Ilfield Frontage") thru **ROWE**. Stay ahead to **EXIT 319**.

WB: Follow **Old Las Vegas Hwy** towards **SANTA FE**. Near EXIT 284, turn **RIGHT** on **Old Pecos Trail (HWY 466)**. When HWY 466 bends west, stay **RIGHT** with **Old Pecos Trail**. Merge **AHEAD** onto **Old Santa Fe Trail**. Cross Paseo de Peralta, and De Vargas St. Turn **LEFT** on **Alameda**. Cross Don Gaspar, and turn **RIGHT** on **Galisteo** (ONE-WAY). Turn **RIGHT** on **Water St** (ONE-WAY). Cross Don Gaspar. At Old Santa Fe Trail/Shelby St, stay **AHEAD** with Water. (**AVOID** left with "Historic 66" sign if driving thru). Turn **RIGHT** on **Old Santa Fe Trail** (MUST) then **RIGHT** back on **Alameda**. This time around, turn **LEFT** at **Galisteo** to leave town.

RV ALERT! Streets downtown are very narrow and crowded: turns are tight. Use your tow car, or park and walk or use the bus (check locally). **EVERYBODY:** The street names and one-way streets are confusing, so expect to get lost! The **one-way** streets require **WB** drivers to circle around to drive old 66. The **earlier route** (EB) used Galisteo to De Vargas to Don Gaspar to San Francisco (but Don Gaspar is One-Way south now). Past the Plaza it turned south on Shelby (now part of Old Santa Fe Trail). By **1931**, the route bypassed the Plaza on Water; by **1933**, it followed the EB tour. See the map at left. **For city attractions and INFO: see NM page-27.**

SANTA FE

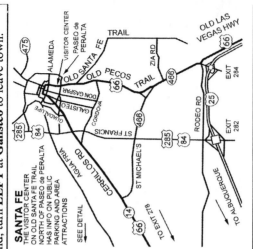

SANTA FE
THE VISITOR CENTER ON OLD SANTA FE TRAIL NORTH OF PASEO de PERALTA HAS INFO ON PUBLIC PARKING AND AREA ATTRACTIONS

SEE DETAIL

SANTA FE DOWNTOWN

EB: Follow **Galisteo** across De Vargas St. Crossing Alameda, be in the **LEFT** lane (becomes One-Way). Turn **RIGHT** on **Water St** (One-Way). Cross Don Gaspar St. At Old Santa Fe Trail/Shelby St, stay **AHEAD** with **Water** (**AVOID** left with "Historic 66" sign unless visiting the Plaza). Turn **RIGHT** (MUST) onto **Old Santa Fe Trail**. Cross Alameda, De Vargas and Paseo de Peralta. At the "Y", **BEAR RIGHT** onto **Old Pecos Trail**. At the stoplight for HWY 466 (St Michaels), turn **LEFT** onto **HWY 466**. Curve to the Rodeo Rd stoplight (right) **BUT** turn **LEFT** onto **Old Las Vegas Hwy** (BEFORE reaching I-25 EXIT 284) and follow the **NE Frontage Rd.**

WB: From downtown **SANTA FE** on Galisteo: At the "Y" veer **RIGHT** onto **Cerrillos Rd (HWY 14).** At the **STOP**, turn **RIGHT** on Manhattan, then **QUICK LEFT** back on **Cerrillos.** Continue southwest on **Cerrillos** towards I-25 **EXIT 278.** Cross under I-25 with **HWY 14.** Turn **RIGHT** on **HWY 599** (towards EXIT 276) **BUT** quickly turn **LEFT** onto the **Frontage Rd,** and follow to **EXIT 267.**

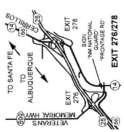

You could spend a lot of time (and cash) in **SANTA FE,** "The City Different" **(SEE:** Directions and maps on **NM page-26).** The whole city is a **"GIFT SHOP ALERT!"** with numerous shops and galleries, plus a heaping' helping of history. City **INFO:** Visitors Bureau: (505) 955-6200. http://www.santafe.org/ or www.santafechamber.com Lodging is more costly on average than in **ALBUQUERQUE,** but the **EL Rey Inn** (1862 Cerrillos) is a good value that dates back to Route 66. expanded over the years into a marvelous, 4.5 acre mini-village with unique southwestern atmosphere. (800) 521-1349. The most historic lodging (but pricier) is the **La Fonda Hotel** at 100 E San Francisco (just off the Plaza). Called "The Inn at the End of the Trail," the La Fonda has incredible multi-story adobe-style architecture. Check the **Federation Guide** for more.

Downtown streets are busy and crowded, so I suggest taking a **Walking Tour** (guided or not) of this compact area. Get brochures and parking info at the **NM Dept of Tourism Visitor Center,** north of Paseo de Peralta at 491 Old Santa Fe Trail, **OR** at the **Chamber of Commerce Office and Visitors Center** located in the **Santa Fe Premium Outlets** (Cerrillos Road and I-25). **NOTE:** RV parking is rather limited downtown. **SANTA FE** brags on its antiquity, with the **OLDEST CHURCH, BELL,** and **HOUSE** in the United States, all located conveniently near Old 66. Also, see the ornate and mysterious **"miraculous staircase"** at **Loretto Chapel. "The Palace of the Governors,"** on the north side of the **Plaza** since 1610, now holds a museum. **Plaza SIDE TRIP:** follow Galisteo up to San Francisco, then use Cathedral Place south to Water or Alameda. The **Plaza** itself is site of the **Soldier's Monument** (1867) and **End of the Trail** marker. If that ain't enough culture, check out the many museums on **"Museum Hill,"** on Camino Lejo, east of Old Pecos Trail, north of HWY 466. For "pop" culture, try **Jackalope,** an outlet for folk art and cool stuff, at 2820 Cerrillos.

EB: At **EXIT 276,** follow the **Frontage Rd** as it curves to stop at **HWY 599:** turn **RIGHT,** then turn **LEFT** on **HWY 14.** Cross under I-25 at **EXIT 278,** and follow **Cerrillos Rd** (HWY 14) northeast, into **SANTA FE.** Cross Hwy 466, US 84/285 and Paseo de Peralta. When Sandoval veers left (at Manhattan) be in the **RIGHT** lane, and stay **AHEAD** with **Cerrillos,** then merge **AHEAD** onto **Galisteo.**

WB: At **EXIT 267**, JOIN **I-25 south** to **EXIT 248**. Exit here, and go west briefly to **HWY 313**: turn **LEFT**. Continue with **HWY 313** south thru **ALGODONES** and **BERNALILLO**. Stay in the **RIGHT** lane at the JCT with **HWY 566** (**AVOID** the left "TO I-25") and stay AHEAD onto **4th St** past the JCT with **HWY 47** (2nd St). Cross under I-40 into **ALBUQUERQUE**.

THE BASE of LA BAJADA HILL

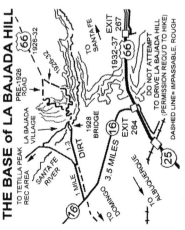

TO TETILLA PEAK REC AREA
PRE-1926 ROAD
1926-32
1930-32
66
TO SANTA FE
LA BAJADA VILLAGE
SANTA FE RIVER
1928 BRIDGE
16 EXIT 264
1 MILE
DIRT
1.3
3.5 MILES
TO DOMINGO
25
TO ALBUQUERQUE
1932-37
66
EXIT 267
TO SANTA FE
DO NOT ATTEMPT TO DRIVE LA BAJADA HILL (PERMISSION REQ'D TO HIKE)
DASHED LINE= IMPASSABLE, ROUGH

SIDE TRIP: La Bajada Hill. Too **treacherous** to drive sans an "experienced" 4WD! To visit the **foot** of this road-building feat, follow **HWY 16** for 3.5 miles west from **EXIT 264**, then **RIGHT** 1 mile. Jog **RIGHT** to join a **rub-board dirt road** for 1.3 miles, over the **1928 Santa Fe River Bridge**. The road bends left to **La Bajada Village**, but the faint path of **1926-'32 '66** curves right, to zigzag drunkenly up steep **La Bajada Mesa**. A **Pre-'66** road carved a long gash across the slope to the left. Some folks hike the hill, but contact the Cochiti Pueblo Natural Resources Manager at (505) 465-2244 (mon-fri 8-4) for **permission** before hand (don't leave valuables exposed, and park/hike at your own risk). On top, "**Dirt 66**" ran to **SANTA FE**, joining Airport Rd over to Cerrillos; but you must return to **EXIT 264**.

Headed west, the impassable path (no trespassing) of **Pre-32 '66** enters the **Santo Domingo Reservation**, to cross the RR at **Domingo** (off HWY 22, west of EXIT 259), where the old trading post recently burned down. Then the faint trace jumps I-40 (west of EXIT 257), to cross a high ridge thru "**BIG CUT**," a notch in the hill visible to the southeast from just **north** of **EXIT 252** (behind the **San Felipe Casino**). From **ALGODONES** thru **BERNALILLO**, **HWY 313** is a nice, scenic drive along the RR, also signed "**El Camino Real**." (see **MAP # 3** on NM page-9 for an overview). South of **HWY 566**, urbanization crowds in as you approach **ALBUQUERQUE**. Some roadside relics look old enough to date back to old '66. **Visually, the El Camino Motor Hotel** is the coolest-looking remnant of tourist days.

EB: Take **4th St north** from **ALBUQUERQUE**, under I-40. Stay **AHEAD** on **4th** thru the JCT with **HWY 47** (2nd St). At the **HWY 556** JCT, turn **LEFT** onto **HWY 313** (AVOID "TO I-25"). Follow **HWY 313** north thru **BERNALILLO** and **ALGODONES**. At the JCT with **HWY 315**, turn **RIGHT** to **EXIT 248**, and join **I-25 North**. At **EXIT 267** (Waldo), join the **Frontage Rd** north to **EXIT 276**.

NM pages-12 and 13

WB: Take **4th** St south to downtown **ALBUQUERQUE**. Turn **LEFT** on **Roma**, then **RIGHT** on **3rd** St. Turn **RIGHT** on **Central**, and **LEFT** back onto **4th** St, At **Bridge Blvd**; turn **RIGHT**, cross the **Rio Grande**, then **LEFT** at the light on **Isleta Blvd**. At the Goff Blvd/Arenal Rd light, turn **LEFT** to stay with **Isleta Blvd** thru **ARMIJO, PARAJITO** and **LOS PADILLAS**. Cross I-25 at EXIT 213.

RV ALERT! 4th to Central Ave to 3rd are tight turns with heavy traffic. **ALT:** Coal to Broadway to Lomas, then back on 4th to Central Ave for more **ALBUQUERQUE** (Post 1937 route)

SEE NM pages-12 and 13 for more **ALBUQUERQUE**

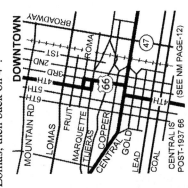

DOWNTOWN

GIANT ALERT #1: At 4th and Marble (north of Lomas) is the 18 foot tall "**Madonna of the Trail** " monument, dedicated in 1928 to "Pioneer Mothers," one of 12 installed along the National Old Trails, and a twin to one in **UPLAND CA**. The Civic Plaza blocks 4th south of Marquette, requiring a short detour north of Central Ave.

Earliest 66 **briefly** took 2nd St south. But **classic Pre-'37 '66**, south of Central Ave, follows **4th** St, past the **Red Ball Café**: "Home of the **Original Wimpy Burger** Since 1922." On Bridge Blvd, don't be fooled: 4th and 8th Streets are separated by only ONE block! **GIANT ALERT #2:** Look to the west for the **GIANT ROADRUNNER** between Blake and Ferris Streets (south of Valdora St). Nearby, the **Blue Castle** fixes busted brakes in a neat old garage made over to resemble a blue, blocky "castle," festooned with knights in armor and "coats of arms." The towns south of **ALBUQUERQUE** blend together, a succession of walled adobe houses among the trees, small farms, and a few old roadside remnants.

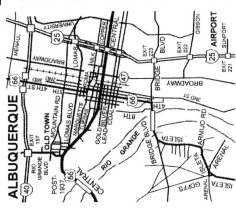

ALBUQUERQUE

EB: Stay **AHEAD** on **Isleta Blvd** thru **LOS PADILLAS, PARAJITO** and **ARMIJO**. Past Valdora St, be in the right lane. At the Goff Blvd/Arenal Rd light, turn **RIGHT** with **Isleta Blvd**. Curve **RIGHT** onto **Bridge Blvd**, then cross the **Rio Grande**. Past 8th St, prepare for a **QUICK LEFT** onto **4th** St (next light). After Gold St, turn **RIGHT** on **Central Ave** in downtown **ALBUQUERQUE**. Turn **LEFT** on **3rd** St. Turn **LEFT** onto **Marquette St** (One-Way), then **RIGHT** on **4th** St, and continue north, past I-40.

NM page-29

WB: South of I-25 EXIT 213, stay **AHEAD** with Isleta Blvd/**HWY 314**. After about **3 miles**, turn **LEFT** on **HWY 147**, across the RR and past **ISLETA PUEBLO** thru the Isleta Reservation. Cross the river and turn **RIGHT** on **HWY 47**, thru **BOSQUE FARMS**, **PERALTA**, and **VALENCIA**. When **HWY 47** branches left, curve **RIGHT** onto **HWY 6** (Main St), and cross the Rio Grande into **LOS LUNAS**. Cross **HWY 313**, then cross I-25, following **HWY 6** all the way past **CORREO**, to join **WB I-40** at **EXIT 126**.
(This is the western **END** of the **PRE-1937 OPTION**: Turn to **NM page-14** to continue **WB** to **MESITA**, and on to **ARIZONA**)

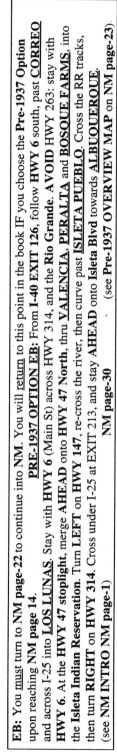

Ancient **ISLETA PUEBLO**, with its enchanting mission church and plaza, is accessed by several side roads from **HWY 147**. Visitors are welcome, but don't trespass, and **DO** obey all Pueblo rules concerning photos, etc. Old 66 passes thru a mix of residences and farms before briefly urbanizing in **LOS LUNAS**. The **Luna Mansion** at **HWY 6** and HWY 314, offers dining in a historic 1881 mansion.

Before 1937, '66 briefly followed **HWY 314** from **ISLETA** to **LOS LUNAS**.

West of I-25, the climb up the sandy slope was easier for early road and railroad builders, than at **ALBUQUERQUE**. Portions of **PRE-1937** 66 follow an abandoned RR alignment. Watch for traces alongside current **HWY 6**, especially where red rock bridge abutments are visible: these are left over from the **AT&SF RR**. West of the **Rio Puerco**, watch closely, between MM 18 and MM 13, for more old road fragments (not drivable: don't trespass on Laguna lands). At **CORREO**, the older road crosses over the tracks, to continue across Laguna Pueblo land (rough, unpaved sections). The **tour route** joins **I-40** (former 4-lane 66) west to **MESITA**.

PRE-1937 OPTION
WEST END

EB: You **must** turn to **NM page-22** to continue into NM. You will <u>return</u> to this point in the book IF you choose the **Pre-1937 Option** upon reaching **NM page 14**.   **PRE-1937 OPTION EB:** From **I-40 EXIT 126**, follow **HWY 6** south, past **CORREO** and across I-25 into **LOS LUNAS**. Stay with **HWY 6** (Main St) across **HWY 314**, and the **Rio Grande**. AVOID **HWY 263**: stay with **HWY 6**. At the **HWY 47** stoplight, merge **AHEAD** onto **HWY 47 North**, thru **VALENCIA**, **PERALTA** and **BOSQUE FARMS**, into the **Isleta Indian Reservation**. Turn **LEFT** on **HWY 147**, re-cross the river, then curve past **ISLETA PUEBLO**. Cross the RR tracks, then turn **RIGHT** on **HWY 314**. Cross under I-25 at EXIT 213, and stay **AHEAD** onto Isleta Blvd towards **ALBUQUERQUE**.

(see NM INTRO NM page-1)   NM page-30   (see **Pre-1937 OVERVIEW MAP** on NM page-23).

Praising Arizona

Route 66 thru Northern **ARIZONA** plays "connects the dots" with history-filled towns across this little-peopled region. This is the place to breathe easy and enjoy the wide-open spaces. **ARIZONA** is famous for scenic beauty, and some rather big HOLES accessed by 66: **Meteor Crater**, **Grand Canyon**, and even **Grand Canyon Caverns**. The rocky landscape of **ARIZONA** is fascinating, especially at famous **Petrified Forest**, while even the bare soil itself possesses a brilliant palate at colorful **Painted Desert**.

ARIZONA offers much first-class driving along Route 66. While there are many abandoned or extremely rough alignments in the eastern portion, gems of old road are scattered along the interstate. Western **ARIZONA** has plenty of terrific '66 to drive, including infamous but not to be missed **Oatman Hwy**. Look for **Arizona Byways** signs marking old '66. **US 66** generally followed the path of the 1857 **Beale Wagon Road** across Arizona, as evidenced by numerous markers along the way. **LUPTON** gives the state a grand start with majestic red cliffs, which quickly peter out in favor of red dirt and distant hills thru **HOLBROOK** and **WINSLOW**. Ahead, the **San Francisco Peaks** loom ever larger as you climb to **FLAGSTAFF** (don't forget **WINONA**). You enter the Coconino National Forest at Canyon Padre, and ride the tall timber thru **WILLIAMS** and the **Kaibab National Forest**. The route drops in elevation passing thru **ASH FORK**, and enters the well-preserved **159 miles** of pristine 2-lane west of EXIT 139, thru **SELIGMAN** and **PEACH SPRINGS**, to **KINGMAN**. The most ruggedly scenic section is **Oatman Hwy**, a roller-coaster ride thru the craggy **Black Mountains** and **OATMAN**. **NOTE**: Mountain and desert driving requires **CARE**. Go **SLOWER** on steep mountain grades. Use lower gears downhill to save on brakes, watch your speed and do not hog the centerline. Park well off the road. In low desert areas, be aware of the **flash flood** danger in low washes, and **DO NOT** drive into water. Just take it EZ, and take the time to savor **ARIZONA**. You too will sing its praises.

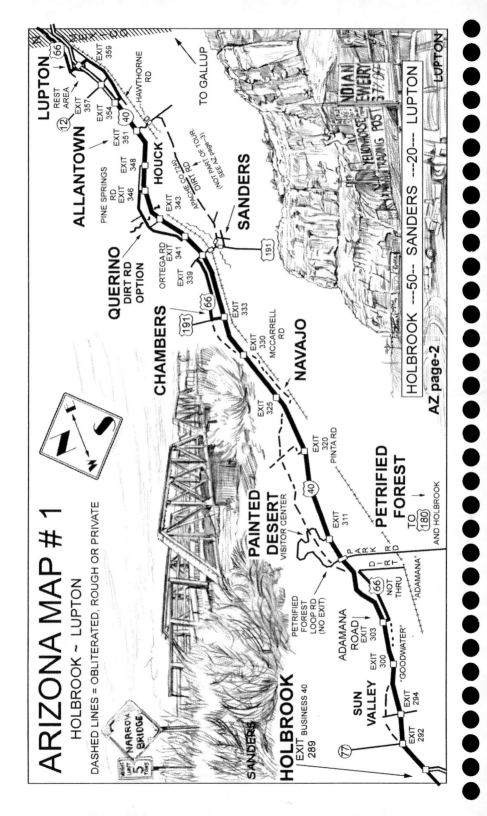

AZ page-3

WB: Cross the state line into **ARIZONA**. At **EXIT 359**, cross under I-40, then turn **RIGHT** on the **South Frontage Rd** thru **LUPTON**. Pass EXIT 357, then **join I-40 WB** at **EXIT 354** (Hawthorne Rd). Pass EXIT 351 (**ALLANTOWN**) and EXIT 348 (**HOUCK**). See the **"DIRT 66" OPTION** at **EXIT 346** (Pine Springs Rd) **OR** continue **WB** on **I-40** past EXIT 341 to **SANDERS.**

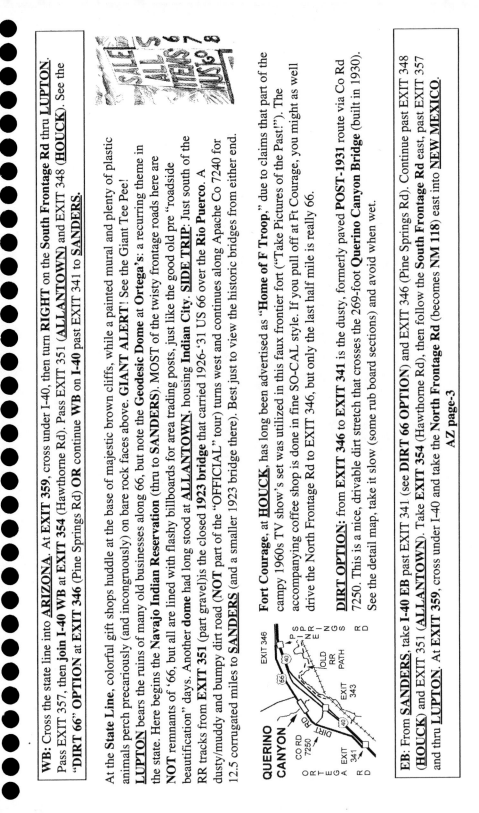

At the **State Line**, colorful gift shops huddle at the base of majestic brown cliffs, while a painted mural and plenty of plastic animals perch precariously (and incongruously) on bare rock faces above. **GIANT ALERT!** See the Giant Tee Pee! **LUPTON** bears the ruins of many old businesses along 66, but note the **Geodesic Dome** at **Ortega's**: a recurring theme in the state. Here begins the **Navajo Indian Reservation** (thru to **SANDERS**). MOST of the twisty frontage roads here are NOT remnants of '66, but all are lined with flashy billboards for area trading posts, just like the good old pre "roadside beautification" days. Another **dome** had long stood at **ALLANTOWN**, housing **Indian City**. **SIDE TRIP**: Just south of the RR tracks from **EXIT 351** (part gravel)is the closed **1923 bridge** that carried 1926-'31 US 66 over the **Rio Puerco**. A dusty/muddy and bumpy dirt road (NOT part of the "OFFICIAL" tour) turns west and continues along Apache Co 7240 for 12.5 corrugated miles to **SANDERS** (and a smaller 1923 bridge there). Best just to view the historic bridges from either end.

QUERINO CANYON

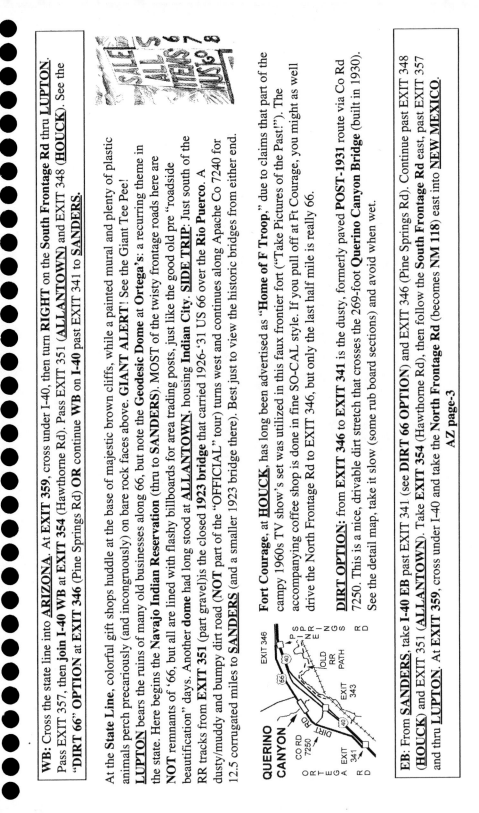

Fort Courage, at **HOUCK**, has long been advertised as **"Home of F Troop,"** due to claims that part of the campy 1960s TV show's set was utilized in this faux frontier fort ("Take Pictures of the Past!"). The accompanying coffee shop is done in fine SO-CAL style. If you pull off at Ft Courage, you might as well drive the North Frontage Rd to EXIT 346, but only the last half mile is really 66.

DIRT OPTION: from **EXIT 346** to **EXIT 341** is the dusty, formerly paved **POST-1931** route via Co Rd 7250. This is a nice, drivable dirt stretch that crosses the 269-foot **Querino Canyon Bridge** (built in 1930). See the detail map, take it slow (some rub board sections) and avoid when wet.

EB: From **SANDERS**, take **I-40 EB** past EXIT 341 (see **DIRT 66 OPTION**) and EXIT 346 (Pine Springs Rd). Continue past EXIT 348 (**HOUCK**) and EXIT 351 (**ALLANTOWN**). Take **EXIT 354** (Hawthorne Rd), then follow the **South Frontage Rd** east, past EXIT 357 and thru **LUPTON**. At **EXIT 359**, cross under I-40 and take the **North Frontage Rd** (becomes **NM 118**) east into **NEW MEXICO**.

WB: Take **EXIT 339** in **SANDERS**. Follow the **North Frontage Rd** west to **CHAMBERS**. Turn **LEFT** on US 191, then join **I-40 WB** at **EXIT 333**. Stay with **I-40 WB** past **NAVAJO** (EXIT 325) and EXIT 311 (**Painted Desert/Petrified Forest**).

SANDERS

SIDE TRIP: Take US 191 south across the RR tracks into **SANDERS**. Just east is the **1923 bridge** that first carried '66 over the **Rio Puerco**, then onto current CO Rd 7240 (see **AZ page-3** and **MAP #1: NOT** part of TOUR). **SCAVENGER HUNT!** What **COLOR** are the bridge girders painted?_____ Just south of the current Rio Puerco Bridge, turn **LEFT** on the paved street for one block, then **RIGHT** to the charming pink and white **66 Diner**. A classic **Valentine Diner**, relocated from **HOLBROOK**, was combined with a house trailer and ingenuity to create a unique café. Also in town is **R B Burnham Trading Post** on US 191.

Remains of old businesses pepper the road to **CHAMBERS**, where an old **Chevron Station** sits on the dead end frontage road west of the exit. Most of the old 66 sections west of here are inaccessible or unadvisable, due to roughness and washouts. Not depicted on this tour, partly due to its fragility and unfortunate exposure to vandalism, is the haunting, crumbling ruin of the former **Painted Desert Trading Post** on the banks of **Dead Wash**. If you visit this site following other guides, please respect the ruins.

A section of abandoned '66 runs thru the **Painted Desert** area of the **Petrified Forest National Park**. **SIDE TRIP**: Two miles north on the Loop Road is the restored 1924 **Painted Desert Inn**. The park road continues south thru the **Petrified Forest. DON'T** pick up petrified wood in the Park. If you have some from outside the park, let the ranger mark it. **ALT WB ROUTE**: After exploring the park, you can connect with **US 180** at the **South** entrance (28 miles south of I-40), then rejoin Route 66 at **HOLBROOK** (but you'll miss cool stuff!). **OR**, you can elect to sample just the northern section of the Park, then rejoin **I-40 WB**.

CAR GAME! "**Billboard FREE for all!**" First person to see the word "**FREE**" on a billboard yells "**FREE.**" First to yell 5 times wins!

EB: Follow **I-40 EB** past **NAVAJO** (EXIT 325). At **EXIT 333**, take US 191 north into **CHAMBERS**. Turn **RIGHT** after a half-mile (just past the post office) on **Apache Co 7060**, which becomes the **North Frontage Rd** to **SANDERS**. JOIN **I-40 EB** at **EXIT 339**.

WB: Follow **I-40 WB** to **EXIT 289** and take **BL-40/Navajo Blvd** into **HOLBROOK**. (how EZ can you get?)

SIDE TRIP: At **EXIT 303** is **Adamana Rd**, a **10-mile** round-trip drive along a paved spur of Route 66 that ends at the site of **Rocky's Pony Express Station** (private). A nice view of the **Painted Desert** is had along the way. On the south side of the exit, go east along **Adamana Rd** for 5 miles, to where it bends south and turns dirt. **Return** to **EXIT 303**.

Back at the exit are a couple of rock shops and the **Painted Desert Indian Center** (a gift shop with Indian cutouts, corrals and old wagons). **GIANT ALERT! Stewarts Rock Shop**, on the northeast side of the exit, has colorful and crazy statues, including a T-Rex eating a woman (female manikins in peril abound), plus a caveman riding an animated dinosaur, among others. The two-headed Dimetrodon east of the exit is theirs, too, as are many colorful billboards worthy of the old days, hawking fossils, meteorites, ostriches and **FREE** petrified wood. **GIFT SHOP ALERT!** This is the type of place my Dad wouldn't stop at!

The only thing left these days at nearby **GOODWATER** is the restored 420-foot timber bridge over "Little Lithodendron Wash," a twin to the decrepit structure over not-so-little "Lithodendron Wash," west of **EXIT 303**. **SUN VALLEY** is a mostly empty housing development platted on the sand east of **HOLBROOK**. At the exit is a former Stuckey's, and an old motel or two plus the **Root 66 RV Park**.

GIANT ALERT(?) Big dinosaur fun once was had at "**International Petrified Forest-Dinosaur Park-Museum of the Americas**" (**NOT** the "real" Petrified Forest Park, but a creative "copy"). One could pay the fee and drive the dirt trail along strange purple hills, among statues of fierce sauroids and fake Indian ruins. Those petrified trees so artfully arranged on the hills were apparently quarried on the property. Unfortunately, it has since closed and been sold for redevelopment. Hopefully the dinosaur statues will remain, or find new homes nearby. One can see for quite a ways from atop the mesa east of **HOLBROOK**, unless the ever-present wind has raised the dust!

EB: From **HOLBROOK**, join **I-40 EB** at **EXIT 289**. Continue past **EXIT 311** (**Painted Desert/Petrified Forest**).

(see **MAP AZ page-2**)

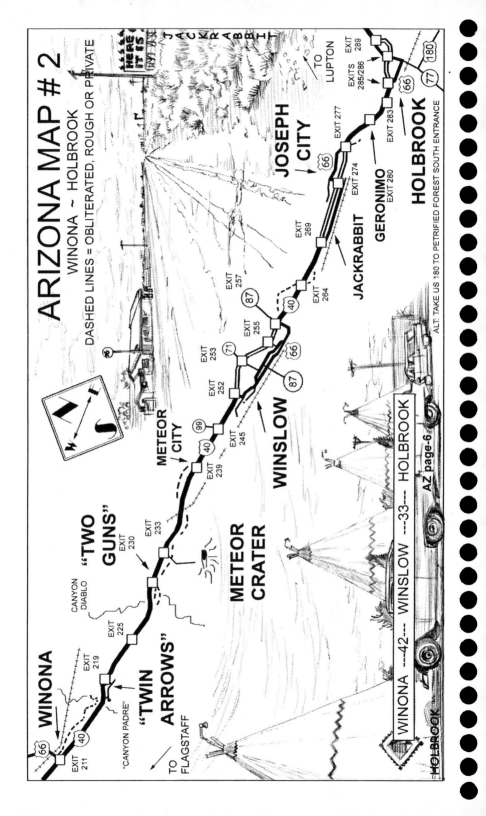

WB: Follow **BL 40/Navajo Blvd** into <u>HOLBROOK</u>. Cross under the middle I-40 EXIT (286). Downtown, turn **RIGHT** on **Hopi Dr.** At **EXIT 285** on the west side, join **I-40 WB** to **EXIT 277**. Exit here and follow **BL 40** into <u>JOSEPH CITY</u>.

HOLBROOK

<u>HOLBROOK</u> was long the headquarters of the extinct **Whiting Bros** chain of discount gas stations. You'll run a gauntlet of statues of other extinct critters just before the east side exit. Many motels and stores, including the Route 66 Motel, cling to the wind-swept mesa above town, but the most FUN place to overnite in town is the wonderful **Wigwam Motel** at 811 W Hopi Dr, owned by the original family since the concrete Teepees were built in 1950. They are bigger on the inside than they look, and feature the original highly polished wood furnishings. Many of the family's old cars are parked by the Wigwams to add a 50's feel. **PHOTO OP!** For reservations (recommended) call (928) 524 3048 after 3pm MST. This is the penultimate in a chain of seven built from 1933 to 1950. <u>SAN BERNARDINO</u>'s Wigwams, the last built, were recently restored, so now you've TWO chances to "Sleep in a Wigwam."

GIANT ALERT! If you haven't seen enough **DINOSAURS**, still more sit near downtown at the **Rainbow Rock Shop**. Nearby at 109 Hopi Dr, **Julien's Roadrunner** offers tin signs, roadside and railroad memorabilia and "Route 66 Stuff" from a mural decorated store. "Looking is FREE!" For good grub, try **Jo and Aggie's Café** at 120 W Hopi.

Those of a historic bent can explore the **Holbrook Visitor Center and Museum** in the former **1898 Navajo County Courthouse** at Arizona and Navajo, with its funky and graffitied pre-fab jail cell (shipped here ages ago by rail). **Local INFO:** 928-524-6558 (Museum) or (800) 524-2459 (CofC).

West of town at EXIT 280, the **Geronimo Trading Post** huddles at the base of a rocky brown bluff. Their signs trumpet the **"World's Largest Petrified Tree."** At 80 tons, I guess that qualifies for a **GIANT ALERT**! The cliffs crowd I-40 to <u>JOSEPH CITY</u>.

EB: Join **I-40 EB** from <u>JOSEPH CITY</u> at **EXIT 277**. At **EXIT 285**, leave I-40, and follow **BL 40/Hopi Dr** into <u>HOLBROOK</u>. Downtown, turn **LEFT** on Navajo Blvd. Cross under EXIT 286. At **EXIT 289**, east of town, join **I-40 EB**.

WB: At **EXIT 277**, follow **BL 40/Main St** into **JOSEPH CITY**. At the access road to **EXIT 274** ("**END AZ BYWAYS**" sign) turn **LEFT** and cross over I-40. Turn **RIGHT** and follow the **South Frontage Rd** past the **JACKRABBIT** to **EXIT 269**. Join **I-40 WB**. At **EXIT 257** (AZ Hwy 87) cross I-40, and turn **RIGHT** with "**Hwy 87 South"/ Historic 66**", past **EXIT 255** and into **WINSLOW**.

JOSEPH CITY, once home to many lively tourist stops like Apache Fort, now hosts little more than a RV park. On east side of town is a **Historic Marker** made of polished petrified wood, bearing a plaque dedicated to the Mormon colonists that settled here in 1876. **SCAVENGER HUNT!** What was **JOSEPH CITY FIRST** known as? _____

SIDE TRIP: For that lonely old Route 66 feeling, be sure to take the dead end section west from the turnoff to **EXIT 274**. This heads along north of I-40, past a feed store which over the years was home to **Hopi Village, Howdy Hanks and Sitting Bull's Indian Store.** The tourist Teepee is still in front, and old **Howdy Hank** himself has been restored and repainted on the west wall (visible from the side road). Further west are the sad remains of "one of the Oldest trading Posts on 66". Those red log walls last served as **Ella's Frontier.** In the 30s and 40s, this was **San Diego Rawson's Frontier Days Trading Post.** Most of the old signs and symbols that once graced this structure are gone, but a few remain to tease the memory.

"If you haven't been to the **Jackrabbit**, you haven't been in the southwest," reads the old postcards. The **Jackrabbit Trading Post** is still a hopping happening alongside 66, but those yellow and black signs that once taunted literally hundreds of miles of Route 66 with the mileage countdown to the place are mostly gone. A large billboard with a black jackrabbit, topped by little rabbit silhouettes, stands proudly across the road, loudly exclaiming "HERE IT IS!" **GIANT ALERT!** Where else can you sit on a giant jackrabbit! **PHOTO OP!** Be sure to check out the **GIFT SHOP** for a variety of roadside souvenirs.

EB: From **WINSLOW**, follow "**Historic 66**" past **EXIT 255**. Cross the Little Colorado River, then turn **LEFT** with Hwy 87 N to **EXIT 257**. Join **I-40 EB** to **EXIT 269**. Take the **South Frontage Road** east past **JACKRABBIT** to **EXIT 274**. Cross I-40 to the "**T**" JCT. Turn **RIGHT** and follow **BL 40/Main St** thru **JOSEPH CITY** to **EXIT 277**: join **I-40 EB** to **HOLBROOK.**

AZ page-8

JOSEPH CITY

TO HOLBROOK

EXIT 277

MAIN

EXIT 274

TO WINSLOW

66 ENDS

EXIT 66/40

TO WINSLOW

WB: Follow **BL 40** into **WINSLOW**. At the east "Y" Historic 66 follows **Third St** One-Way WB thru downtown past Kinsley St. On the west side of town, join **I-40 WB** at **EXIT 252**.

WINSLOW

In **WINSLOW**, follow the signs to the **Old Trails Museum** on Kinsley between 2nd and 3rd, which is usually open Tues thru Sat from 1-5 pm, featuring old west, road and railroad history.

PHOTO OP! At Kinsley and 2nd is the "**Standing on the Corner**" statue, dedicated to the classic Eagles song "Take it Easy" (which often can be heard wafting from across the street at **Roadworks**, a convenient and well-stocked **gift shop**). A mural painted on the building behind the statue depicts a "girl in a flat bed Ford," as if reflected in a shop window. Hopefully this will be saved after a recent fire gutted the structure. Local INFO: 928-289-2434.

2nd **St** is the older way thru town, so to enjoy **WINSLOW** fully you should drive

both directions, as either street has plenty of relics of relics of roadside 66. Old gas stations, cafes, and motels abound. On the corner of Barry and Second, for example, sits a recognizable Conoco cottage-style station. A former **Whiting Bros** may still be identified by its red and yellow stripes, near the east "Y."

WINSLOW is justifiably proud of the restored **La Posada Hotel** at 303 E Second, an ornate former Harvey House built in 1928. Check out the southwestern style lobby, or try one of their charming rooms for the night (928) 289-4366. Two old **Valentine diners** sit on Second and Third; the "**Highway Diner**" in original-looking red and white livery, and the "**Santa Fe Diner**," whose porcelain panels are now disguised with recent additions. Barry St, which goes north to I-40 EXIT 253, is also signed as "Beale Wagon Route," commemorating the ancestor of the roads and railroad across northern Arizona. Route 66 dead ends on the west end of town, past EXIT 252. An older 2–lane remnant runs along closer to the RR nearby.

EB: Take **EXIT 252** on the west side of **WINSLOW**, and follow **BL 40**/"**Historic 66**" east into town. At the west "Y" bear **RIGHT** with **Second St** (One-Way EB) thru downtown, then follow **BL 40** out of town.

WB: Follow **I-40 WB** from <u>WINSLOW</u>. Continue west past EXIT 245 (Hwy 99), EXIT 239 (METEOR CITY) EXIT 233 (METEOR CRATER) EXIT 230 (TWO GUNS) and EXIT 219 (TWIN ARROWS) to EXIT 211 at <u>WINONA</u>.

TWIN ARROWS

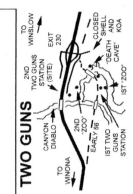

TWO GUNS

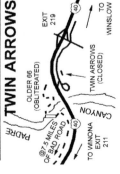

Watch for still another geodesic dome (topped by a rainbow), this time at **Meteor City** off Exit 239. "Wide-angle" **PHOTO OP**! Here is the **"World's Longest Map of Route 66"** (as seen on TV!) Further west, the actual **METEOR CRATER** is the site of a tremendous meteor impact, which left a **HUGE** hole in the desert, well worth a look. **GIFT SHOP ALERT.** Closer to I-40, yet another white-domed business was featured in the movie *STARMAN*. http://www.meteorcrater.com/

TWO GUNS was a storied tourist town on the edge of **Canyon Diablo**. Past an old concrete arch bridge lie crumbling rock ruins of gas stations, two roadside zoos (hence the oft photographed sign: "**Mountain Lions**") and infamous **Apache Death Cave** (I toured the cave years ago when **TWO GUNS** enjoyed a brief resurgence...not recommended now!). Once you could get guided tours of the area, but all of this, including the KOA and Shell station, is now **closed** and on **PRIVATE PROPERTY.** The old ruins can be hazardous, and there are lots of nails scattered about, so please play it **safe** and just view the ruins from the exit.

GIANT ALERT! TWIN ARROWS was once an attractive establishment, with its red/white Valentine diner, and namesake gigantic arrows thrust into the soil. Now boarded up, the remains are easiest reached for photo purposes by **EB** travelers: just take the off ramp for **EXIT 219** and there you are. **WB**, take the **EXIT 219** overpass to the South Frontage Rd, then go west. You'll have to circle back (plans may be afoot to move the buildings to <u>FLAGSTAFF</u>). Nearby, another ancient **1914 concrete bridge** arches over **Canyon Padre**, north of I-40. **Unfortunately**, the only access is via a 15-mile round-trip on a **VERY** rough and decrepit section of old 66, east from EXIT 211. This is **NOT** your casual vacation side trip, and **not advised for first-timers.**

EB: From **EXIT 211** at <u>WINONA</u>, follow I-40 EB past EXIT 219 (TWIN ARROWS), EXIT 230 (TWO GUNS), EXIT 233 (METEOR CRATER), EXIT 239 (METEOR CITY) and EXIT 245 (HWY 99), then take **EXIT 252** on the west side of <u>WINSLOW</u>.

(see **MAP 2 AZ page-6**)

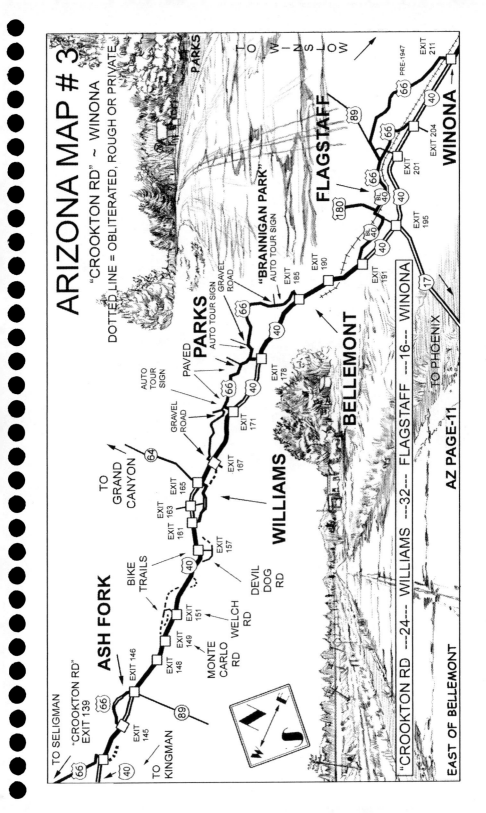

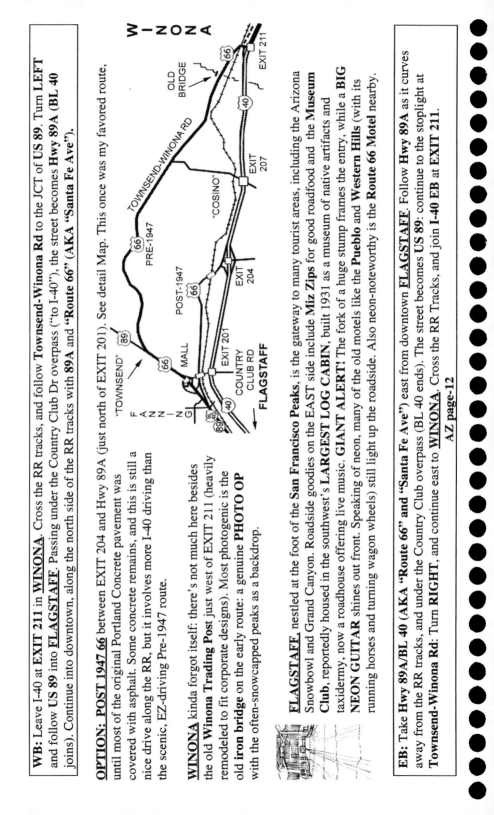

WB: Leave I-40 at **EXIT 211** in **WINONA**. Cross the RR tracks, and follow **Townsend-Winona Rd** to the JCT of **US 89**. Turn **LEFT** and follow **US 89** into **FLAGSTAFF**. Passing under the Country Club Dr overpass ("to I-40"), the street becomes **Hwy 89A (BL 40** joins). Continue into downtown, along the north side of the RR tracks with **89A** and **"Route 66" (AKA "Santa Fe Ave")**.

OPTION: POST 1947 66 between EXIT 204 and Hwy 89A (just north of EXIT 201). See detail Map. This once was my favored route, until most of the original Portland Concrete pavement was covered with asphalt. Some concrete remains, and this is still a nice drive along the RR, but it involves more I-40 driving than the scenic, EZ-driving Pre-1947 route.

WINONA kinda forgot itself: there's not much here besides the old **Winona Trading Post** just west of EXIT 211 (heavily remodeled to fit corporate designs). Most photogenic is the old **iron bridge** on the early route: a genuine **PHOTO OP** with the often-snowcapped peaks as a backdrop.

FLAGSTAFF, nestled at the foot of the **San Francisco Peaks**, is the gateway to many tourist areas, including the Arizona Snowbowl and Grand Canyon. Roadside goodies on the EAST side include **Miz Zips** for good roadfood and the **Museum Club**, reportedly housed in the southwest's **LARGEST LOG CABIN**, built 1931 as a museum of native artifacts and taxidermy, now a roadhouse offering live music. **GIANT ALERT!** The fork of a huge stump frames the entry, while a **BIG NEON GUITAR** shines out front. Speaking of neon, many of the old motels like the **Pueblo** and **Western Hills** (with its running horses and turning wagon wheels) still light up the roadside. Also neon-noteworthy is the **Route 66 Motel** nearby.

EB: Take **Hwy 89A/BL 40** (AKA **"Route 66"** and **"Santa Fe Ave")** east from downtown **FLAGSTAFF**. Follow **Hwy 89A** as it curves away from the RR tracks, and under the Country Club overpass (BL 40 ends). The street becomes **US 89**: continue to the stoplight at **Townsend-Winona Rd**: Turn **RIGHT**, and continue east to **WINONA**. Cross the RR Tracks, and join **I-40 EB** at **EXIT 211**.

AZ page-12

WB: Follow 89A/BL 40 west thru downtown **FLAGSTAFF**, curving under the RR tracks. Bear **RIGHT** with **BL 40/Route 66** at the "Y" with S Milton Rd. Continue west to **EXIT 191**, and join **I-40 WB** thru **BELLEMONT** (EXIT 185).

Downtown **FLAGSTAFF** has a variety of old buildings housing interesting shops and cafes. Towering over all is the **Hotel Monte Vista** neon sign. On the south side between San Francisco and Beaver is the **Visitor Center** in the Amtrak Depot. **SIDE TRIP:** Before 1934, '66 crossed the RR on **Beaver**, then turned **RIGHT** on **Phoenix** and **LEFT** on **Mikes Pike** to **Milton Rd**. Beaver is **ONE-WAY** now, so this is best done WB. Several old motels survive here, including the **Downtowner**, a hostel with a great sign.

Local INFO: (928) 779-7611. www.flagstaff.az.us

GIANT ALERT! **Granny's Closet**, a great restaurant on Milton, is the site of the former **Lumberjack Café**. This was home to the very **FIRST** of the GIANT so-called "**Muffler Men**," an axe-wielding **Paul Bunyan** installed in 1962, ancestor to the three Illinois giants. Granny's currently displays their own rendition of Tall Paul, but whither the original? **Northern AZ University** has TWO identical giants (honoring their "Lumberjacks" team). Perhaps Paul didn't venture very far?

FLAGSTAFF DETAIL

PRE-'34 66 VIA MIKES PIKE, PHOENIX AND BEAVER (BEAVER IS NOW ONE-WAY SB)

BELLEMONT

POST 1931 (BECOMES GRAVEL) TO PARKS
SWATH OF POST 1921
OPTIONAL ROUTE VIA 1931-41 ROUTE (PART GRAVEL), **RECOMMENDED**
EXIT 185
DEAD END WEST (POST 1941)
DEAD END EAST
PINE BREEZE INN

BELLEMONT sat idle for years, but new development has eroded much '66 feel. **DEAD END SIDE TRIPS:** Old 66 runs for about 2 miles to the west (before getting ROUGH). To the east, the road (now paved over in blacktop) passes by the former site of an old Whiting Bros Station, filmed for the movie "**Easy Rider**." The old concrete emerges here, to dead end after a bumpy 0.7 of a mile. **Route 66 Roadhouse** and a HD dealer are near the EXIT. See **GRAVEL OPTION** to **PARKS** on **AZ page-14!**

BELLEMONT (EXIT 185). Take **EXIT 191**, curve under I-40, then **RIGHT** on **BL 40/ "Route 66"** into **FLAGSTAFF**. At Milton Rd, turn **LEFT** with Hwy **89A/BL 40/ "Route 66."** Go under the RR tracks, then curve into downtown.

EB: Follow **I-40 EB** thru **BELLEMONT** (EXIT 185). Take **EXIT 191**, curve under I-40, then **RIGHT** on **BL 40/ "Route 66"** into **FLAGSTAFF**. At Milton Rd, turn **LEFT** with Hwy **89A/BL 40/ "Route 66."** Go under the RR tracks, then curve into downtown.

WB: Follow **I-40 WB** past **BELLEMONT**. From **I-40 EXIT 178**, go north to the JCT with **CO RD 146**: Turn **LEFT** thru **PARKS**. At the access road for **EXIT 171**, turn **LEFT** to join **I-40 WB**. Pass **EXIT 167**, and take **EXIT 165** (see **GRAVEL OPTIONS** 1 and 2)

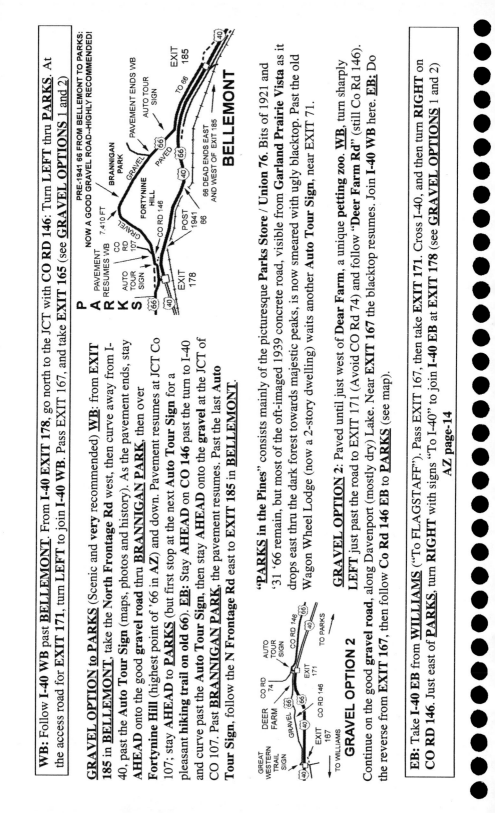

P — PRE-1941 66 FROM BELLEMONT TO PARKS:
A — NOW A GOOD GRAVEL ROAD–HIGHLY RECOMMENDED!
R
K
S

BELLEMONT

GRAVEL OPTION to PARKS (Scenic and very recommended) **WB:** from **EXIT 185** in **BELLEMONT**, take the **North Frontage Rd** west, then curve away from I-40, past the **Auto Tour Sign** (maps, photos and history). As the pavement ends, stay **AHEAD** onto the good **gravel road** thru **BRANNIGAN PARK**, then over **Fortynine Hill** (highest point of '66 in **AZ**) and down. Pavement resumes at JCT Co 107; stay **AHEAD** to **PARKS** (but first stop at the next **Auto Tour Sign** for a pleasant **hiking** trail on old 66). **EB:** Stay **AHEAD** on **CO 146** past the turn to I-40 and curve past the **Auto Tour Sign**, then stay **AHEAD** onto the **gravel** at the JCT of CO 107. Past **BRANNIGAN PARK**, the pavement resumes. Past the last **Auto Tour Sign**, follow the N Frontage Rd east to **EXIT 185** in **BELLEMONT.**

GRAVEL OPTION 2

"PARKS in the Pines" consists mainly of the picturesque **Parks Store / Union 76**. Bits of 1921 and '31 '66 remain, but most of the oft-imaged 1939 concrete road, visible from **Garland Prairie Vista** as it drops east thru the dark forest towards majestic peaks, is now smeared with ugly blacktop. Past the old **Wagon Wheel Lodge** (now a 2-story dwelling) waits another **Auto Tour Sign**, near **EXIT 71.**

GRAVEL OPTION 2: Paved until just past the **Dear Farm**, a unique **petting zoo**. **WB:** turn sharply **LEFT** just past the road to EXIT 171 (Avoid CO Rd 74) and follow **"Deer Farm Rd"** (still Co Rd 146). Near **EXIT 167** the blacktop resumes. Join **I-40 WB** here. **EB:** Do

Continue on the good **gravel road**, along Davenport (mostly dry) Lake. Near **EXIT 167**, then follow **Co Rd 146 EB** to **PARKS** (see map).

EB: Take **I-40 EB** from **WILLIAMS** ("To FLAGSTAFF"). Pass **EXIT 167**, then take **EXIT 171**. Cross I-40, and then turn **RIGHT** on **CO RD 146**. Just east of **PARKS**, turn **RIGHT** with signs "To I-40" to join **I-40 EB** at **EXIT 178** (see **GRAVEL OPTIONS** 1 and 2)

WB: At **EXIT 165**, turn **LEFT** and pass under I-40 to follow **BL 40** into **WILLIAMS**. Follow **Railroad Ave (BL 40 WB) ONE-WAY** thru **WILLIAMS** (double back to drive **BOTH** One-Way Streets). Continue out to **I-40 EXIT 161**, and join **I-40 WB.**

WILLIAMS has the distinction of being the very **LAST** US 66 town bypassed, on Oct 13, 1984. **Scavenger Hunt!** What is the "fun" slogan painted on the RR overpass above BL 40/ Route 66 just west of EXIT 165? _____ Of the ONE-WAY streets thru town, the original route was via **"Route 66."** The **WB** street, **Railroad Ave**, came along in 1955. The town is so compact you should drive **BOTH**. It's traditional for overnighters to stroll downtown in the evening, but you may need a coat, even in summer! Along the way, check out Pete's **Gas Station Museum**, with his father's 1950 Ford in front, and gas collection inside. **GIFT SHOP ALERT!** City INFO: 928-635-1418.

SIDE TRIP:
EARLY 66 VIA:
RODEO, AIRPORT, EDISON
AND GRAND CANYON BLVD.

WILLIAMS

For eats, try **Rods Steakhouse** (look for the big Neon Bull) or **Twisters 50's Soda Fountain (The Route 66 Place).** **Old Smokey's Restaurant** still serves biscuits and gravy under their Mountain Man sign. Plenty of classic sleep-overs survive (many with neon). Check the Federation Guide. Two of the most unusual are the **Red Garter Bed and Bakery**, in an 1897 bordello (look for the "manikin of the evening" leaning out a window) on Railroad, and the **"Old West Main St**," an old motel recently remodeled into a "false-front" frontier town.

One of **WILLIAMS** major attractions is the **Grand Canyon Railway**, which offers train rides in restored 1880s coaches (usually pulled by a vintage steam engine) to the canyon for day visits, or overnight (get room reservations for the Rim 6 months in advance!) Near the historic 1908 log depot is the **Frey Marcos Hotel** (Harvey House). INFO: (800) THE TRAIN.

EB: From **EXIT 161**, take **BL 40** into **WILLIAMS**. Follow **"Route 66" EB ONE WAY** thru downtown (double back to drive **BOTH** One-Way Streets). Continue east with **BL 40** to **EXIT 165**, and join **I-40 EB** ("to Flagstaff").

(see MAP #3 AZ page-11)

WB: Take **I-40 WB** from **WILLIAMS.** Use **EXIT 146** (AZ Hwy 89 S) but turn **RIGHT** with **BL 40** thru town ONE-WAY WB on **Lewis**, then re-join **I-40 WB** at **EXIT 144**. Take **EXIT 139**, and follow "Crookton Rd" to **SELIGMAN.**

SIDE TRIP: If you've brought your mountain bike along, two sites in the Kaibab National Forest offer **BIKE TRAILS** on sections of abandoned '66! South of the **Devil Dog Rd exit**

MONTE CARLO RD — DEVIL DOG RD — WELCH RD — ASH FORK HILL

(#157) is the **first Bike Trail sign**, directing you along the **1922 & '32 Routes**, thru thick woods. Cars can take the short stretch west from **Forest Rd 108** to the I-40 tunnel (turn back here). From I-40, down the steep escarpment of infamous Ash Fork Hill, (smell the overheated brakes!) take **EXIT 151** (**Welch Rd**) north for the **second Trail sign**. This tour follows the precariously perched **1922 alignment** along a steep hillside, before returning by the **1932 road**, from near the **Monte Carlo Truck Stop** (respect private property: DO NOT LITTER!). Safeguard any valuables left in your vehicle. Remnants of the old roads also run uphill, cut off at the freeway (**VERY ROUGH!**).

The I-40 bypass wasn't kind to **ASH FORK** (famous for flagstones) as few businesses still line its pair of ONE-WAY streets. Here the WB street, **Lewis**, is the oldest. Among the points of interest in town is **Desoto's Beauty and Barber Shop**, housed in an old gas station. **PHOTO OP!** A cool **1958 Desoto** perches on the roof, a real purple (and white) dinosaur of an auto. Next door, in a pink and blue building, is the "**Route 66 Grill.**" A few architecturally interesting old motels (one with cobblestone walls) rest alongside Lewis Street. For eats, the **Ranch House Café** at 111 E Park is recommended. Note the abandoned RR alignment running alongside I-40 headed west from town.

ASH FORK

PINE IS A FRAGMENT OF OLDER 66

← TO SELIGMAN/TO WILLIAMS →

EB: Join **I-40 EB** at **EXIT 139**. Take **EXIT 144**, cross under I-40, and follow **BL 40** thru **ASHFORK** ONE-WAY EB on **Park** (double back to drive Lewis too) then re-join **I-40 EB** at **EXIT 146**. Take **EXIT 161**, and follow **BL 40 EB** into **WILLIAMS**.

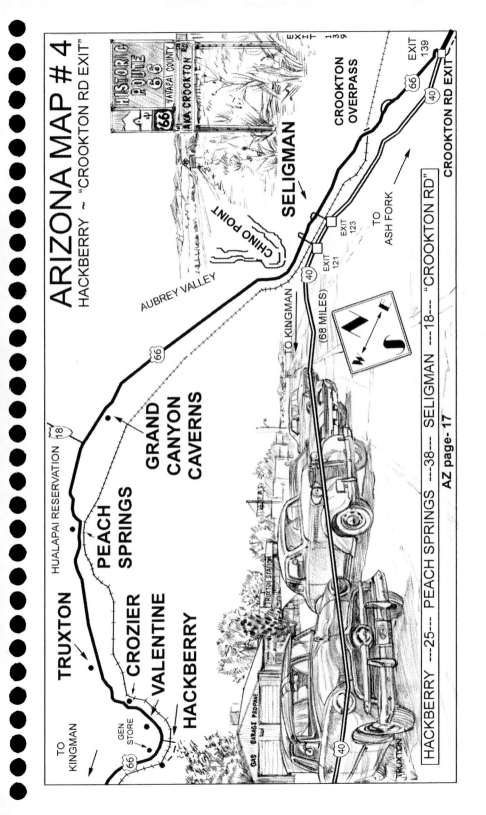

ARIZONA MAP # 4
HACKBERRY ~ "CROOKTON RD EXIT"

HISTORIC ROUTE 66

66 AKA CROOKTON

AKA CROOKTON YAVAPAI COUNTY

EXIT 139

SELIGMAN

CROOKTON OVERPASS

66

40

CROOKTON RD EXIT

CHINO POINT

EXIT 123

TO ASH FORK

AUBREY VALLEY

40

EXIT 121

TO KINGMAN

(68 MILES)

N W S E

66

TO KINGMAN

GEN STORE

66

TRUXTON

CROZIER

VALENTINE

HACKBERRY

PEACH SPRINGS

GRAND CANYON CAVERNS

HUALAPAI RESERVATION

18

GAS GARAGE PROPANE

TRUXTON

TRADING STATION

40

40

HACKBERRY ---25--- PEACH SPRINGS ---38--- SELIGMAN ---18--- "CROOKTON RD"

AZ page-17

WB: Follow "Crookton Rd"/"Historic 66" from **EXIT 139**. Cross over the RR tracks. Cross over the east side I-40 access road. At the east side of town, follow the **WB lane** as it curves to the **RIGHT**, then STOP, and turn **LEFT** into **SELIGMAN**.

EXIT 139 is the **eastern gateway** to a golden stretch of about 159 (almost) uninterrupted miles of pristine, EZ-driving Route 66. "Go WEST, young man," and you'll reach **TOPOCK** on the Colorado River WITHOUT setting tires on I-40 (you DO have to cross under it twice). Recently rebuilt "**Crookton Rd**" follows alongside the bygone railroad as it climbs steadily into the hills. **OPTION**: About **6 miles WB** from **EXIT 139** you can elect to turn **RIGHT** onto "**Old Crookton Rd.**," a short loop of **slightly rough older 66** that curves below a hillside (which the newer road carves thru).
EB: turn **LEFT** almost 2 miles east of the RR (before the descent). At "**Crookton Crossing**" are a pair of overpasses over the railroad tracks. The **unused** span makes a good platform for train spotting. Look for more abandoned **1920s and '30s roadbed** alongside current **Historic 66** on the way into…

SELIGMAN, the birthplace of the **Historic Route 66 Association of Arizona** and home of the **Annual Fun Run**. Each spring hundreds of cars of every stripe cruise downtown, before heading out to **TOPOCK** (or visa versa). Take the time to visit association founder **Angel Delgadillo** (as seen in commercials) at his former barbershop, now the **Route 66 Visitor Center. GIFT SHOP ALERT**! To the east is the world's famous **Snow Cap**. This has long been the funniest food spot on '66, as the late **Juan Delgadillo** (Angel's brother) played a gamut of jokes and tricks on his customers, including false doorknobs, "squirting" catsup bottles and "slightly used napkins." Each visit to his outlandishly decorated diner was a colorful experience, including a sign proclaiming "**Dead Chicken**" and a customized, flamboyant parade car parked out front. Despite Juan's untimely passing in 2004, his family intends to keep up the comical tradition, and the good food. Town INFO: (928) 422-3352. arizonan.com/Seligman/index.html (**SELIGMAN** continues on **AZ page-19**)

SELIGMAN

TO PEACH SPRINGS

"CROOKTON RD"

MAIN

EARLY 66
RAILROAD AVE

WB: STOP
THEN LEFT

EB: BEAR
RIGHT

TO ASH FORK

WEST
I-40
ACCESS

EXIT
123

EXIT
121

TO KINGMAN
(68 MILES)

EB: On the east side of **SELIGMAN**, bear **RIGHT** with the sign "**To Crookton Rd/ Historic 66**" (AVOID the I-40 access road that branches off left). Cross over the I-40 access road. Cross over the RR tracks. At **EXIT 139**, join **I-40 EB** to **ASH FORK**.

SELIGMAN part 2: Though small, this travel-town offers many places to spend the night. The **Route 66 Motel** (928) 422-3204 is often recommended, as are others in the Federation guide. Check out the Supai Motel's superb neon sign (rooms are hard to find during the Annual Fun Run, so reserve well ahead). Other choices for road food (not literally, one hopes) are the **Roadkill Café**, or the **Copper Cart Restaurant**. An old-time place for liquid refreshment is **Black Cat Cocktails**. **SIDE TRIP**: Mention must be made of the **early route** thru town, which came in from the east on **Railroad Ave** (past the still-standing Delgadillo Pool Hall and the site of a couple of old-time brothels), then turned north, just before the empty Fred Harvey Hotel and Café (1900-1954) on **Main St**.

As for the abandoned route west out of **SELIGMAN**, look under the RR trestle west of town to peek at a **1920s rock culvert**. This faint dirt route (edged with rocks and the remains of an old flivver) can also be seen from atop the west side **BL 40** overpass. At **Chino Point**, the road and RR squeeze around the sharp "point" of the **Aubrey Cliffs** before entering **Aubrey Valley**. Just west of the base of the hills, the 1930s route is visible as it veers off for a few miles on the north. Further on, the **Calvary Baptist Institute** was once and old motel.

TO CHINO POINT

SELIGMAN

1920S CULVERT

"DIRT 66"

66

66

TO EXIT 121

Grand Canyon Caverns (formerly **Dinosaur Caverns**) was another place my Dad would not stop at (We **ALMOST** did in 1969, 'till he found it was situated a whole MILE off of 66)! The slight detour for the cave tour (and restaurant) is well worth the time (I MADE Dad stop on a 1981 trip). **GIANT ALERT**! The great green **Allosaurus** (?....can't be a **T-REX** with three fingers!) still poses out front for obligatory snapshots. **GIFT SHOP ALERT**! At the JCT with AZ 66 is the recently refurbished **Caverns Inn** (928) 422-4565. **SCAVENGER HUNT**! What **COLOR** is the big Cavern dinosaur's **BELLY**?

EB: Follow **AZ 66** from **PEACH SPRINGS** (becomes "**Historic 66**" at Yavapai Co Line). Approaching **SELIGMAN**, follow "**Historic 66**" under the west-side I-40 access road, into town.

(see **MAP 4 AZ page-17**)

AZ page-19

The steep hill east of **PEACH SPRINGS** offers a quick view of the distant **Grand Canyon**. This town is the headquarters of the **Hualapai Indian Reservation**. The Hualapai Tribal Forestry Dept is housed in a cobblestone former trading post (that predates 66) on the north side of the road, while a picturesque old gas station/garage (Osterman's Shell from 1932) remains on the south. Modern **Hualapai Lodge** offers lodging and the **River Runner's Resort** restaurant (928) 769-2230. Arrange for tours of the **Lower Grand Canyon** here.

Wooden markers welcome you to tiny **TRUXTON**, (est. 1951) home to the **Frontier Motel and Café**, the nifty neon sign of which was recently restored with matching funds from the **Route 66 Corridor Preservation Program.** (928) 769-2238 **PHOTO OP!** On the west side, a weather-beaten **1950 Ford** supports a bi-directional sign pointing to **LA and Chicago**. In front stands a pole festooned with boards pointing the way to all the towns named on the song "**Route 66**" (they even remembered **Winona**!).

Further west, 66 drops down into **Crozier Canyon**, where the wide-open spaces surrender to craggy slopes. Just west of milepost 89, old 66 veers off across a concrete bridge (posted) before passing by a row of tin roofed tourist cabins visible in the floodplain of **Crozier Creek** below. The **LAST** paving on US 66 in **ARIZONA** occurred along here circa 1937, shortly after workers blasted big bites from out of the hills above the RR tracks for the improved path of Route 66.

The old **VALENTINE** Post Office (famous for Valentine's Day postmarks) is long gone, but the **Valentine Indian School** although long disused, is still standing. The "Non-Indian" school, a one-room bldg "across the tracks," still stands nearby. A few roadside remnants cling to the flanks of Old Mother Road, including Chief's Motel and an ancient Union 76 station. The boulder-strewn slopes of the hillsides here were threatened until recently by an unfortunate mining effort, but the rugged beauty endures.

EB: Follow **AZ 66** east from **HACKBERRY**, thru **VALENTINE**, **TRUXTON** and **PEACH SPRINGS**.

AZ page-20

(see **MAP 4 AZ page-17**)

P E A C H — PEACH
S P R I N G S — SPRINGS

DIAMOND CREEK RD

66

BIA 19

TO TRUXTON

TO TRUXTON

TO S·E·L·I·G·M·A·N

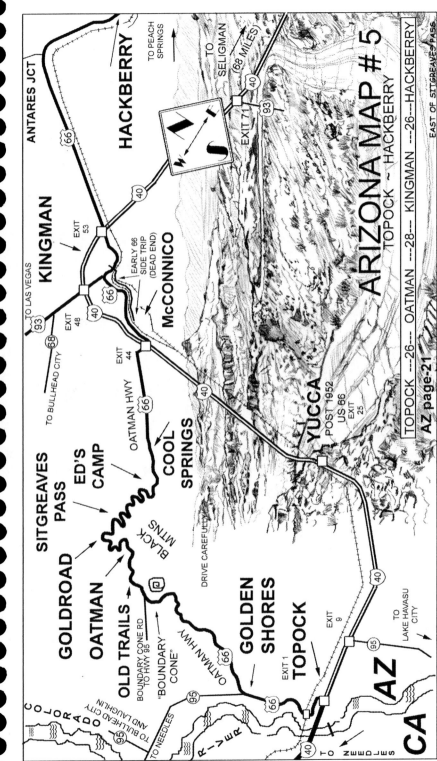

ARIZONA MAP #5

TOPOCK ~ HACKBERRY

TOPOCK ---26--- OATMAN ---28--- KINGMAN ---26---HACKBERRY

AZ page-21

EAST OF SITGREAVES PASS

WB: Take AZ 66 thru **HACKBERRY**, around **Antares Curve**, and under EXIT 53 into **KINGMAN** on BL 40/Route 66/Andy Devine.

Old **HACKBERRY** rests south of the railroad on "**Dirt 66**," but the **Hackberry Gen Store** offers a great stop on **AZ 66**. This was the former haunt of famed Route artist **Bob Waldmire**, now operated by the **Pritchards**, who have kept up the tradition to make this a place that makes the brake lights glow. **PHOTO OP!** There is a passel of cool old stuff to see outside, including rusty old sedans, vintage gas pumps and signs, and a bright red '56 Corvette. **GIFT SHOP ALERT!** Plenty to see (and buy) on the inside, too. **Guys**, check out the "tastefully" decorated men's room!

West of **HACKBERRY**, AZ 66 and the RR negotiate long "**Antares Curve**," centered on the junction with Antares Rd. Here, near the Kozy Corner Trailer Court and an A Frame structure that once housed a popular restaurant, is a **GIANT ALERT!** Delightfully out of place in the desert is a 14 foot tall "**Tiki**" (or Easter Island) **Idol** head! Why? Why not.

KINGMAN

The way west is fast and straight into **KINGMAN**, where you encounter I-40 for the first time in miles. **Be advised**: Going either WB or EB, this is a good location to top off your **gas tank**. Old 66 thru town is variously signed as "**Route 66**" and "**Andy Devine**," (to honor an old-time actor). Many chain motels cluster near the exits, while classic Route 66 lodging remains along the route, complete with neon signs (**NOTE**: as elsewhere, some places **RAISE** room rates during events).

A water tower with a huge "**Historic Route 66**" shield welcomes you to a downtown full of photogenic architecture, dominated by the tall "Hotel Beale" signs. Nearby is the vintage **Hotel Brunswick**, a three-story stone structure built in 1909. The second floor balcony offers a view of '66 and the railroad tracks (if I can sleep thru the train noise, then so can you). Rooms are clean and rates are reasonable, plus a restaurant is downstairs (928) 718-1800. For a vintage motel, you might check out the **Hill Top Motel**, on the hill east of downtown, at 1901 E Andy Devine. Nearby the 1943 **City Café** is now the **Hot Rod Café** (more **KINGMAN** on **AZ page-23**).

EB: In **KINGMAN**, cross under EXIT 53: stay **AHEAD** with **AZ 66** along the RR Tracks. Follow **Antares Curve** to **HACKBERRY**.
AZ page-22

On the west side of downtown, in a historic 1907 building, is the **Powerhouse Visitor Center**, the head-quarters of the **Historic Route 66 Association of AZ**. Make time for the fantastic **Route 66 Museum** upstairs, open 7 days a week. It's worth the small charge to view the quality displays, including dioramas of a **dustbowl family** and earlier sojourners in a prairie schooner, plus murals, wall-sized quotes from *The Grapes of Wrath*, large maps of old 66, scrapbooks, and a bullet-nose Studebaker. **GIFT SHOP ALERT!** INFO: (928)753-5001. Noteworthy is the nearby **Mohave Museum** for regional history.

Across '66 is **Locomotive Park**, featuring a majestic black **Santa Fe steam locomotive and a red caboose**. PHOTO OP! My family posed here in 1962…you should too. At the west end of the park is a monument dedicated to the **Beale Wagon Route**, with wagons and camels on top (camels were used in experiments with desert travel). **SCAVENGER HUNT!** According to the marker, what **YEAR** did the railroad come to **KINGMAN**? _____

KINGMAN DETAIL

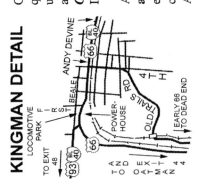

SIDE TRIP: This paved round trip of almost **6 miles** provides an enjoyable, scenic drive down OLD 66 towards __McCONNICO__. From downtown __KINGMAN__, cross the tracks on **4th St**. A few streets south, follow the **main road** as it curves **RIGHT** onto **Old Trails Rd**. Follow the **SHARP** turn **LEFT** under the **RR trestle**, then **SLOW** and watch out for the **NARROW** squeeze between blocks of boulders on a blind curve. Imagine meeting a truck here on some dark night in the 1930s. After a pleasant drive between the two branches of the RR tracks, along **Perfume Canyon** (named for the sewage treatment plant), the road ends at **Route 66 Motocross Raceway**, so turn back to rejoin current Route 66 (which descends the canyon on the opposite side) at 4th St in __KINGMAN__.

WB: Go under I-40 at **EXIT 44** (follow the "**Historic 66 Oatman Hwy**" sign). Stay **AHEAD** from I-40, and turn **LEFT** to follow **Oatman Hwy.** (22 miles to **OATMAN**) Climb the mountain grades past **COOL SPRINGS** and **ED's CAMP** to **SITGREAVES PASS**.

ADVISORY: The Oatman Hwy section is **HIGHLY** recommended, but **VERY** steep and crooked, with deliciously scary drops! **No trucks over 40 feet. Huge RV's** should take **I-40**, the **POST-1952** route (or use your tow-car). See **AZ page-1** for mountain driving tips.

The drive across the drainage of **Sacramento Wash** is one of the most laid back on 66. No turns, no stops, just ease along at 45mph and watch the ragged ramparts of the **Black Mountains** loom ever closer. Stop at the pullout to read the **Back Country Byway sign** for history and tips ("...lookout for **wild burros** and **bighorn sheep** in the road."). The first sign of life on the mountain is recently rebuilt **COOL SPRINGS**. This 1926 store and camp had reverted to stone rubble, before being rebuilt the first time for the movie "*Universal Soldier*." Not much was left of the set after Van Damme was thru. Fortunately, Ned Leuchtner, a real estate agent from Chicago, had a vision (and Dennis Dechenne had the skills) to restore this "cool" place to life, basing the restoration on old photos. Those old Mobilgas pumps look fine under the rock canopy.

Up the hill resides another old-time place, intact but closed and forbidden to tourists. Ed Edgerton, an old prospector who forsook the "Mother Lode" to mine "the Mother Road", started **ED'S CAMP**. Here grows possibly the ONLY (living) **Saguaro cactus** on Route 66! (No, they don't grow in KS, OK, TX or NM, despite what Hollywood sez). For free advertising, Ed spelled out "Ed's Camp" with white rocks on the side of a thimble-shaped hill near his roadside empire.

The road **REALLY** gets hairy west of Ed's, with hairpin curves and sheer drops coming hot and heavy. Note the interesting variety of stone or cable guardrails (or the LACK thereof) that offer faint comfort. Near **Milepost 30**, a wide spot on the shoulder offers a place to park, and over 30 rock steps lead up to **Shaffer's Fish Bowl Springs**, a man-made basin that collects water from a seep. Flowers appear in season (as do bees). Please respect the fragile beauty of this area (and be careful!). The view of the switchbacks downhill is tremendous (and often imaged). **PHOTO OP!**

EB: Descend from **SITGREAVES PASS**. Pass by **ED'S CAMP** and **COOL SPRINGS** on Oatman Hwy. Approaching I-40 **STOP**, then turn **RIGHT** ("To I-40") and cross under I-40 at **EXIT 44**. Turn **LEFT** on the **Frontage Rd** towards **KINGMAN**.

Don't waste a "sigh of relief" on reaching 3550 foot high **SITGREAVES PASS**," for now's the time for the dizzying drop **DOWNHILL** (watch those brakes!). On the east side of the pass are a foundation and a few pipe guardrails belonging to on old Ice Cream stand (yes, roadside enterprise conquered even this remote pass). To the west, another wide spot offers a grand view of crags, cliffs and remnants of old mining days. A bit further, a gravel road takes off along a spur of rock. You can walk this out to see a great vista of **three states** (AZ, CA and NV), IF it isn't too hazy.

A series of tight hairpins take you down to the level of old **GOLDROAD**, a long-gone gold mining town. To see what is buried **deep** under Route 66, try the **Gold Road Mine Tour**. **GIFT SHOP ALERT**! (928) 768-1600. Bare rocky peaks provide a rugged backdrop for rustic **OATMAN**, which once mined for gold, but now digs for tourist dollars with shops and cafes, staged gunfights and live music all crammed into its one burro-lined street. Feed the wild burros carefully, as they bite (what they do to the sidewalks is worse)! The circa 1902 **Oatman Hotel and Café** is the most authentic place in town, with good food (buffalo burgers) and atmosphere. During the Fun Run, old 66 is jammed bumper to nerf bar with all sorts of colorful street rods and hot rods. Park and walk a while. Your brake-foot needs rest. INFO: (928) 768-6222. www.oatmangold.com/

Thankfully, they repaved the road between **OATMAN** and **GOLDEN SHORES**, after neglect had rendered it nearly defunct. Today's drive is pleasant at **45 mph**! Many tight curves on the ridges can fool you at higher speeds. Shaggy trees offer a temporary green respite in the last stretch before **TOPOCK**, the Colorado River and the bridges to **CALIFORNIA**. Relief is short lived, as the desert resumes on the other side of the river. The **Topock Gorge Marina** offers true relief for thirst and hunger. **EB** drivers, see the **advisory** on **AZ page-24** (especially **RV**'ers) and the **Back Country Byway** kiosk north of **GOLDEN SHORES**. It's a trip you won't soon forget.

(see Map 5, AZ page-21)

AZ page-25

CALIFORNIA OR BUST!

This was the **Battle Cry** for generations of westward bound travelers, starting with the Gold Rush days, and stretching into the 21st Century. Dirt-poor **Dust Bowl Okies**, with hopes and belongings tied to a beat up jalopy. Wanna-be celebrities with movie stars in their eyes, bound for **HOLLYWOOD** with only a bus token and their dreams. Vacationing families heck-bent for **Disneyland**, with a backseat full of whining kids. **Route 66** was their road of choice.

The Mother Road's swath across **SOUTHERN CALIFORNIA** offers a stark contrast between the vast, wide-open spaces of the arid **Mojave Desert** and the tightly packed humanity of the **LA Basin**. Spindly palm trees add a vertical dimension, and a bit of exotica, to most towns along the way, while sagebrush, broom weed, tamarisk and spiky Joshua Trees decorate the desert. Separating these extremes is the "tear on the dotted line" fracture of the San Andreas Fault.

SAN BERNARDINO is the gateway to the metro **LOS ANGELES** area. **Foothill Blvd** was once lined with orange groves and vineyards, now strip malls and houses spring from the rich soil. This corridor still has much of Old 66 to enjoy, with the **San Gabriel Mountains** a continuous backdrop. **LA** was an early adopter of the freeway culture. The infamous **Arroyo Seco Parkway** was the first such east of the Mississippi, and much of the "Drive-In, Thru and Around" culture was birthed on or near the Twin Sixes.

California driving requires attention, whether in desert or city. Watch for tailgaters impatient with out of state slowpokes, and traffic jams in the city. In desert climes, beware of **flash floods** and heat. Carry water and watch your **gas gauge**! Either starting or ending your trip here, may you find **YOUR** Route 66 dreams in sunny **CALIFORNIA.**

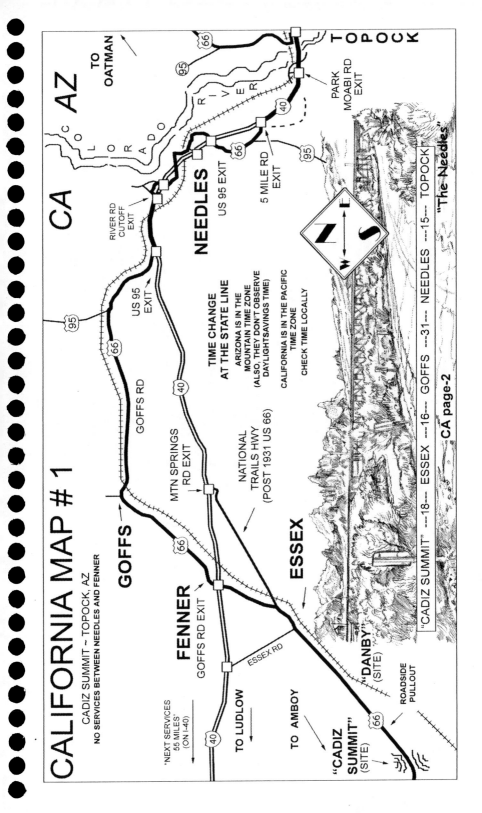

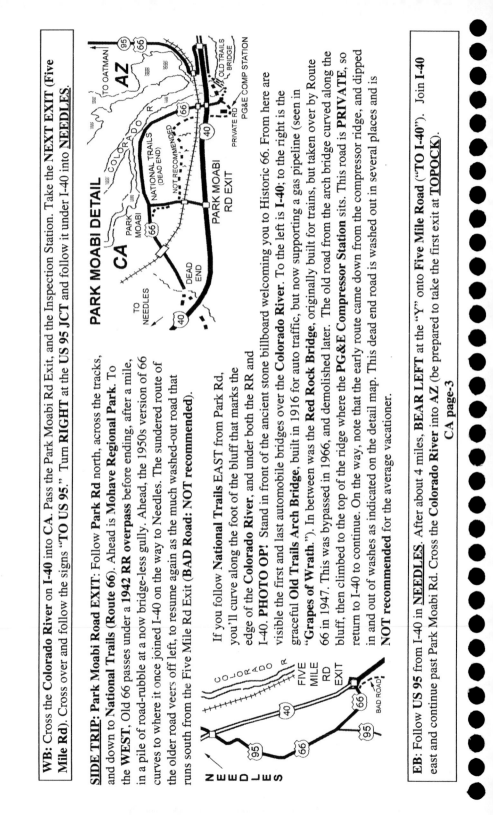

SIDE TRIP: Park Moabi Road EXIT:

Follow **Park Rd** north, across the tracks, and down to **National Trails** (Route 66). Ahead is **Mohave Regional Park**. To the **WEST**, Old 66 passes under a **1942 RR overpass** before ending, after a mile, in a pile of road-rubble at a now bridge-less gully. Ahead, the 1950s version of 66 curves to where it once joined I-40 on the way to Needles. The sundered route of the older road veers off left, to resume again as the much washed-out road that runs south from the Five Mile Rd Exit (**BAD Road: NOT recommended**).

If you follow **National Trails** EAST from Park Rd, you'll curve along the foot of the bluff that marks the edge of the **Colorado River**, and under both the RR and I-40. **PHOTO OP!** Stand in front of the ancient stone billboard welcoming you to Historic 66. From here are visible the first and last automobile bridges over the **Colorado River**. To the left is **I-40**; to the right is the graceful **Old Trails Arch Bridge**, built in 1916 for auto traffic, but now supporting a gas pipeline (seen in "**Grapes of Wrath.**"). In between was the **Red Rock Bridge**, originally built for trains, but taken over by Route 66 in 1947. This was bypassed in 1966, and demolished later. The old road from the arch bridge curved along the bluff, then climbed to the top of the ridge where the **PG&E Compressor Station** sits. This road is **PRIVATE**, so return to I-40 to continue. On the way, note that the early route came down from the compressor ridge, and dipped in and out of washes as indicated on the detail map. This dead end road is washed out in several places and is **NOT recommended** for the average vacationer.

N E E D L E S

WB: Pass under I-40 at the US 95 JCT and follow **Broadway** into **NEEDLES**. At the Y with Front St, bear **LEFT** with **Broadway** thru downtown. Past J St, curve with **Broadway** across the RR tracks, then turn **LEFT** on **Needles Hwy**. Pass under I-40, then curve **RIGHT** and cross I-40. At the "**Y**," bear **LEFT** with **National Old Trails Hwy**, to **River Road Cutoff**. Turn **LEFT, then join I-40 WB.**

PHOTO OP! On the east side of **NEEDLES** is the oft-imaged sign for the vintage **66 Motel**. Nearby is the official "**Welcome Wagon**," a reconstructed freight wagon bearing the town name, the perfect place to pose. For cool desert architecture, check out the Ford Dealership and a nearby mission style-church along Broadway, among others. The imposing former **Masonic Temple** (with three Moroccan-arch doorways) at Broadway and F St dates back to 1929. It later became a theatre, and has been undergoing renovation.

SIDE TRIP: Front St carried **early 66** along the RR tracks, then did a square jog around the **El Garces**, the huge Harvey House being restored. **NEEDLES** has long been a railroad town, and train spotters will enjoy the view of the railroad yard along Front St. West of downtown on Front St, a small park features a few old railroad boxcars and a **Santa Fe caboose. SIDE TRIP:** The older route crossed under the railroad on **K St**, thru a narrow and low underpass (**8-foot vertical clearance**). It turned west on **Spruce** to N St (now Broadway) but you must jog up to Walnut to connect now. For eats, try the **Burger Hut** at Broadway and D, a long-time fast food haunt. **Fender's River Road Resort** at 3396 Needles Hwy (north of I-40 on the west side) is a small riverside motel/camp with a nice neon sign (plus a "license-plate tree"). Check them out for yourself.

EB: Take the **River Rd Cutoff Exit**, cross over I-40, then quickly turn **RIGHT** onto **National Old Trails Hwy**. Merge **AHEAD** onto **Needles Hwy**, and cross under I-40. Turn **RIGHT** on **Broadway**, then cross over the RR Tracks, and follow **Broadway** past J St and thru downtown **NEEDLES**, to the JCT with I-40. Cross under I-40 and follow **US 95** from town.

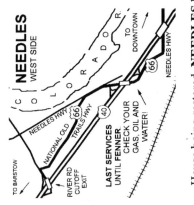

NEEDLES
WEST SIDE

LAST SERVICES
UNTIL FENNER
CHECK YOUR
GAS, OIL AND
WATER!

N E E D L E S

DOWNTOWN DETAIL

WB: Follow **I-40 WB** from **NEEDLES**. Take the next EXIT ("To Las Vegas") and follow **US 95** north. Just before the RR XING, turn **LEFT** on **Goffs Rd**. Cross the RR tracks into **GOFFS**. Curve around with **Goffs Rd**, and head to **FENNER**. Pass under I-40, and continue to the STOP at **National Trails Hwy**: turn **RIGHT** thru **ESSEX** and "**DANBY**" to the mountain pass at "**CADIZ SUMMIT**"

CAR GAME! Don't get lost in the vast **Mojave Desert**! Thankfully, there are **Route 66 Shields** painted on the pavement. Tell the kids to watch carefully for them, lest ye go astray! **First** to spot **each sign** gets 10 points…100 points wins!

Route 66 took two routes west of **NEEDLES**. The **Post 1931** road, now covered by **I-40**, charges boldly up and over the **South Pass** of the **Sacramento Mountains**. An 11-mile stretch connects **ESSEX** with the **Mountain Springs Rd Exit** of I-40. The **early** road follows the railroad over an easy-driving little-trafficked no-grade curve above the mountains. Just north of old 66 on Lanfair Rd in **GOFFS** is the restored 1914-era **Goffs Schoolhouse**. Inside the one-room school are exhibits of the cultural history of the **Mojave Desert**. Outside are displays of mining machinery, old vehicles, and two windmills. The complex is usually open by appointment only, but the outside areas and a historical marker can be viewed from the gate. Check the **Mojave Desert heritage & Cultural Association's** website: www.mdhca.org, or call (760) 733-4482.

SCAVENGER HUNT! Who was the architect for the Goffs school? _____

FENNER, at the I-40 Exit, has the only gas and food services for miles. **ESSEX** still has a post office and the remains of the **Wayside Market**, but the public well that once provided "**FREE WATER**" to thirsty US 66 is dry. A few miles west of town begins what I call the "**Route 66 Public Art Corridor**." From here to **AMBOY**, hundreds of travelers have written their **NAMES**, with rocks bottles and miscellany, on the dirt berm along the north side of 66. Be careful of heat stroke and snakes if you choose to add your own ("McClanahan" is just too darn long). Along the way, "**DANBY**" is the fenced-off site of an old station/cabins complex dating to the 1930s. More "**Public Art**" is up ahead at the ruins of "**CADIZ SUMMIT**".

EB: From the mountain pass at "**CADIZ SUMMIT**," proceed on **National Trails Hwy** thru "**DANBY**" and **ESSEX**. About 2 miles further, turn **LEFT** on **Goffs Rd** (BEFORE reaching the RR overpass). Cross under I-40, then pass thru **FENNER** to **GOFFS**. Curve around to cross the RR tracks, and follow **Goffs Rd** east to US 95. Turn **RIGHT**, then follow **US 95** to **I-40** and **NEEDLES**.

(see **MAP # 1** on CA **page-2**)

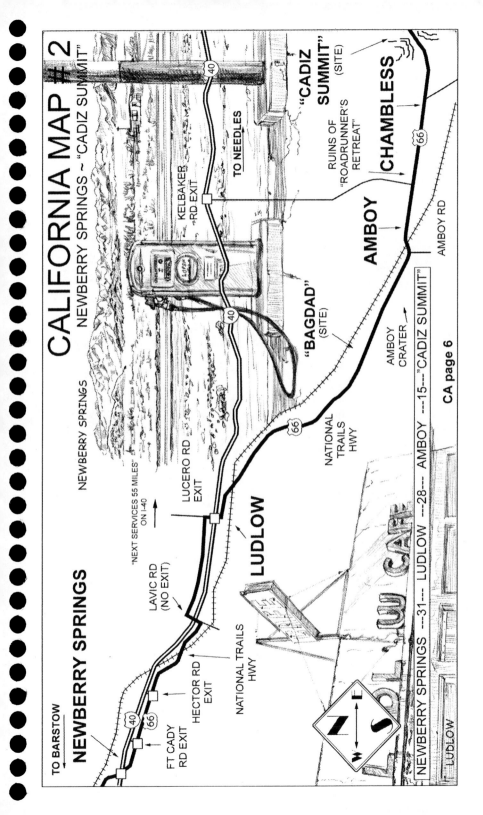

CALIFORNIA MAP #2
NEWBERRY SPRINGS ~ "CADIZ SUMMIT"

TO BARSTOW →

NEWBERRY SPRINGS

NEWBERRY SPRINGS

"NEXT SERVICES 55 MILES" ON I-40 →

LAVIC RD (NO EXIT)

FT CADY RD EXIT

HECTOR RD EXIT

NATIONAL TRAILS HWY

LUDLOW

LUCERO RD EXIT

KELBAKER RD EXIT

TO NEEDLES

"BAGDAD" (SITE)

"CADIZ SUMMIT" (SITE)

RUINS OF "ROADRUNNER'S RETREAT"

CHAMBLESS

AMBOY

AMBOY RD

AMBOY CRATER

NATIONAL TRAILS HWY

LULU CAFE

LUDLOW

N W S E

NEWBERRY SPRINGS ---31--- LUDLOW ---28--- AMBOY ---15---"CADIZ SUMMIT"

CA page 6

WB: Descend thru the pass at "**CADIZ SUMMIT**" and pass by **CHAMBLESS** and the Kelbaker Rd JCT, then continue thru **AMBOY**. Cross the RR tracks, then stay **AHEAD** with **National Trails Hwy** past the JCT of Amboy Rd, towards **LUDLOW**.

Look carefully on the south side of the road (between Danby and Cadiz Summit) for a restored roadside "rest area" pullout. Tablets describe the history and geology of the area. "**CADIZ SUMMIT**" was the site of a café/station/garage and cabins complex, perched just before the pass thru the **Marble Mountains**. Only low walls, foundations and the cinder-block ruin of the garage remain, all heavily encrusted with more "**public art**." I don't encourage graffiti, but this has been the tradition here for many years. This is an eerie place, feeling like a set for one of those post-apocalyptic movies, (the coming of I-40 WAS doomsday for businesses like these) with remains of old autos, campfires, assorted unidentifiable junk, evidence of "parties" and a lonely, pink cross on a nearby peak.

Down the hill, the now-shuttered **Chambless Market** once shaded its gas pumps with a huge awning, under which the temperature was still a balmy 122 degrees when my Dad had a tire fixed once. **GIANT ALERT!** West, in "**East Amboy**," are the well-preserved ruins of the **Roadrunner's Retreat Café and Station**, with its immense neon sign depicting a **GIANT ROADRUNNER**. Dodge filmed a commercial here in 1988, but for the Route 66 place that must hold the record for appearances in commercials, videos, and movies, check out **Roy's Café and Motel** in **AMBOY**, begun in 1927 by Roy Crowl and operated by the late **Buster Burris** for decades since 1938. In the spring of 2005, **Roy's** was purchased by the founder of Juan Pollo Restaurants, who is restoring the place to its past glory. Gasoline (at reasonable prices for the remote area) and restrooms are available. **Roy's** remains a "can't miss" site (you can't miss it because there is not much else in **AMBOY** except the Post Office!).

Backing up a bit, between the **Roadrunner** and **Roy's**, watch for more "**Public Art**" in the "**SHOE TREE**," a lonely scrub at the edge of a wash, liberally festooned with cast-off footwear of every type (including someone's red high heels). Bring your OWN contribution!

EB: Curve with **National Trails Hwy** to cross the tracks into **AMBOY** (avoid the turn onto "Amboy Rd"). Pass the JCT of Kelbaker Rd, and stay ahead thru **CHAMBLESS**, then climb the pass to "**CADIZ SUMMIT**".

WB: Cross the RR tracks, then follow **National Trails Hwy** into **LUDLOW**. At Lucero Rd, turn **RIGHT**, and cross under I-40 (see ALERT). Turn **LEFT** on the **North Frontage Rd** (National Trails Hwy). At **Lavic Road**, turn **LEFT** across I-40 (no exit) then **RIGHT** back on **National Trails Hwy**. Cross the RR tracks, then pass **Hector Rd** (exit) and **Ft Cady Rd** (exit) into **NEWBERRY SPRINGS**.

ALERT: The road between **LUDLOW** and **Ft Cady Rd** (near Newberry Springs) can be very **ROUGH** in places. An alternate is I-40. The road between **LUDLOW** and **AMBOY** is a **BIT** harsh in places (especially at bridges), but this latter section is a "must-drive" and NOT bad enough to skip, so just "drive 55" and enjoy. About 4 miles of road east of LUDLOW have been repaved.

Visible for miles near **AMBOY** is the cone of **Amboy Crater**, a US Dept of the Interior National **Landmark**, whose lava flow crosses Route 66 a bit west. A lone, scraggly tree north of '66 marks the site of **"Bagdad"**, a vanished "ghost town" once host to the "real" **Bagdad Café**, the inspiration for the cult-movie of the same name. Another long-gone site nearby is "**Siberia**," where only hard-to-spot foundations remain.

Many picturesque roadside ruins reside in **LUDLOW**, including the former **"Ludlow Café"** (east side on the north) and an old garage. Recommended for good grub is the **Ludlow Café/Coffee Shop**, with its genuine "Googie"-style coffee shop architecture and friendly staff. Check out the view from inside thru the angled stained glass window, and the display of old mining carts out front. **SCAVENGER HUNT!** What is the date on the "Ludlow Mining Co" cart?   Next door is the small **Ludlow Motel** (the Federation Guide once said: "no frills but very clean"). Check in at the Chevron (760) 733-4338. West of **Lavic Rd** '66 passes thru the lava runoff from **Pisgah Crater** and along the edge of the white expanse of **Troy Dry Lake**. There is actually water in **NEWBERRY SPRINGS**, named for the springs at the foot of the mountain that crowd '66 on the south. Also in town is a relic of the former **Whiting Bros Gas Station** chain (AKA "Dry Creek Station") preserved, complete with pumps, behind a fence. Another spot on your "must-stop" list, the current **Bagdad Café** of movie fame, (formerly the Sidewinder Café) draws a worldwide clientele for eats and stories: the defunct motel from the film is right next door (760) 257-3101.

EB: See ALERT. Follow **National Trails Hwy** past Ft Cady Rd (exit) and **Hector Rd** (exit). Cross the RR tracks, then, at **Lavic Rd** (no exit) turn **LEFT** and cross I-40. Turn **RIGHT** to continue on **National Trails Hwy** to Lucero Rd. Turn **RIGHT**, cross under I-40, then **LEFT** on National Trails Hwy into **LUDLOW**. Cross the tracks east of town and continue towards **AMBOY**.

(see MAP # 2 CA page 6)

CALIFORNIA MAP # 3

"CAJON JCT" ~ NEWBERRY SPRINGS

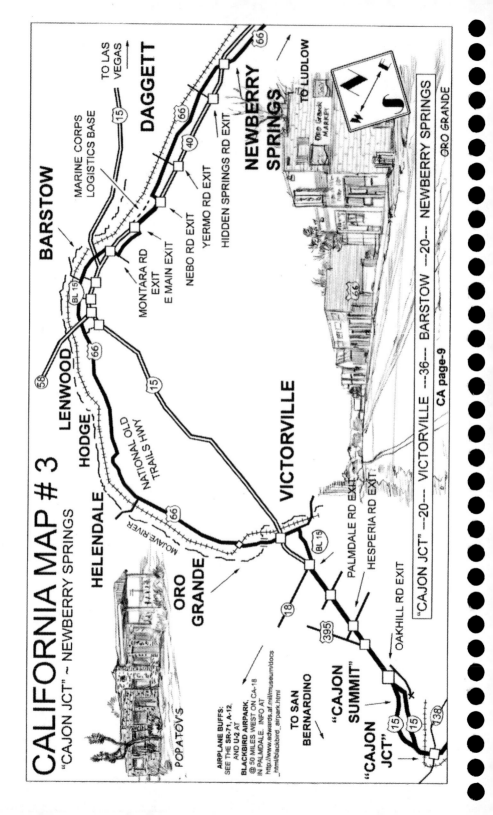

BARSTOW

DAGGETT

TO LAS VEGAS

MARINE CORPS LOGISTICS BASE

15

66

40

NEWBERRY SPRINGS

TO LUDLOW

Rio Grande MARKET

MONTARA RD EXIT

E MAIN EXIT

NEBO RD EXIT

YERMO RD EXIT

HIDDEN SPRINGS RD EXIT

BL 15

58

LENWOOD

66

HODGE,

15

NATIONAL OLD TRAILS HWY

VICTORVILLE

HELENDALE

66

MOJAVE RIVER

ORO GRANDE

BL 15

PALMDALE RD EXIT

HESPERIA RD EXIT

18

395

OAKHILL RD EXIT

POPATOV'S

AIRPLANE BUFFS:
SEE THE SR-71, A-12,
AND U-2 AT
BLACKBIRD AIRPARK.
@ 50 MILES WEST ON CA-18
IN PALMDALE. INFO AT
http://www.edwards.af.mil/museum/docs
_html/blackbird_airpark.html

TO SAN BERNARDINO

"CAJON SUMMIT"

"CAJON JCT"

15

15

138

"CAJON JCT" ---20--- VICTORVILLE ---20--- NEWBERRY SPRINGS

VICTORVILLE ---36--- BARSTOW ---20--- NEWBERRY SPRINGS

CA page-9

ORO GRANDE

WB: Take National Trails Hwy thru **NEWBERRY SPRINGS** and under I-40. Past **DAGGETT**, follow the curve **LEFT** onto **NEBO RD**, and join **I-40 WB**. Take the **NEXT EXIT** ("Marine Corps Logistic Base"). Turn **LEFT** under I-40, then **RIGHT** on the South Frontage Rd (E Main). At Montara Rd, turn **RIGHT**, cross under I-40 (avoid left lane) and follow **BL 15/Main St** into **BARSTOW**.

Just west of Minneola Rd is the angular canopy for the former **CA Inspection Station**, now a haven for miscellaneous "stuff." You also pass the defunct **Solar 2 power plant**, which once used multiple mirrors in experiments to convert solar heat into energy (solar energy is surely in abundance around here).

At the junction of Daggett Yermo Rd in nearby **DAGGETT** is a cute little building. This structure, with its sharply peaked triangular roof and lower sides that curve out and tuck under, was once a café. Next door is a garage building with the odd name "Mugwumps." **SIDE TRIP:** North of the railroad here (cross on **"Daggett Yermo Rd"**) are several photogenic old buildings on **Santa Fe St** (the older route), including the still-open **Desert Market**, an empty hotel, and the **Daggett Garage**, which according to its historic marker, dates back to the 1880s. **Scavenger Hunt!** What is the date on the front of the Desert Market? _____ I remember eating at the now closed Daggett Café as a kid on vacation, and innocently taking the waitresses' tip! (sorry!). **NOTE:** Daggett was NOT named for the robot dog in *Battlestar Galactica* (original version)! Likely the other way 'round.

DAGGETT YERMO RD · SANTA FE ST · **DAGGETT** · 66 · 40 · "A" ST · NEBO RD EXIT · HIDDEN SPRINGS RD

Old 66 bounces up and down thru a series of dips west of **DAGGETT**, but soon runs into an obstacle: the **Marine Corps Logistics Base**. Security concerns have closed the east gate, enforcing a brief return to I-40 at Nebo Rd, before following old 66 into **BARSTOW**.

EB drivers: It's a **VERY GOOD IDEA** to gas up before leaving **BARSTOW**.

BARSTOW EAST SIDE · NATIONAL TRAILS HWY · DOWNTOWN · TO LAS VEGAS · 15 · MAIN · MONTARA RD EXIT · E MAIN EXIT · E MAIN · MARINE CORPS LOGISTICS BASE · 40 · NEBO RD EXIT · TO DAGGETT

EB: Follow Main St east from **BARSTOW**. Cross under I-40 (in the **LEFT LANE**): turn **LEFT** at the stoplight onto **E Main St** (South Frontage Rd). At the **NEXT EXIT** (Marine Corps Logistics Base), join **I-40 EB**. Take the **NEXT EXIT** and turn **LEFT** under I-40 on Nebo Rd. Curve onto **National Trails Hwy** and along the tracks thru **DAGGETT**, then under I-40 into **NEWBERRY SPRINGS**.

CA page-10

WB: Follow **Main St/BL 15** across I-15 and thru downtown **BARSTOW**. Pass First St, then follow **BL 15/National Trails Hwy** west from town, past L St and under Hwy 58. Stay **AHEAD** with **National Old Trails Hwy** thru **LENWOOD**.

BARSTOW owes its existence to the railroads. In fact, the current location of downtown was dictated by the **Santa Fe** in 1925, when the whole town had to be moved to current Main St, so the railroad yards could be expanded. Left behind, north of the railroad yards, was the 1910s-era **Casa Del Desierto**, the former **Harvey House**. Here are a railroad museum and the **Route 66 Mother Road Museum**, a truly first class collection of displays and artifacts of road and region. Fri-Sun 11-4 or appt: http://www.route66museum.org/ or (760) 255-1890. **SIDE TRIP**: From Main, follow **First St** north over the railroad yard, then curve down and turn off **RIGHT** to the museum. **GIFT SHOP ALERT!**

A variety of vintage motels line Main. The **El Rancho** was built from railroad ties salvaged from the defunct Tonopah and Tidewater RR. My favorite is the **Route 66 Motel**, (195 W Main) with its great **NEON SIGN** and courtyard display of old cars, including a Nash piloted by a scary Howdy Doody puppet. Conditions in the 1920s-era stucco cabins are VERY simple and spartan (no phone), but usually clean and quiet (and cheap). The office is full of road-related clippings, photos and goodies. Their guest book lists bunches of Europeans, who enjoy the old-road ambiance, but you should check a room first if not used to older motels. They aren't perfect (760) 256-7866. Food choices in town range from fast food (including a humongous McDonalds with a railroad theme) to a classic **Bun Boy**. The **Palm Café** has a nifty neon sign, plus a palm tree or two. West of town, the Route 66 Apartments in **LENWOOD** are an "adaptive reuse" of a former motel. Rustic remnants of roadside businesses abound all along the way west to **VICTORVILLE**. I-15 was once 4-lane 66, but the 2-lane rules!

EB: From **LENWOOD**, follow **National Old Trails Hwy** under Hwy 58 and past L St onto **Main St** in **BARSTOW**. Follow Main **St/BL 15** thru downtown, then cross I-15 and curve down towards the Montara Rd underpass at I-40.

The directions are **EZ** on this stretch of '66, so is the driving: most of the 'Vegas-bound traffic stays on I-15. Enjoy the slower pace here, and if someone's in a hurry, just pull off and let them fly by, while you enjoy the many relics of Route 66 while cruising across sandy, sagebrush dotted hills, beside the **Santa Fe Railroad** and the tree-lined, mostly-dry course of the **Mojave River**.

It's easy to miss **HODGE**. Marking the town of **HELENDALE** is the **Helendale Market. GIANT ALERT!** Just west is a sign for **Newton's Towing**, bearing a ponderous **PARROT**, the mascot for the old **"Polly"** gasoline brand. The vintage gas prices shown **(REG: 18.9 ETHYL 21.9)** will make you cry for the good old days when "Polly" was "cheep!"

Among the numerous roadside remains is a stone residence adapted from the old **Sage Brush Inn**, about 1.5 miles west of **HELENDALE**. Here **Sagebrush Annie** ran a roadhouse that reportedly raised eyebrows and rumors. **FOLK ART ALERT!** Further west, between **Cardigan Rd** and **Turner Rd**, a fenced desert lot is now home to "**Bottle Tree Ranch**." Elmer Long's artistic creation, composed of countless colorful bottles arrayed on "trees," is intermixed with '66 signs and other artifacts (in the tradition of Miles Mahan). **SAD NEWS: "Popatov's Service Station**," yet another picturesque stone business that stood abandoned along 66, was recently demolished. At **Bryman Rd** is a billboard pointing out the turnoff to **Roy Rogers Double R Bar Ranch**, the late movie cowboy's hideaway, now owned by the Enriquez family (annual open house). www.Royrogersranch.com

East of **ORO GRANDE** is a tight squeeze thru a narrow **1925-era RR underpass** and then the Riverside Cement Plant (which explains all the parked cars coated with white dust). The old storefronts of "downtown" <u>ORO GRANDE</u> line one side of old 66. The **Mohawk Mini Mart** may be closed, but "**Club 66**" offers "happy hour" from a bright yellow building with an expressive rounded facade. Thirsty for antique shopping? Check out the false-fronted **Route 66 Antique Station**, complete with old fire truck and caboose.

WB: Follow National (Old) Trails Hwy from **ORO GRANDE**, across the **Mojave River**. Stay **AHEAD** under I-15 and enter **VICTORVILLE** on **D St** (BL 15). At the stoplight for **7th St**, turn **RIGHT**, thru downtown. Cross Mojave Dr and La Paz Dr on **7th St/BL 15**. At the HWY 18/Palmdale Rd Exit, cross the overpass and curve off right to join **I-15** southbound ("To San Bernardino").

A majestic 1930 **"Modified Baltimore Truss" Bridge** (you bridge fans know what that means, right?) carries '66 over the **Mojave River** (which actually shows some water here at times). Especially ornamental are those ornate guardrails along the curved approach to the steel bridge. Before you reach I-15, be sure to slow down for **Emma Jean's Holland Burger**, a well preserved (both inside and out) vintage truckstop café. Friendly staff (only a stranger once) and fine roadfood, PLUS: a scene from "Kill Bill" was filmed here. (760) 243-9938 (Hmmmmm…pancakes!)

VICTORVILLE is home to many relics of 66. You'll sure want to spend some time in the great **California Route 66 Museum** on D St between 5th and 6th St. On hand are many exhibits, a gallery, research library and travel info. **GIANTESS ALERT!** The museum has carefully preserved relics from the late **Miles Mahan's "Hulaville" Museum"** (AKA Mahan's Half Acre), a long-gone open air folk-art exhibit of artfully arranged bottles, strange and humorous signs, and a **15 foot tall Hula Dancer** (rescued from a restaurant). She now shimmies her grass skirt inside the museum, along with a model of Hulaville itself. Too bad for the Illinois **Giants** that she is clear on the other end of 66. If they met, giant romance could bloom. **GIFT SHOP ALERT!** Use the alley behind the museum and between 5th and 6th St to reach the parking lot. Http://www.califrt66museum.org or (760) 951-0436.

Check out the **New Corral Motel**, with its rampant neon stallion, before grabbing the superslab towards **SAN BERNARDINO**. If you like fast jets check **MAP # 3** for info on the **Blackbird Airpark** in **Palmdale**. It's not on 66, but 50 miles is an eyeblink in an **SR-71** at Mach 3!

EB: At the HWY 18/Palmdale Rd EXIT, follow the **BL 15/Historic 66** signs onto the **Frontage Rd**. Before the light, get in the **RIGHT LANE**, then **RIGHT** with **BL 15** and **7th St** into **VICTORVILLE**. Follow **7th St** past Mojave Dr into downtown. Turn **LEFT** on **D St** (BL 15). Stay **AHEAD** under I-15 on **D St/ National (Old) Trails Hwy**. Cross the **Mojave River** into **ORO GRANDE**.

There's **NO** avoiding **I-15** for a while. Take comfort in the fact that the freeway overlaps the path of **4-Lane 66** between **BARSTOW** and **CAJON PASS.**

At the JCT of US 395, the **Old Outpost Café** is an old-timer, as is the **Summit Inn**, just off the **Oakhill Rd Exit** at the top of **Cajon Pass.** Besides **"Ostrich Burgers,"** the Summit has lots of cool "stuff" to admire. An earlier incarnation of the **Summit Inn** was located on the original **Cajon Summit** of Route 66, which was higher than I-15, in between the WB and EB lanes. Intact sections of **1920s** and **'30s era pavement** survive near the summit (unreachable).

SIDE TRIP: Follow **Mariposa Rd** south from the **Summit Inn** to its end, where a sandy **Forest Rd** turns left uphill. If you **cautiously** drive this a short way to a turnout, you will be able to see the **1930s pavement** on the other side of the EB lanes, and a nice view of the railroad far below in the valley. Note: a **Forest Adventure Pass**, available at Circle K Stores, is required to park and hike anywhere in the forest.

UPPER CAJON PASS

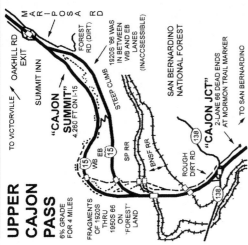

TO VICTORVILLE OAKHILL RD EXIT

M A R I P O S A   R D

SUMMIT INN

FOREST RD (DIRT)

"CAJON SUMMIT"
4,260 FT ON I-15

6% GRADE FOR 4 MILES

FRAGMENTS OF 1920S THRU 1950S 66 ON "FOREST" LAND

STEEP CLIMB

1920S 66 WAS IN BETWEEN WB AND EB LANES (INACCSESSIBLE)

SAN BERNARDINO NATIONAL FOREST

EB
WB
15
15

SP RR

BNSF RR

CAJON JCT DEAD ENDS AT MORMON TRAIL MARKER

"CAJON JCT"
2-LANE 66 DEAD ENDS AT MORMON TRAIL MARKER

ROUGH DIRT RD

138

138

TO SAN BERNARDINO

BACK on I-15, EB tourists can catch a glimpse of the **1920s road** from below, as a faint shelf that curves in and out along the hills above. This 1920s road, narrowly paved with chunks of rocks embedded in asphalt, was a terror, with sharp, blind curves, sheer drops and no shoulders. The **1930s 2-lane** that followed was, in turn replaced by **4-Lane 66**, and then **I-15's WB lanes.** Today the white knuckles are found on truckers careening downhill (or on drivers stuck behind slow trucks crawling up). Note the **"Runaway Truck Ramps"** on the downgrade stretch, and watch your speed. **Scattered fragments of 1920s-1950s '66** lie on "Forest" land, as shown on the detail map. The dirt road in is rough and sandy. Hours would be required to scout all these bits thru the brush (**NOT advised**).

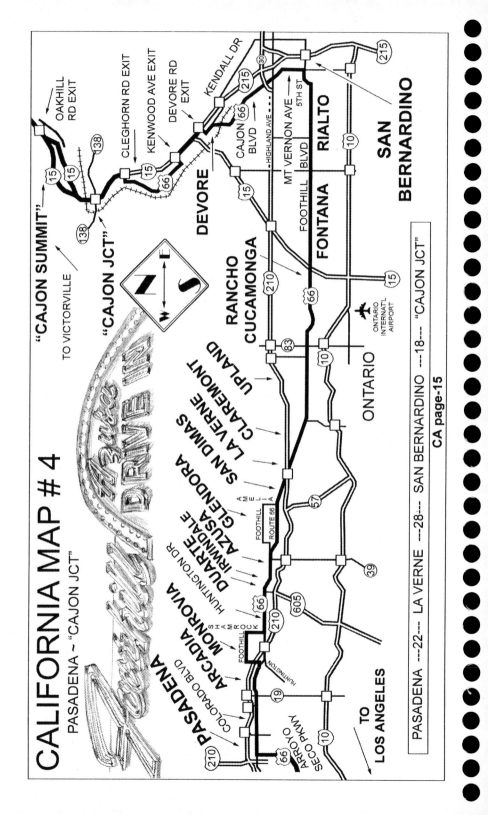

CALIFORNIA MAP # 4

PASADENA ~ "CAJON JCT"

"CAJON SUMMIT"

TO VICTORVILLE

"CAJON JCT"

OAKHILL RD EXIT

CLEGHORN RD EXIT

KENWOOD AVE EXIT

DEVORE RD EXIT

KENDALL DR

DEVORE

CAJON BLVD

HIGHLAND AVE

MT VERNON AVE

5TH ST

RIALTO

FOOTHILL BLVD

FONTANA

SAN BERNARDINO

RANCHO CUCAMONGA

UPLAND

CLAREMONT

LA VERNE

SAN DIMAS

GLENDORA

AZUSA

IRWINDALE

DUARTE

HUNTINGTON DR

ARCADIA

MONROVIA

SHAMROCK

FOOTHILL

HUNTINGTON

COLORADO BLVD

PASADENA

ARROYO SECO PKWY

TO LOS ANGELES

ONTARIO

ONTARIO INTERNATL AIRPORT

AMELIA

FOOTHILL

ROUTE 66

PASADENA ---22--- LA VERNE ---28--- SAN BERNARDINO ---18--- "CAJON JCT"

CA page-15

WB: Follow **I-15** south from "**CAJON JCT**" (at Hwy 138) to the **Cleghorn Rd EXIT**. At the foot of the off ramp, turn **RIGHT** and curve **LEFT** onto **Cajon Blvd** southbound. About 6 miles further, at the barricades, turn **LEFT** onto **Kenwood Ave** to **I-15**.

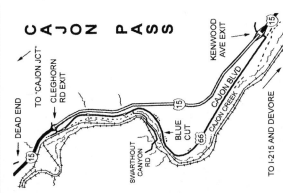

SIDE TRIP: Long before paved roads and railroads, this pass was an important corridor, including an early toll road and the **Mormon Trail**. On the east side of "**CAJON JCT**," turn south on the frontage road (2-lane 66), which dead ends at the **Mormon Trail Marker** (actually a copy of an earlier one).

The **Cleghorn Rd EXIT** leads to a great stretch of 66 to drive. **Cajon Blvd** ends just to the north, but south, the former 4-Lane winds its way along **Cajon Creek**, thru the rugged topography created by the infamous **San Andreas Fault**. Some classic old bridges cross normally dry gulches along the way. **SCAVENGER HUNT!** What is the **DATE** on the old bridge just south of **Cleghorn Rd?** _____

Swarthout Canyon Rd was the site of an old **Migrant Workers Camp** during the **Depression**. Further along, the **Blue Cut** is named for the blue-gray colored rock that Cajon Creek cuts thru. The immediate area of **Blue Cut** includes a wide, tree-shaded spot on the creek bank, with a historical marker. This was **ONCE** a great place to picnic or watch trains. Unfortunately, it is now at times a haven for "illicit activity." I wouldn't worry, but I do suggest admiring the rugged scenery as you drive on past this **short** stretch. To the south along the curve, a stone wall guards the drop to the creek, while the former EB lanes of 4-Lane 66 crowd the rock-strewn hillsides. Many remnants of 1920s and '30s roadway lie in the flats, long abandoned due to floods. Some are on private property, others are buried or hard to get to (or out of...I got stuck once). Enjoy Ma Nature while you can, as you are briefly forced to join the freeway again, headed towards **SAN BERNARDINO**.

EB: Take the **Kenwood Ave EXIT** from **I-15**. Turn **LEFT**, cross under **I-15**, then turn **RIGHT** on **Cajon Blvd**. After about 6 miles, veer **RIGHT** from Cajon Blvd to pass under I-15 at the **Cleghorn Rd EXIT**, and join **I-15 NB** thru "**CAJON JCT**" (at Hwy 138).

CA page-16

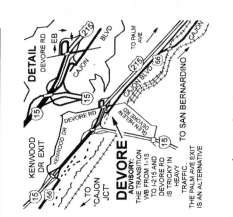

WB: Join **I-15 SB**. **QUICKLY** move to the **middle/left lanes** (signs: "Riverside/San Bernardino I-215"). **I-15** splits right: **BEAR LEFT** with **I-215**, but **QUICKLY** take the **NEXT** off ramp (signs: "Devore Rd/Glen Helen Park Right Lane" and "Historic 66 Next Right"). Once the offramp merges with the other road **QUICKLY** get in the **RIGHT LANE** and **EXIT** again to **DEVORE**. Turn **LEFT** on **Cajon Blvd**, and cross Devore Rd. At the "**Y**" with Kendall Dr, **BEAR RIGHT** with Cajon Blvd under the RR tracks. Pass under the "Highland Ave" overpass, then **STOP**, carefully curve **RIGHT** to the Mt Vernon stoplight, and turn **LEFT** into **SAN BERNARDINO**.

Cajon Blvd continues in **DEVORE**, with plenty of old businesses to watch for. A mile south of the RR overpass, look back north towards the silos. The narrow concrete slab extending out of the curve is the original 66, paved well before 1926. This crossed the RR at grade, connecting to **Kendall Drive** before proceeding. This is possibly the only example of this type of Route 66 pavement left! North of **DEVORE**, more period road exists, but it is rock and asphalt.

In **SAN BERNARDINO**, **Mt Vernon Ave** is home to several vintage motels, but these were bypassed long ago, and cater now to "long term" trade. This urban street bears many reminders of old cafes, gas stations and garages. The **Mitla Café**, circa 1937, is a great Mexican food place. As you head south on **Mt Vernon**, watch as the **Santa Fe Smokestack** looms ever larger ahead.

EB: Take **MT VERNON Ave NB**. Past 19th St, get in the **RIGHT** lane. Mt Vernon curves left: **STAY AHEAD (AVOID Mt Vernon)**, then curve under Highland Ave onto **Cajon Blvd**, along the RR tracks. Pass under the RR tracks. At **Glen Helen/ Devore Rd** in **DEVORE**, turn **RIGHT**. Cross over I-215, and turn **RIGHT** immediately. Loop back northward, then **AVOID** the right-turn lane and join **I-215 NB**. I-215 merges with **I-15**. At the "**Kenwood Ave Next Right**" sign, merge into the **RIGHT-Hand** lane. **EXIT** at Kenwood Ave.

WB: In **SAN BERNARDINO**, follow Mt Vernon Ave across 6th St, then get in the **RIGHT** lane, and turn **RIGHT** on **5th St/ CA HWY 66**. Follow **5th St** as it curves **LEFT** to 4th St, straightening out to become **Foothill Blvd** westbound. Follow **Foothill Blvd** thru **RIALTO** and **FONTANA** into **RANCHO CUCAMONGA**, crossing under I-15. Stay **AHEAD** on **Foothill Blvd**.

Fast food fans should investigate the **McDonalds Museum** north of downtown **SAN BERNARDINO** on E St at 14th, once the site of the world's first McDonalds, begun in 1948. From here, the **McDonald Brothers** branched out and evolved their **"SPEEDEE SERVICE SYSTEM"** and the Golden Arches, years before Ray Kroc bought out the fledgling chain. On display are artifacts and collectibles from the early days, plus Route 66 items (909) 885-6324. A **Route 66 Cruisin Hall of Fame Museum** is **planned** for downtown: watch http://www.route-66.org for updates. Also downtown on 4th is the 1928 era **California Theatre**. City INFO: (909) 885-7515.

Located just east of the **RIALTO** city limits are the concrete Tee Pees of the classic **Wig Wam Motel**. This beloved icon has recently come under the care of owners dedicated to preservation. Renovated and refreshed, the Wigwams, one of two such motels on 66, and the last of the chain built, are a testament to the re-emergence of Route 66 (909) 875-3005. **Scavenger Hunt!** What is the shape of the **El Camino Real** marker on the south at Riverside and Foothill in **RIALTO**? _____ City INFO: (909)875-5364.

Foothill Blvd west from **RIALTO** is a mix of shopping centers and older buildings that once were garages, gas stations and cafes. Many of the old motels have lost their neon, but some still show a bit of **SO-CAL** charm, with quaint names and prime examples of bungalow courts. This portion is also **CA State Hwy 66**, although most signs are of the "Historic 66" variety. **GIANT ALERT! FONTANA** is home to **"Bono's Historic Orange,"** perhaps the last of the **Giant Orange Stands** that once lined **CALIFORNIA** roads. **Bono's Restaurant** itself is an icon dating from 1935, at 15395 Foothill Blvd. City INFO: (909) 822-4433.

EB: In **RANCHO CUCAMONGA**, follow **Foothill Blvd** under I-15, and thru **FONTANA** and **RIALTO** into **SAN BERNARDINO**. Where 4th St continues ahead out of Foothill, curve around **LEFT** onto **5th** St. Past Roberts St, turn **LEFT** on **Mt Vernon Ave**.

CA page-18

WB: Follow **Foothill Blvd** west thru <u>**RANCHO CUCAMONGA**</u>, <u>**UPLAND**</u> and <u>**CLAREMONT**</u>. (avoid turn-only lanes)

As you motor east or west on **Foothill**, keep an eye open for the many instances of the **Route 66 Shield** proudly displayed on businesses along the entire stretch. There's plenty of cool Route 66 stuff to see and eat in <u>**RANCHO CUCAMONGA**</u>. The historic **Sycamore Inn** (dating way back to 1848) at 8318 Foothill Blvd was originally a stagecoach stop. Down the road at 8189 Foothill is **the Magic Lamp Inn**, a 1957 restaurant with ornate "Arabian Nights" décor. **GIANT ALERT!** The neon sign depicting a **Giant Aladdin's Lamp** will rub you the right way! City INFO: (909) 987-1012.

GIANT ALERT 2: Between Center Ave and Hermosa St, watch out for the toothsome tin terrors at **Route 66 Memories**, an antique shop whose yard is crammed cheek to toothy jowl with fantastic metal sculptures of **DINOSAURS**. Ranging from a rowdy T-Rex and Triceratops to a placid Apatosaurus (Brontosaurus to you cave men), these metal monsters are some of the most lively and "personable" of any I've seen. Takes me back to my dino-fanatic childhood. **GIFT SHOP ALERT!** This area was once home to orange groves and vineyards. Two of the former wineries, the **Virginia Dare Winery** (at Haven Ave), and the **Thomas Vineyards** (at Vineyard Ave) have been adapted for use as shops.

<u>**UPLAND**</u> has revitalized its section of '66, with retro-décor added to spice up the strip malls, as in the Route 66 Shopping Center. **GIANT ALERT #3 and 4!** Look for the **Giant Route 66 Coffee Cup** on the north, just west of Euclid. Also, at Euclid and Foothill, is the **Madonna of the Trail** statue, depicting a rugged pioneer mother and children, one of 12 across the country (Albuquerque also) honoring those sturdy women who had to listen to months of "How much longer?" and "When will we be there?" from the backseat of the covered wagon. In a similar "go-west" vein are the Buffalo Burgers at the **Buffalo Inn** (circa 1929) at 1814 W Foothill. City INFO: (909) 931-4108.

The tree-lined drive thru <u>**CLAREMONT**</u> is green and soothing. **Wolfe's Market**, run for 4 generations by the Wolfe family, began in 1917, moving to its current spot, on the south side of Foothill, in 1935. City INFO: (909)624-1681.

EB: Follow **Foothill Blvd** thru <u>**CLAREMONT**</u>, <u>**UPLAND**</u> and <u>**RANCHO CUCAMONGA**</u>. (avoid turn-only lanes)

WB: Take **Foothill Blvd** thru **LA VERNE**; pass under I-210 (middle lane) and continue thru **SAN DIMAS** to **GLENDORA**. Foothill becomes "**Route 66**" (formerly Alosta). Past Citrus, follow the curve right, then straighten out WB on **Foothill Blvd** again, thru **AZUSA**.

Many newer places are adopting an old look along **Foothill**, like the Retro-styled Shell station east of I-210 in **LA VERNE**." **La Paloma Café**, with its long, mission style facade and neon sign, is no latecomer. The **Foothill 66 Gas Station** at Gary is usually priced reasonably. East of Amelia, at the edge of **SAN DIMAS**, is **Pinnacle Peak Steakhouse**, with a big bovine on the roof and cut-off ties on the walls.

GLENDORA offers an **OPTION**: See the **detail map** for the older alignment via Amelia Ave, Foothill Blvd and Citrus Ave. Amelia is a beautiful palm-tree lined street, while Foothill passes thru lushly landscaped walled residential estates. Tall slender palms compete with short trees trimmed into rounded "gumdrop" shape. Watch for the **Altadena Dairy** and **Tommy's Burgers** along this 5-mile section.

The **tour route** has more 66-related sites, as many businesses show 66 pride in their names or signs. Among them are Route 66 Plaza and Route 66 Mural. A tuxedo store even has a neon 66 shield. Between Glendora and Pasadena Streets, **Alosta Ace Hardware** has a nifty **Route 66 Mural** on their west wall. **Flappy Jack's Pancake House** at 640 W Route 66 is decorated in '66 style, while the **Golden Spur** has a "kickin" neon sign in the form of a **BIG BOOT (GIANT ALERT)**!

AZUSA boasts the photogenic tile and stucco architecture of their 1932 **City Hall and Auditorium**. At the junction of Foothill and "Route 66" is the site of the old **Foothill Drive-In Theatre**. The walls surrounding this former fresh-air cinema are down, the land destined to house facilities of Azusa Pacific University. The **neon marquee**, however, is reportedly slated for preservation.

EB: Follow **Foothill Blvd** east thru **AZUSA**. Follow the curve **RIGHT** onto "**Route 66**" (formerly Alosta) into **GLENDORA**. Stay ahead as **Foothill Blvd** resumes thru **SAN DIMAS** and **LA VERNE**. Cross under I-210; stay ahead with **Foothill** thru **CLAREMONT**.

WB: Follow **Foothill Blvd** west from **AZUSA** thru **IRWINDALE** (Foothill becomes **Huntington Dr**) and **DUARTE** into **MONROVIA**. Cross **Mountain Ave**, then turn **RIGHT** on **Shamrock Ave**. Turn **LEFT** on **Foothill Blvd**. Cross **First Ave**, then turn **LEFT** on **Santa Anita Ave**. Cross under I-210, then turn **RIGHT** on **Colorado Blvd**. Curve uphill and join **Colorado Place** WB at the light. Follow the curve onto **Colorado St**, and head into **PASADENA**.

West of **IRWINDALE** (the San Gabriel "River" runs thru it) is **DUARTE**, home to the **Justice Brothers Racing Museum** at 2734 E Huntington Dr, west of Las Lomas (9-5 weekdays: FREE admission). For the racing and old car buff, the museum features a variety of vintage racing vehicles, plus memorabilia and miscellany. The cars are so colorful the kids will love them. **GIFT SHOP ALERT**! (800) 835-8784. **DUARTE** also hosts an annual **Route 66 Parade**. Info: (626) 357-3333. **Huntington Drive** here is landscaped with "bell-shaped" trees, and the center median bears replica mission bells that serve as "City of Duarte" markers.

A jewel of an antique gas station survives in **MONROVIA** on **Shamrock** at Royal Oaks, in front of **Dale's Garage**. Vintage gas pumps and classic style in an attractive setting make this a real **PHOTO OP!** Scenes from a movie about the Lindberg kidnapping were filmed here. Up on **Foothill Blvd**, that is **NOT** a lost "Aztec temple" at Magnolia Ave, but the unique **1925 Aztec Hotel**, designed in "Aztec ruins" style. **OPTION:** The later route along **Huntington Dr** has its share of sites, including the **Pottery Ranch**, a long-time outlet with a vintage neon sign. At the corner of Santa Anita and Huntington in **ARCADIA** is an example of California drive-in style. Currently a Denny's, this exotic structure, with its folded plate roof and central tower complete with windmill, was the last of the Van de Kamp's restaurant chain on '66. **ARCADIA** is most famous for the **Santa Anita Park and Racetrack.**

EB: Take **Colorado St** east from **PASADENA**. Curve onto **Colorado Place**. Pass **Harvard Dr**, then, at the light, veer **LEFT** onto **Colorado Blvd**. Past the RR underpass, turn **LEFT** on **Santa Anita Ave**. Cross under I-210 (AVOID right lane), then turn **RIGHT** on **Foothill Blvd**. Cross **California Ave**, then turn **RIGHT** on **Shamrock**. At **Huntington Dr**, turn **LEFT**, thru **DUARTE**, **IRWINDALE** (becomes **Foothill Blvd**) and into **AZUSA**.

(see MAP # 4 CA page-15)

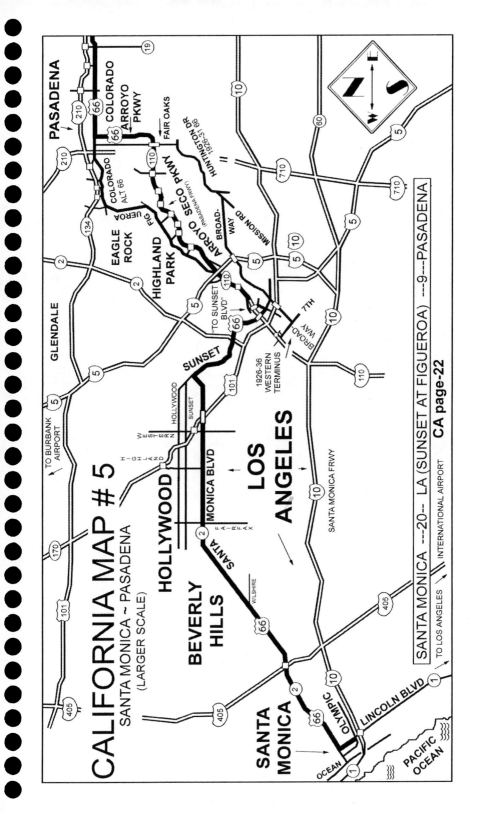

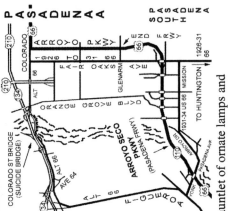

If you've watched the annual **Tournament of Roses Parade**, you've seen the flower-flocked floats "float" right down '66 along **PASADENA**'s stretch of **Colorado Blvd**. This attractive city is chock-full of preserved architectural styles and varieties of popular culture, in a typical SO-CAL mix. "National Register of Historic Places" listings abound. On the "Pop" side, the **"Out of the Closet"** thrift store has a great neon sign (and **CLEVER NAME**), as does **Whistle Stop Trains**, while **Cameron Seafood** has a **big neon fish**. Old motels abound, of which the **Saga Motor Lodge** comes recommended as a well-preserved 1950s motel (800) 793-7242. A car dealership on Colorado retains an ornate facade of the days when **Packard** was the luxury king. Local Info: (626) 795-3355.

SIDE TRIPS: **Route 66** followed many routes to reach **LA** from **PASADENA**. Scattered on these alignments are some choice cultural sites. Check out the majestically curved 1913 **Colorado St Bridge** (AKA: **"Suicide Bridge"**) that spans the **Arroyo Seco** (dry river). Follow **Colorado** west from the **Arroyo Parkway** intersection, across the freeway. Once thru the Orange Grove Blvd stoplight, **AVOID** the Hwy 134 W onramp by bearing **LEFT** with Colorado Blvd to pass between the gauntlet of ornate lamps and guardrails that line the bridge. Ahead is the **"ALT" 66** route via Figueroa, which later joins the **Arroyo Seco Parkway** past Ave 26 in **HIGHLAND PARK**. On this route is the 1924 **Highland Theatre**; nearby are the **Southwest** and **Heritage Square Museums**. Local info: (323) 246-0920. On **1926-'31 US 66**, along **Fair Oaks Ave** (south of Arroyo Seco Pkwy at Mission St) is the 1915-era **Fair Oaks Pharmacy** (as seen on TV)! The **1925 Rialto Theatre** is nearby. At **Fairview** and **Mission St** (on the **1931-34 Route**) is the former **El Centro Market**, the first **Drive-Thru** market, now renovated. The original **1926-'31 Route** continued south on Fair Oaks to Huntington, then joined **Mission Rd** briefly to pick up **Broadway** all the way to 7th St in downtown **LA**: the original **Western Terminus** of **Route 66** (before it moved to **SANTA MONICA** in 1936). See **Piotrowski**'s book for more!

WB: Stay in the **CENTER** lane of the **Parkway** until past the I-5 interchange. Cross under the College St Overpass, then take **EXIT 24B** right ("To Sunset Blvd"). At the STOP, angle **LEFT** onto **Figueroa Terrace** (follow the signs for "Sunset Blvd"). Turn **LEFT** onto **Alpine St** and cross the freeway, then bear **RIGHT** onto **Figueroa**, and **RIGHT again** onto **Sunset Blvd** in <u>**LOS ANGELES**</u>.

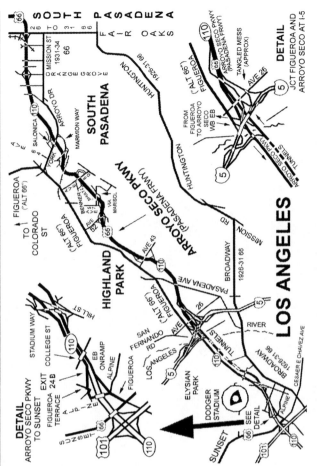

The scenic and historic 1940 **Arroyo Seco Parkway** (AKA **Pasadena Freeway** and CA Hwy 110), the first "freeway" west of the Mississippi, is infamous for traffic. Built as a landscaped parkway intended for slower speeds, the Arroyo's curves and scanty exit ramps cause back ups and wrecks at modern velocity. The Arroyo, for all its flaws, is well worth driving, and the most direct way to <u>LA</u>. Thanks to road warrior **Scott Piotrowski**, here's the straight scoop on surviving the Arroyo. **NOTE**: This is **LA**: there will **ALWAYS** be traffic!!! The **best** time to take the **Arroyo Seco Pkwy** to <u>LA</u> is the **afternoon.** Try to drive from <u>LA</u> to <u>**PASADENA**</u> from about 10 am to 1 pm. Try to keep up to 55 mph, but slow down for the big curves. The **EB lanes**, thru the four ornate **TUNNELS**, are the most scenic option. Efforts are underway to restore the Parkway to its 1930s appearance. **OPTIONS**: The map shows alternate routes of '66 via Figueroa or Huntington.

EB: Turn **LEFT** on **Figueroa** from Sunset. Stay **AHEAD** in the **RIGHT LANE** to join the **Arroyo Seco Pkwy** (Pasadena Fwy). Stay in the far **RIGHT** lane thru the 4 tunnels, then move to the **CENTER LANE** past the last tunnel, and stay there to <u>**PASADENA**</u>.

WB: Follow **Sunset Blvd** west from Figueroa in **LOS ANGELES**. Cross the 110 Freeway. Cross Hyperion Ave. Past Sanborne, get in the **LEFT** lane, and turn **LEFT** at the next chance onto **Manzanita** (also signed **Santa Monica Blvd**. A difficult turn if traffic is heavy). At the STOP, turn right with **Santa Monica Blvd** (AKA: CA Hwy 2). Continue thru **WEST HOLLYWOOD** to **BEVERLY HILLS**.

ADVISORY: Santa Monica Blvd from Sunset thru **WEST HOLLYWOOD** is a congested city strip, with heavy traffic. **Drive Carefully!**

There is just TOO much to do in the **LA** area. To start mining info, check the Los Angeles Chamber at www.lachamber.org or (213)580-7500. From Sunset Blvd, sports fans can take Elysian Park Ave to visit **Dodger Stadium**. **GIANT ALERT**! Nearby, **Sunset** cruises the colorful **ECHO PARK** area, where another sport is enacted ad infinitum atop **Jensen's Recreation Center**, as the enormous animated bowler on the antique sign hurls strike after illuminated strike. For a bite, try **Millie's** "Home of Good Food" since 1926, on the south side, just east of Maltman St.

LA conjures up images of neon-lined streets, and some still shine. To shed more light on the subject, visit the **Museum of Neon Art** at 501 W Olympic. INFO: www.neonmona.org. Car buffs may wish to visit the **Petersen Automotive Museum** at 6060 Wilshire Blvd (at Fairfax: take Wilshire Blvd east from 66 in Beverly Hills). Three floors of auto history are portrayed in "streetscapes." www.petersen.org

HOLLYWOOD

DETAIL

BEVERLY HILLS

LOS ANGELES

TO PASADENA
(SEE CA page-24)

From **Santa Monica Blvd**, the famed **Hollywood Sign** is visible at times on the north. Also north of 66 runs **Hollywood Blvd** and the continuation of **Sunset**. Up here, you'll find the famous corner of **Hollywood and Vine**, plus sites like **Grauman's Chinese Theatre**, and the **Egyptian Theatre**. INFO: http://www.hollywoodchamber.net/ (323) 469-8311 for these and other movie-related locales. On old 66 in **W HOLLYWOOD**, the **last route** of US 66 ('53 to '64). Speaking of **HOLLYWOOD**, **Barney's Beanery** (third oldest eatery in LA). Speaking of **HOLLYWOOD**, the **last route** of US 66 ('53 to '64) used the **Hollywood (101) Freeway** from the Arroyo Seco Pkwy up to Santa Monica Blvd.

EB: Take **Santa Monica Blvd** thru **WEST HOLLYWOOD**. Cross 101 Frwy. Continue on **Santa Monica Blvd** past Hoover St, then curve **RIGHT** past Manzanita, and merge **AHEAD** thru the Sanborne light onto **Sunset Blvd**. Continue past the 110 Frwy to **Figueroa**.

WB: Continue on **Santa Monica Blvd** (Hwy 2) thru **BEVERLY HILLS** and **WEST LA**. Cross under I-405 into **SANTA MONICA**. Cross 9th St, then get in the **LEFT** lane, and turn **LEFT** on **Lincoln Blvd** ("To I-10") to **Olympic Blvd**, the **END**" of US 66.

Check out the **BEVERLY HILLS** sign at Doheny Dr. Of architectural note are the **Art Moderne Police Station** and the domed **City Hall**. **$$$ ALERT**! The route crosses high-zoot **Rodeo Drive** along the way. At Wilshire, **Trader Vic's** has a long history of Polynesian ambiance. Approaching **SANTA MONICA**, scattered signs of past Route 66 life begin to emerge from the urbanscape.

WB Drivers: Congratulations on being true **Road Warriors**! After touring **SANTA MONICA**, use **I-10** to access the freeway system and begin your homeward trip. **Thanks** for driving **Route 66**! Come back again, real soon! **AIRPORTS: Los Angeles International** is south of **SANTA MONICA** (via I-405 to Century Blvd, or Lincoln Blvd/Hwy 1 to Sepulveda). Other airports are at **SANTA MONICA** (via I-405 to Century Blvd, or Lincoln Blvd/Hwy 1 to Sepulveda). Other airports are at **Burbank** (via I-5 north) or **Ontario** (off I-10 just west of I-15, near **SAN BERNARDINO**).

SIDE TRIPS: The "**Official**" end of 66 at **Olympic** is rather unsatisfying. For a **better finish** to your voyage, visit the "**Unofficial**" end of '66, the **Will Rogers Hwy Marker**, in **Palisades Park**, at the "**T**" intersection of **Santa Monica Blvd** and **Ocean**. The 14-block park tops a sheer bluff, lined with exotic palms and shrubs, overlooking the **Pacific Ocean**. The marker is a great **PHOTO OP** to mark the end of your trip, as is the neon **Santa Monica Yacht Harbor Sign**, the gateway to the attractions of the **Santa Monica Pier**, at **Colorado and Ocean**. The long row of tall hotels that line the inland side of Ocean mirror the line of skyscrapers that mark the east end of 66. Some of these, like the **Georgian Hotel** with its light blue walls and ornate trim, give the street an appropriate "**ocean**" feel. **RV ALERT**! The streets here are rather tight and crowded. Might be time to use the tow car (or park and walk). City INFO: www.smchamber.com or (310) 393-9825.

EB: To **BEGIN** at the **Western Terminus**: Take **I-10** (**Santa Monica Freeway**) west almost to its end and **EXIT** onto Olympic Blvd, to Lincoln Blvd, in **SANTA MONICA** ('66 "began" here at the JCT of Hwys 1 and 2). Turn **RIGHT** on Lincoln Blvd and continue to **Santa Monica Blvd** (**Hwy 2**): turn **RIGHT**. Continue thru **WEST LA** and **BEVERLY HILLS** into **WEST HOLLYWOOD**.

(see CA INTRO CA page-1)   CA page-26   (see MAP #5 CA page-22)

SANTA
MONICA

P A L I S A D E S   P A R K

SANTA
MONICA
PIER

OCEAN

OCEAN AVE

OLYMPIC BLVD

LINCOLN BLVD

SANTA MONICA BLVD

COLORADO

TO LA

RECOMMENDED READING

These are books that have proven helpful to me in my research, or that will enhance your Route 66 experience. Where possible, I have included the author's website for the self-published books so that you may order directly from them. (asterisked books may be purchased from the Federation website). Look on the web for reviews and further information.

GUIDEBOOKS: IL: *Traveling the New, Historic Route 66 in Illinois** by John Weiss www.il66authority.com

MO: *Missouri US 66 Tour Book* by C.H. (Skip) Curtis www.birthplaceofroute66.com/bk2.html

OK: *Oklahoma Route 66** by Jim Ross /Ghost Town Press www.66maps.com

Official Oklahoma Route 66 Association Trip Guide www.oklahomaroute66.com

NM: *New Mexico Route 66 on Tour. Legendary Architecture from Glenrio to Gallup* by Don J. Unser Museum of New Mexico Press

AZ: *Route 66 Across Arizona: A Comprehensive Two-Way Guide for Touring Route 66* by Richard K. and Sherry G. Mangum Hexagon Press

CA: *Guide To Historic Route 66 in California* by Vivian Davies and Darin Kuna CA Historic Route 66 Association www.wemweb.com/chr66a/catalog.html

LA AREA: *Finding the End of the Mother Road: Route 66 in Los Angeles County** by Scott Piotrowski/ Route 66 Productions www.66productions.com

ENTIRE ROUTE: *Route 66 Dining & and Lodging Guide** An indispensable guide. GET ONE! National Historic Route 66 Federation www.national66.org

Route 66 Map Series* 8 maps of the whole route, by Jim Ross and Jerry McClanahan Ghost Town Press www.66maps.com (also publisher of the *Bones of the Old Road* video, featuring Jim and Jerry)

Route 66 Adventure Handbook* Drew Knowles Interesting places and attractions along 66 www.ExitHere.net

Route 66 for Kids A small, hand-produced booklet with good suggestions for kids by Emily Priddy www.kidson66.com

The Complete Route 66 Guidebook and Atlas by Bob Moore and Rich Cunningham. Two book set. Not for beginners.

ADDITIONAL READING: *Route 66: The Mother Road** by Michael Wallis (75th Anniversary Edition)

The Federation News Magazine of the National Historic Route 66 Federation. Jerry has written many articles for them (and will continue).

Images of 66 Vols #1 and #2 by David Wickline. Great albums of modern photos along the Route.

Route 66 Remembered by Michael Karl Witzel

Route 66: The Empires of Amusement and Route 66: The Romance of the West by Thomas Arthur Repp Mock Turtle Press

American Road Magazine My Route 66 Kicks dept.
www.americanroadmagazine.com

Route 66 Magazine www.route66magazine.com Check for back issues with Jerry's articles, from 1994 thru 1999. Some featured his ROOTIE ™ cartoon.

WEBSITES: There are many websites devoted to Route 66. Try an internet search and see what comes up (wow). The sites below are helpful:

www.mcjerry66.com Jerry McClanahan's Route 66 gallery website and home to the EZ66 GUIDE updates.

www.national66.org National Historic Route 66 Federation. Online store, links to other Route 66 websites and more.

www.route66photographs.com Shellee Graham's and Jim Ross' exceptional roadside images

www.route66egroup.info/index.html Yahoo Route 66 E- Group. Lots of timely 66 info, up to the minute news, links and chit chat.

www.route66guidebooks.com A site that lists all the Route 66 guidebooks currently in print.

ROUTE 66 ASSOCIATIONS: Great resources for info on Route 66 and events. Dedicated people, all. Consider joining one or more!

Route 66 Association of Illinois www.il66assoc.org

Route 66 Association of Missouri www.missouri66.org
Route 66 Association of Kansas (Riverton) Email: route66@kans.com
Kansas Historic Route 66 Association (Baxter Springs) www.ksrt66association.us

Oklahoma Route 66 Association oklahomaroute66.com

The Old Route 66 Association of Texas
www.barbwiremuseum.com/TexasRoute66.htm

New Mexico Route 66 Association www.rt66nm.org

Historic Route 66 Association of Arizona www.azrt66.com

The California Route 66 Preservation Foundation www.cart66pf.org

California Historic Route 66 Association www.route66ca.org

ACKNOWLEDGEMENTS

Many members of the Route 66 community have shown me great hospitality and generosity in my 20 years of researching Route 66.

Jim Ross, Scott Piotrowski and David Clark were especially helpful in preparing this guide by sharing their wealth of knowledge in their areas of expertise, plus their gracious hospitality (can't forget Carol and Julie, either). Scott ushered me around the complex Pasadena to LA area (which is well documented in his excellent book *Finding the End of the Mother Road: Route 66 in Los Angeles County*) and David did the same on his end of '66, the Chicago area (covered in detail in his two exceptional books *Exploring Route 66 In Chicagoland* and *Route 66 In Chicago*). Jim is, of course, my valued collaborator on The Route 66 Map Series (which we have updated and improved) and the Bones of the Old Road video, neither of which would exist without his vision. His ability to organize and categorize Route 66 research inspired my own to greater heights.

Other fine folk that aided my research, or are great Route 66 people that offered moral support over the years include, but are not limited to (in no particular order): John Weiss. Delbert and Ruth Trew. Pat and Virgil Smith. Thomas and Becky Repp. Johnny "V" Meier. Kathy Anderson. Shellee Graham. Becky Ransome. Jon Robinson. Laurel Kane of Afton Station. Steve Rider. Frank Maloney. Akkey Takeuchi. Bob "Crocodile" Lyle. Carl Johnson. Cheryl Nowka. Dan Harlow. Bob Waldmire. David Rushing. Dawn Welch at the Rock Café. Sue Preston at Seaba Station. Debrah Hodkin. Don Holland. Emily Priddy. Eric Finley. Jeff Jensen. Mike Ward. Kathy Miller. Greg Laxton. Bob Harmon. Jim Conkle. Jim Powell. Marian Clark. Linda and Rocky Drake. Mark Potter. Bill and Linda Fernau. Michael Taylor. Ramona Lehman at the Munger Moss Motel. Michael and Suzanne Wallis. Rich Henry. Jeff Meyer. Pat and Jennifer Bremer. Ron Jones. Ken Turmel. Glenda and Tommy Pike. John Turnbull. Kathy Miller. Fran Houser at the Midpoint Café in Vega. Dale and Hilda Bakke. Guy Randall. Skip Curtis. Drew Knowles. Elaine Downing. The members of the Route 66 E-Group. (Please forgive me if I've forgotten anyone).

I cannot forget all the dedicated volunteers at the many Route 66 museums and associations, and the many business owners along the highway who work hard to keep our Route 66 icons alive. They are the backbone of the Route 66 renaissance.

And of course, David and Mary Lou Knudson, without whom this guide would not have been possible.

This book is dedicated to my mother, Reba McClanahan (for years of moral support in my Route 66 endeavors) and my father, Don McClanahan (for driving us on those Route 66 vacations while my kid brother Steve and I drove him nuts.)